ENDORSEMENTS

'Renton writes with the range and forensic eye that has made him such a vital commentator on the political right and its history'.

Lawrence Black, *Professor of Modern History,*
University of York, UK

'In a refreshing reversal of leftist histories that seek primarily to celebrate, David Renton's study is based on the premise that "we cannot understand the history of English socialism without understanding the people who resisted that form of politics". He encourages socialists to reflect on how they communicate and engage with those they seek to persuade or overcome'.

Matthew Worley, *Professor of Modern History,*
University of Reading, UK

'Detailed, well-researched and authoritative'.

Paul Jackson, *Professor in the History of Radicalism &*
Extremism, University of Northampton, UK

HORATIO BOTTOMLEY AND THE FAR RIGHT BEFORE FASCISM

Horatio Bottomley and the Far Right Before Fascism examines Bottomley's life and politics, and what made him one of the great figures of Edwardian life.

During the First World War, his magazine *John Bull* sold two million copies a week. Bottomley addressed huge crowds urging them to wage a war of extermination against ordinary Germans. The first chairman of the *Financial Times*, the inspiration for Toad in *The Wind in the Willows*, Bottomley was also a major figure in post-1918 politics, urging Conservative voters to dump their leaders and try something new. This carefully researched biography, the first new life of Bottomley for 50 years, shows how he began on the centre-left of Edwardian politics and then moved to the margins, becoming a leading figure on the Edwardian far right, and pre-empting the non-fascist far right of our own days.

This book will appeal to scholars and students with interests in political history, fascism and the far right.

David Renton is a British historian and barrister. His other books include *Labour's Antisemitism Crisis: What the Left Got Wrong and How to Learn From It* (Routledge 2022), *No Free Speech for Fascists: Exploring "No Platform" in History, Law and Politics* (Routledge 2021) and *Never Again: Rock Against Racism and the Anti-Nazi League 1976–1982* (Routledge 2019).

Routledge Studies in Fascism and the Far Right

Series editors
Nigel Copsey, Teesside University, UK and Graham Macklin, Center for Research on Extremism (C-REX), University of Oslo, Norway.

This book series focuses upon national, transnational and global manifestations of fascist, far right and right-wing politics primarily within a historical context but also drawing on insights and approaches from other disciplinary perspectives. Its scope also includes anti-fascism, radical-right populism, extreme-right violence and terrorism, cultural manifestations of the far right, and points of convergence and exchange with the mainstream and traditional right.

Titles include:

For more information about this series, please visit: www.routledge.com/Routledge-Studies-in-Fascism-and-the-Far-Right/book-series/FFR

HORATIO BOTTOMLEY AND THE FAR RIGHT BEFORE FASCISM

David Renton

Dear Mark,

I wanted to thank you for all your help with H.B.. It's a much stronger book for your assistance.

Best wishes,

David

Routledge
Taylor & Francis Group

LONDON AND NEW YORK

Cover image: © Sophie Carapetian

First published 2023
by Routledge
4 Park Square, Milton Park, Abingdon, Oxon OX14 4RN

and by Routledge
605 Third Avenue, New York, NY 10158

Routledge is an imprint of the Taylor & Francis Group, an informa business

British Library Cataloguing-in-Publication Data
A catalogue record for this book is available from the British Library

Library of Congress Cataloging-in-Publication Data
Names: Renton, Dave, 1972- author.
Title: Horatio Bottomley and the far right before Fascism / David Renton.
Description: Abingdon, Oxon; New York, NY : Routledge, 2023. | Series:
    Routledge studies in Fascism and the far right | Includes
    bibliographical references and index.
Identifiers: LCCN 2022022063 (print) | LCCN 2022022064 (ebook) | ISBN
    9781032306537 (hardback) | ISBN 9781032304373 (paperback) | ISBN
    9781003306085 (ebook)
Subjects: LCSH: Bottomley, Horatio, 1860–1933. | Bottomley, Horatio,
    1860–1933—Political and social views. | Great Britain—Politics and
    government—1910–1936. | Capitalists and financiers—Great
    Britain—Biography. | Journalists—Great Britain—Biography.
Classification: LCC DA566.9.B6 R46 2023 (print) | LCC DA566.9.B6 (ebook)
    | DDC 328.41/092 [B]—dc23/eng/20220509
LC record available at https://lccn.loc.gov/2022022063
LC ebook record available at https://lccn.loc.gov/2022022064

ISBN: 978-1-032-30653-7 (hbk)
ISBN: 978-1-032-30437-3 (pbk)
ISBN: 978-1-003-30608-5 (ebk)

DOI: 10.4324/9781003306085

Typeset in Bembo
by codeMantra

CONTENTS

1

INTRODUCTION

The subject of this book is 19th- and 20th-century political life, and the part in it played by one person, celebrated in his time but almost forgotten today: the journalist, politician and businessman Horatio Bottomley. Bottomley has drifted out of our collective memory, and we are the poorer for this. He was a press magnate, and his magazine *John Bull* was the best-selling news weekly of its time,[1] with two million readers during the Great War. *The English Review* called him a "Prince of Fleet Street", and wrote: "He owned a racing stable. To quite a million of good people he shone like a star".[2] The music-hall singer and comedian Mark Sheridan dedicated a song to him: "*Who's the wisest man in town? Who's the judge without a gown? Mr Bottomley – John Bull!*"[3] An anonymous pamphleteer described him as the "finest orator in the Kingdom… the first lay lawyer in the land… a fine sportsman… a fearless and independent politician". And the effect of the prose is not altogether diminished when we reveal that these compliments appeared in a document printed by Bottomley himself.[4]

On Bottomley's telling, the most remarkable part of his life story was the speed of his rise from penury to plenty. In his memoir *Bottomley's Book*, published in 1909, he made repeated proud allusion to his harsh upbringing, despite seeming ashamed of its particulars. When he tells of his uncle Austin Holyoake's funeral[5] – where he first encountered his mentor Charles Bradlaugh – he describes himself as coming up from "school", and talks later of leaving this school to travel up to London.[6] But the school goes unnamed – it was in fact an orphanage. Nor did things improve with any speed: the solicitor who employed Bottomley at the age of 14 was a drunkard whose managing clerk was sentenced to hard labour for fraud.[7] Elsewhere in the memoir Bottomley chides one-time Liberal leader Lord Rosebery for subsequent disloyalty to his party: "Come amongst us and do your work. You have all the advantages of name and wealth and power".[8] Readers were intended to contrast all these advantages – name *and* wealth *and* power –

DOI: 10.4324/9781003306085-1

with their own humble beginnings as he imagined them, and indeed with his own: "We members of the general public", "we men in the street".[9]

Bottomley was made by the politics of the 1870s and early 1880s. This book shows how, in the aftermath of Chartism's defeat, socialists (including members of Bottomley's immediate family) had battled to save as much of the Chartist programme as they could, by reinventing themselves as secularists, as republicans, even as spiritualists. It describes how left-wing ideas were reinvigorated in the 1880s, and how the Liberal Party, which had once been broad enough to include at its left end advocates of trade unionism and of workers' co-operation, so lost the support of these voters that rivals on its left were able to supplant it, leading to the formation of today's Labour Party. The book describes the animosity that socialists stirred up in their opponents, from Victorian clergymen to Edwardian factory owners... and in Horatio Bottomley. We cannot understand the history of English socialism without understanding the people who resisted that politics – in the 1830s, and since.

When he stood for Parliament Bottomley's leaflets described him as the "man of Destiny, who never went to Eton or Oxford, but was educated in the University of Life and is all the better for it".[10] Bottomley promised if elected to fight for the poor and dispossessed. Yet the closer we look at his left-wing credentials the less impressive they seem. He would respond with fury to the rise of socialism and workers' unions in the dying days of the Victorian era. Neither could be allowed to block his own path to power.

As well as a politician, Bottomley was a businessman and speculator, with vast sums passing through his hands. Hundreds of millions of pounds were invested in his companies. Yet even the monies purporting to fund Australian gold mines financed no pumps and no excavations. Nor did any of his wealth ever trickle down to the working-class voters that Bottomley expected to back him. Rather, it was their role to subsidise him.

This book is a study in political movement. It explains how Bottomley could travel, in incremental steps, from being a loyal supporter of the most left-wing position available in late Victorian politics, which was a left Liberalism then known as "Radicalism", to becoming an ally of the Conservatives, and then moving further right still. By 1914 he was a leader of the Edwardian far right, obsessed as it was with feminism, with the conspiracies of homosexuals and/or Jews, and with the rise of trade union power.

This book also takes seriously Bottomley's own self-image when he was at his height, this man who treated the John Bull cartoon on the masthead of his own magazine as a kind of mirror. From the *John Bull* platform, during the course of the war, Bottomley demanded that people of German descent should no longer be allowed to walk British streets unmolested. *John Bull*'s readers would be called on to hate "Germhuns" and "Austrihuns". Elsewhere the left was calling for the revolutionary overthrow of the ruling class. According to Bottomley those to be detested included politicians and civil servants – and those to be violently attacked included foreign-born neighbours, pacifists and socialists.

Bottomley was sent on a tour of the Western Front, and then to review the fleet. It was suggested that he help the government manage the wartime food supply. Lloyd George called him into his office, but never, despite the excitement of his boosters, into the cabinet. So he waited for the call and England waited with him – and yet the call never came.

In Bottomley's mind, he was Dick Whittington: he had begun poor, he had become rich. His life had started in obscurity. Now, millions knew its every detail. At any moment, his ascent would have to be crowned by this final victory, the reward of government office. Yet studied in detail, his life is by no means a heroic narrative. With Bottomley, there were always too many highs and too many lows; the final defining moment of arrival remained always just beyond his grasp.

If readers today know his name at all, it is because he was at last convicted of fraud, and sentenced in May 1922 to seven years in prison. Today we see him as the manipulator of a generation's desire to do good by their country and to pay off its war debts. But to the watching public of his time, Bottomley was a great business leader. Often accused of wrongdoing, he had been repeatedly vindicated in court. His many victories before the law convinced millions that he must be honest, and that their limited savings could be invested with him. This spell lasted until his overreach, when the fraud of his Victory Bond Club was proven and he suffered a fall from which he could not recover.

There have been eight biographies of Horatio Bottomley, though it is 50 years[11] since the publication of Alan Hyman's, the most recent. This present account, to a greater extent than any predecessor, treats Bottomley as he saw himself – as a politician. As he saw it, the business side of his career was always subordinate to the parliamentary. It was a means towards the greater goal, funding him until he could secure a seat in the House of Commons. His life's unifying theme was his desire to establish himself there, and to exert political power.

As a tribune of the people, his views took the form of a contempt towards those on his left, beginning as a mere unfocused dislike and increasing into hatred. As with others who walked a path from left to right in the 1920s–30s, Bottomley's trajectory was directed against his younger self. The milieu that he was born into, as careful study shows, was one of skilled workers, atheists and co-operators, and advocates of votes for women. This was a generation trying to introduce fairer ways to organise economic life. To set Bottomley's rise towards business and political success in the context of this early backdrop is to grasp that his rise was far from simple. Among the poor there are always people of talent and habits of solidarity – but against both them and their values he would rage for the rest of his life.

Notes

1 My thanks to the staff of the Bishopsgate Institute, Hackney, London Metropolitan, National and Parliamentary archives, and the British Library at Colindale and

St Pancras for their help. Gratitude is also owed to the friends with whom I have discussed this book including Ian Birchall and Naomi Care, to Mark Sinker for his editorial input, and to Anne, Sam, and Ben. A century later, there is only one news magazine in Britain that reaches even a tenth of *John Bull's* sale. In winter 2020–21, the best-selling news weeklies in Britain were *Private Eye* with an average of 230,000 sales and *the Economist* with 130,000 sales. C. Tobbitt, 'News and current affairs magazine ABCs: The Week Junior thrives under lockdown', *Press Gazette*, 11 February 2021.

2 *The English Review*, July 1922.
3 Written and sung by Mark Sheridan, 1915.
4 H. Bottomley, *Who is Mr Bottomley?* (London: Horatio Bottomley, 1915).
5 H. Bottomley, *Bottomley's Book* (London: Odhams Limited, 1909), p. 165.
6 Bottomley, *Bottomley's Book*, p. 90.
7 Bottomley, *Bottomley's Book*, p. 4.
8 Bottomley, *Bottomley's Book*, p. 119. A Liberal lord, Rosebery had been Prime Minister from 1895–96; after his resignation he had since the turn of the century become gradually estranged from the younger and more Radical wing of the party, though he still had a following. The irony is that Bottomley seems to be attacking him for positions on war and empire that he, Bottomley, would soon fervently embrace.
9 Bottomley, *Bottomley's Book*, p. 115.
10 A. Hyman, *The Rise and Fall of Horatio Bottomley: The Biography of a Swindler* (London: Cassell, 1972), p. 192.
11 Bottomley, *Bottomley's Book*; R. Blaythwayt, *Horatio Bottomley: The Man as He is Today* (London: Odhams, 1916); R. Bigland, *Bottomley!!!* (Birmingham: Farwood Publishing, 1922); 'Tenax' (E. Bell), *The Rise and Fall of Horatio Bottomley* (London: David Weir, 1923), p. 12; H. J. Houston, *The Real Horatio Bottomley* (London: Hurst & Blackett, 1923); S. T. Felstead, *Horatio Bottomley* (London: John Murray, 1936); J. Symons, *Horatio Bottomley* (London: The Cresset Press, 1955); and Hyman, *The Rise and Fall*.

2
FATHERS, REAL AND IMAGINED

Through his mother Elizabeth Holyoake, Horatio Bottomley was connected to writers and campaigners at the centre of great events. His maternal uncle was George Jacob Holyoake, a socialist, an atheist and an advocate of workers' co-operatives. George Jacob was the first of the family to settle in London, where his sister Elizabeth joined him. After her death, George Jacob acted as Horatio's guardian, presenting the young Horatio with a model to emulate of the campaigning journalist's career. This chapter will also trace two further influences on Horatio's early life: his father William, a shipwright and then a tailor's foreman, and Charles Bradlaugh, journalist, pamphleteer and advocate of left-wing politics, including atheism. By the time Bottomley as a 14-year-old boy first encountered Bradlaugh, he had supplanted Holyoake as the effective leader of the Victorian Radicals. So high was Bradlaugh's rise that Bottomley believed him a greater figure than Holyoake – and even convinced himself that Bradlaugh was in fact his own unacknowledged father.

George Jacob Holyoake: the rising artisan

Bottomley's maternal uncle George Jacob Holyoake was born in 1817 at No. 1 Inge Street, Birmingham, a spacious, airy house near the Fox Tavern,[1] at the southern edge of the city. Water came from a pump in the family's yard.[2] The neighbour at No. 2 sold cakes and tarts from a "low, broad, bow window". At No. 5 sat a second neighbour behind voluminous green silk curtains, selling charms that removed warts. A third, at No. 12, was a baker who allowed the Holyoake children to warm their own pies in his oven.[3]

The Holyoakes were a family of "artisans",[4] which is to say skilled workers, sometimes self-employed, sometime employed as high-waged craftsmen.

DOI: 10.4324/9781003306085-2

Around them lived others of the same class: brass founders, gold-beaters, stocking weavers and watch-makers. In 1824, the Combinations Act began to permit union activity, which led to a successful strike by London shipwrights.[5] With Britain rapidly becoming an industrial power, her labour aristocrats could expect a salary of thirty shillings or more a week.[6]

Horatio's grandfather, George Jacob's father George Herbert Holyoake, worked at the Eagle Iron Foundry, one of two dozen in Birmingham,[7] which made pots, safes, weights, garden rollers, gear wheels, gates and fire hearths. On Sundays, George Herbert dressed in a brown overcoat, cloth breeches and white top boots. He was "tall and comely". A proud man, he refused to remove his hat in the presence of his employers.[8] Aged ten, George Jacob began working at this same foundry: "I must have been very young then, as I remember asking my father to let me hold his hands as I went along by his side in the early morning; and his hand, enclosing mine, was a new sensation of pleasure, and seemed to put fresh life into me".[9] For the next 13 years, Holyoake worked with white iron and burnished steel.

Horatio's grandmother Catherine had a "grave, impressive face". She "wished her children to be honest, truthful and pious", and took them to services at the Congregational Church on Carr Lane where they learned that mankind was divided into an elect destined to salvation, and a remainder set for hell. As the priest John James explained:

> What turned Adam and Eve out of paradise? Sin. What destroyed God's own city, and scattered his chosen people over the face of the earth? Sin. What brought disease, accidents, toil, care, war, pestilence, and famine into the world? Sin.[10]

In 1829, George Jacob's baby sister Eliza died at home. To the loving brother, the fault was also that of the church authorities, who had summonsed Catherine for late payment of rates, causing her to be out of the home as Eliza breathed her last. This began a period of tragedy for the family, with another sibling Louisa dying in 1832.

Horatio's mother Elizabeth was born the year of Louisa's death. We can imagine her watching as her older brother George Jacob grew into a confident young man. He left home each morning at six, travelling to work with their father. In his work breaks he forged a miniature steel fire-grate and brought it home, where it shone on his mother's shelf. He attended chapel with his mother on Fridays and Sundays, and taught for a while at a Congregationalist Sunday School.[11] At the age of 17, he began attending meetings at Birmingham's Mechanics' Institution, which housed a library with 3,000 volumes, a reading-room, and a museum of mechanical models and scientific specimens,[12] having been established for the "'Promotion of Knowledge among the Working Classes', by the cheap instruction of the members in the principle of the arts they practise, and in various branches of science". In the evenings George Jacob would return home deep in conversation with his tutor and friend Hawkes Smith.

At the Institution he learned of the factory reformer Robert Owen, who promoted working-class education and the founding of self-sufficient "Villages of Co-operation", inspired by Owen's previous model community of New La-nark, which had flourished by replacing child labour with education and limiting hours of work. New Lanark broke with the established apprenticeship system, creating a virtuous cycle in which work was well paid but the workers were productive.[13] Owen was one of the few prominent thinkers of that time who believed that the new productive techniques associated with industry would be taken up everywhere. This argument was appealing to socialists: that society's evolution ensured the rise of the working class and the victory of their philoso-phy. Decades before, Owen had penned a letter to the Governments of Europe and America. "New scientific power, and the rapid increase in knowledge among all classes of men", he wrote, would change the world. The capture of informa-tion by the great majority of people would prove to them "the absolute necessity which has thus arisen from them to give different direction to their powers, and will inform them also, how the change is to be affected".[14]

At the Eagle Iron Foundry, George Jacob's fellow workers were nervous in the presence of their master, dressing in cheap clothes, so that he would not cut their wages.[15] Yet signs of change were coming. In 1833, father and son travelled to Worcester to watch the first steam train to depart Birmingham for Coventry, at an extraordinary eight miles an hour.[16] The new transport system would make England seem smaller and would also increase the demand for skilled workers. If the present still belonged to the bosses, the future belonged to labour.

The Owenite newspaper *The Pioneer* told its readers to break apart the great houses of the rich and to share their wealth universally: "At a very early period, we shall find the idle possessor compelled to ask you to release him from his worthless holding".[17] Holyoake began attending an Owenite meeting-house on Well Lane.

Owen called for the transformation of education. "Every pupil", he wrote, "shall be encouraged to express his or her opinion". Religious instruction would not be imposed on anyone. Everyone would be encouraged to learn, irrespective of their career or their parents' standing: "All shall be treated with equal kind-ness". As it would be four decades before women were able to obtain university degrees, perhaps the most striking demand was that "Both sexes shall have equal opportunities of acquiring useful knowledge".[18]

In June 1836, George Jacob heard Owen speak for the first time. In January 1837, aged 19, he recorded in his diary that he himself "spoke for the Owenites" at a meeting.[19] He was elected to the Committee of the Birmingham Mechanics' Institute. Around this time fellow Owenite Frederick Hollick[20] wrote to him from London, warning that the London left was far behind its counterpart in the Midlands and the North: "The worst lecture I ever delivered in Birmingham would be thought a prodigy here".[21]

In February 1838 Holyoake joined Owen's new Association of All Classes of All Nations. He also participated in the Chartist movement, which was demanding a vote for every man, for annual parliaments, for the secret ballot, for payment of MPs and for reform of electoral districts. A petition to this end, delivered to Parliament by Birmingham's Radical MP Thomas Attwood, had been signed by 1.3 million people. Holyoake attended their rallies in Birmingham[22] and that same year married another Radical, a farmer's daughter,[23] Ellen Williams. He walked to Derbyshire. "Over the foundry walls where I worked had come gleams of the sun, which had made me long to see the outlying world on which it shone unconfined. Now I was in that world: happy days were those, for my heart was as light as my purse".[24]

In 1840, the Owenites thanked Holyoake for collecting funds to enable the purchase of a socialist chapel in Lawrence Street. In August he lectured in Worcester, after which the Owenites there invited him to join them as a full-time worker.[25] The socialists in the town offered him 16 shillings a week, enough to feed his wife[26] and their daughter, Madeline.

In 1841, the Owenites made him a "social missionary" in Sheffield, and his salary doubled, to £80 per year.[27] The Owenite headquarters was in Sheffield's Rockingham Street, with a school with 50 pupils which held meetings in the evening and at weekends. Holyoake's circle widened to take in those of more moderate view than his own.[28]

This same year Holyoake's friend Charles Southwell was also made a social missionary to the Bristol district. Southwell had been a bookseller, and had also fought for the liberal Spanish Queen Isabella against an uprising by her reactionary opponents (named "Carlists" for their preferred ruler, Don Carlos, Count of Molina). The first issue of Southwell's newspaper *The Oracle of Reason* had sold six thousand copies, in large part because of the atheism which ran alongside its socialism.[29] In it the Bible was described as the "idol of all sorts of blockheads, the glory of knaves, and the disgust of wise men. It is a history of lust, sodomies, wholesale slaughtering and horrible depravity".[30]

Southwell was arrested and charged with blasphemy. Holyoake demanded that the Owenites support him. William Galpin, General Secretary of the Owenites, replied with tepid reassurance that the Owenite Central Board would "not fail to assist Mr Southwell all they can". Nevertheless, Southwell's chosen course of confronting the Church "was in direct opposition from what the Board have always advocated".[31]

In January 1842, Southwell was convicted, fined £100, and sentenced to 12 months' imprisonment. In Sheffield, Holyoake renounced all religion. He had been "born pious, and nursed in orthodoxy", but any beliefs he had once held "in the humanising tendency of Christianity" had been destroyed. "The persecution of my friend has been within these few weeks, the cradle of my doubts, and the grave of my religion... my faith is no more".[32]

Holyoake left Birmingham to help Southwell. In May, he addressed a meeting of the Cheltenham Mechanics' Institution on the topic of "Home Colonisation": this was the Owenite proposal that poverty be resolved not (as the government proposed) with emigration, political repression and the workhouse, but rather with a positive programme of public works taking the form of self-sufficient working-class villages.[33] Around 100 Chartists and socialists were present to hear him. A Mr Maitland (a "teetotaller, and sort of local preacher"[34]) noted that Holyoake's speech had made no mention of chapels. Did the socialists, asked this hostile questioner, see no role for religion in their future society?

At first Holyoake stuck to the Owenite script, acknowledging that he had avoided all talk of God in the body of his speech. But why was he here, if not to help his friend Southwell? He cited the £20 million pounds gathered by the Church every year in taxes and continued:

> I appeal to your heads and your pockets if we are not too poor to have a god? If poor men cost the state so much they would be put like officers on half-pay. I think while our distress lasts it would be wise to do the same with the Deity.[35]

Holyoake then talked of Southwell in Bristol jail, and called the Bible "a viper".[36]

On 26 May, after a meeting with Southwell in Bristol, Holyoake saw the *Cheltenham Chronicle*'s third-page report on his lecture on Socialism, under the title "ATHEISM AND BLASPHEMY". Socialism, yelled the newspaper, was "more appropriately termed, Devilism", and it highlighted what it portrayed as a threat to put God on half-pay, demanding Holyoake be prosecuted for blasphemy. These good Christians boasted that they had three journalists to testify that these exact words had been spoken.[37]

Back in Cheltenham, Holyoake was arrested.[38] A collection was organised in Sheffield by fellow socialist and Chartist Julian Harney. "Fervent", wrote Harney, were the wishes of the people for "your triumph over your persecutors".[39]

Holyoake's trial began in August 1842.[40] He was permitted to speak for nine hours in his defence, expounding the doctrines of socialism as well as of atheism,[41] and appealing to the principle of free speech: "What can we think of the morality of a law which prohibits the free publication of opinion?"[42] At the end of the hearing the jury, composed of seven gentleman farmers and four shopkeepers,[43] took just two minutes to find him guilty. The judge sentenced him to six months imprisonment, to endure solitude, gruel and coarse bread.[44] After eight weeks he learned news worse than all this: the death from fever of his daughter Madeline.[45]

1842 also saw another great wave of Chartist activity: a second petition was signed, this time by three and a half million people, there were strikes in the Midlands and the industrial North and riots in the potteries (with 116 men and women imprisoned), and Feargus O'Connor and almost every member of the national executive was prosecuted.

On release Holyoake toured Gloucester and Cheltenham before giving a lecture in Rochdale to the Socialist Society, on the merits of Owenite land colonies and co-operation. The following year, 28 skilled artisans, with Owenite socialists prominent among them, would establish the first modern cooperative society, the Rochdale Equitable Pioneers Society.[46]

In 1846, having settled in London, Holyoake founded his own newspaper, its first issue declaring: "*The Reasoner* will be Communistic in Social Economy – Utilitarian in Morals – Republican in Politics – and Anti-theological in Religion".[47] This communistic social economy was a reference to Owenism, and early articles addressed themselves to supporters of the movement: "As for those who have no courage themselves, let them not discourage others. The late retardation of our views has opened our eyes, not damped our ardour".[48]

Several Holyoakes worked on *The Reasoner*, including George Jacob's brother Austin. Among its earliest guarantors (with a donation of five shillings) was one "E. H."[49] – in all likelihood Horatio Bottomley's future mother, their sister Elizabeth, 14 years old and still living with her parents at No. 1 Inge Street in Birmingham.

Meanwhile Holyoake was moving ever closer to the centre of events. When Chartism and the battle for the People's Charter surged again in 1848, he had become one of its best-known speakers.[50] On 10 April, some 20,000 Chartists marched from Kennington Common in South London, along a route lined by 200,000 more or less sympathetic spectators. The government signed up 85,000 special constables to prevent disorder, equipped the Bank with artillery and placed 7,000 soldiers all around Westminster.[51]

But after this peak the campaign declined. The press attacked it, insisting that the petition's numbers had been inflated. Mocked and humbled, the Chartists too came to believe in their defeat. Feargus O'Connor, their best-known leader, became an alcoholic. In 1852, he struck three of his fellow MPs, after which he was held in an asylum. The same year Robert Owen converted to spiritualism. He had never stopped believing that human beings could live under fairer conditions; he now presented the dead as their allies in that struggle, titling one pamphlet, *The Future of the Human Race; or a Great Glorious and Future Revolution to Be Effected Through the Agency of Departed Spirits of Good and Superior Men and Women.*[52]

Defeat also had an impact on *The Reasoner*. In its first years, it had presented itself as just another Owenite newspaper, albeit the boldest, reporting on disagreements with the movement and discussing the fates of the socialist full-timers. The longer the paper continued, however, the more that its hostility to Christianity dominated, and references to socialism became rarer. *The Reasoner* is where George Jacob coined the term "secularism" for his mature philosophy, arguing that the existence of god could never be known for sure, so that all vestiges of religion[53] must be purged from the state. To sustain an audience, Holyoake and his comrades repackaged themselves as free-thinkers rather than the socialists they had once been.

William Bottomley: from artisan to mechanic

Thanks to the activities of Horatio's uncle George Jacob, the Holyoakes are well documented. The same cannot be said for the Bottomleys. They had lived in Bradford, Halifax, Leeds, Stockport and Manchester through the 19th century, but the census records just one with this surname in London:[54] William, Horatio's father, who grew up on Oxley Road in Bermondsey, four miles from Bethnal Green. He was three years older than Horatio's mother Elizabeth, and also from a large family, the third child of Samuel Bottomley, a shipwright, and Hanna, with four younger siblings to follow.[55]

In 1841 William was just 13 years old. He too is listed on the census as a shipwright. This was a sought-after career deep into the 1840s. The Admiralty gave preferential treatment to London shipyards, where wages were high because workers were paid on "gang contracts", in which workers recruited one another and yard-owners negotiated with them as groups.[56]

Nevertheless, not long afterwards, William would reject the family profession to train as a tailor. Like shipwrights, tailors were artisans, and this doubtless seemed an upward move at the time, not least since tailors were also the custodians of the upward rise of others. Trabb in *Great Expectations* is probably the best-known tailor in Victorian fiction. The protagonist Pip has come into a great sum of money. As a new customer, Pip is measured by Trabb "as if I were an estate and he the finest species of surveyor".[57] When Pip leaves Trabb's shop he feels confident and rich in his new attire. William Bottomley, we may assume, expected to witness and enable many similar transformations.

Yet by the 1840s the numbers of self-employed tailors were falling, their work undertaken by employees and by women. In documents he was listed as a "tailor's foreman".[58] At the front of the workshop, prospective customers were shown samples and fitted by a master tailor. In the back the sewing tailors – anything from two or three to a dozen "journeymen" and "seamstresses" – carried out the master's orders.[59] As foreman, William's task was to convey orders from front of shop and to ensure they were accurately completed in the back.

The 1850s would be a wretched time to work in this industry. Charles Booth, ship-owner, reformist, chronicler of the Victorian London poor, reported that wages were depressed, as journeymen tailors worked ever more often out of their own homes, their wives and daughters expected to contribute unpaid. A journeyman could supplement his wages by passing off his women's work as his own – but the masters responded by cutting piece-rates, and home-working (so Booth reported[60]) became the worst-paid of all work. It was known as "sweating", the ancestor of the modern term "sweatshop labour".

Tailors attempted to resist these reductions. By the early 1850s, an Association of Working Tailors had been founded, which claimed some 2,000 of London's 18,000 tailors as recruits. It owned a model workplace on Castle Street East, near London's Oxford Street. Here was the workers' co-operation that had enthused Owen and Holyoake. With no owner to profit from the co-operative,[61] the work would be good and the wages high (7–14 shillings per coat).[62] Middle-class visitors gave their support, including the novelists Thomas Hughes (of *Tom Brown's Schooldays*) and Charles Kingsley (*The Water-Babies*). Yet artisans criticised the Association: its officials were said to employ hireling labour, and would not share profits.[63]

The news of Elizabeth's engagement to William King Bottomley was welcomed by the Holyoakes. Her brother Horatio had emigrated after the Chartists' defeat to Australia's gold belt, and now lived at Ballarat, in Victoria. On 22 April of that year, he responded with delight to a letter from William about the forthcoming marriage, and wrote to his mother Catherine, joking about the felicity of William's middle name: "I little expected there would ever be a King in the family... I hope he will govern over his dominions with honour and integrity".[64]

In 1857, aged 29 or 30, not long after the birth of his daughter Florence, William was taken to Bethlehem hospital at St. George's Fields in Southwark, the original "Bedlam",[65] in the grip of an unknown mental illness, before returning to work the following year.

By the 1860s, tailors were facing a second enemy: mechanisation. Singer, the leading manufacturer of US-made sewing machines, was selling 10,000 machines in Britain a year.[66] Till now, even the poor had dressed themselves in hand-made clothing,[67] but it was increasingly possible to buy cheaper machine-made clothes. Jobs were threatened and prospects were poor. Those with savings could perhaps reinvent themselves as masters, but William was a mere foreman. With the birth of his son Horatio in 1860, the pressures on him must have grown.

Charles Bradlaugh: the white-collar Radical

In the second half of the 1850s, Elizabeth Holyoake was attending the secularist lectures at Islington's Hall of Science.[68] One speaker there was George Jacob's successor in the secularist movement Charles Bradlaugh, a rising star in the movement and beyond. Karl and Jenny Marx were refugees in London from the failed 1848 revolution in Germany, and Jenny may well have attended some of the same lectures as Elizabeth. As Jenny told her husband, Bradlaugh was becoming a "tower of strength to the working-class movement".[69]

Sixteen years George Jacob's junior, Bradlaugh was born in Hoxton in 1833. The Bradlaughs were not workers but clerks, Charles senior clerking for a solicitor, with his son as the firm's errand-boy from age 11–13. As an ardent young Christian approaching confirmation, Charles junior was asked to write an essay showing how the 39 Articles of the Church of England grew out of New Testament teachings. Young Bradlaugh discovered a series of inconsistencies between church teaching and the gospels, and asked for advice. He was suspended from his congregation for three months and reported to his parents, who threw him out of his home. So he turned to the atheists he had seen preaching in Hackney's Victoria Park. His first public lecture was organised by Austin Holyoake, with George Jacob in the chair. Bradlaugh was 17, though he "looked more like 14 as he stood up in a youth's round jacket", recalled George Jacob, but "he spoke with a readiness, confidence and promise".[70]

Around the time of Horatio's birth in 1860, the rivalry was heating up, as the young Bradlaugh expanded out of his London patch for a wider compass, to speak in the secular halls of Sunderland, Bradford, Doncaster and Bolton.[71] His message was that the movement had erred. They should not rest at calling for the removal of religion from public life. They should go further, insisting that there was no God and that religion was mere superstition. Holyoake was a limited public speaker, without a "bold voice" or "good presence".[72] Once militant, he was now a member of the cautious older guard.[73] Bradlaugh replaced him as President of the London Secular Society,[74] and founded *The Investigator* as a rival to *The Reasoner*.

The work they were both doing was much the same, but Bradlaugh had greater success. Holyoake's response was to nurture friendships outside the atheist milieu, including with one well-known fellow enthusiast for the subordination of religion, for votes for women, and for trade unions and worker co-operatives, John Stuart Mill.[75] For some time Mill had been sending Holyoake small gifts of money, terming himself a "friend of freethinking opinions".[76] Soon he went further, sending Holyoake the proofs of his book *On Liberty*, at the same time begging the agitator not to admit he had seen the text early: "It is likely enough to be called an infidel book in any case; but I would rather that people were not prompted to call it so".[77]

Such high-profile support must have been gratifying, but in the spring of 1860, Holyoake suffered a collapse that would incapacitate him for a year.[78] Elizabeth would need her brother's support when Horatio was born, but George Jacob was in no fit state.

William and Elizabeth

In Holyoake's engagement diary for 1860, the sentence "Bessie has a boy"[79] is the first recorded mention of the new child. The name Horatio came from his maternal uncle in Ballarat, and his middle name William honoured his father. The birth certificate shows that he was born on 23 March 1860 at 16 St Peter Street, Bethnal Green. The house was a terrace building of brick, with doors and windows in the shape of Greek arches, and Bethnal Green, though it bordered on the wealthy City of London, was then a poor district, the centre of sweat-shop production in shoemaking, furniture-making, and tailoring, with a settled population that sometimes remained in the borough for generations.[80] The sky-line was dominated by the nearby church of St Peter with St Thomas. Tall and overpowering, in a pseudo-Norman style, this grey brick edifice loomed over a neighbourhood with a reputation for religious dissent. At the church's consecration,[81] jeering crowds had allowed an ox to run loose, and for years the diocese complained of hostility.

By 1860 William and Elizabeth had been married for five years. Their first child, Grace Madeline,[82] known in the family as Florence, was three years old, and they had relocated to Field Road in Forest Gate, fleeing east as their savings ran out. In 1863, William had two further relapses, and the second was fatal.[83] He was buried on 14 July 1863,[84] at just 36 years old. Asked how his father died,

Horatio Bottomley refused to acknowledge any mental illness and claimed he had died of "consumption", which is to say tuberculosis.[85]

The presiding minister at the funeral was Thomas Stallybrass,[86] a Congregationalist.[87] Long afterwards, Horatio would recall standing at his father's graveside, peering into a large hole, into which he threw a bunch of flowers. Then the earth was thrown into the ground.

> Whenever I hear rain beating on an iron roof, I live over again the few minutes I stood by my father's grave. I cannot remember the name of the cemetery, but if you could take me to the gates of it, I could walk directly to the grave.[88]

Beyond William's wages, Elizabeth had no paid work, and relied on the support of her brothers. In principle, George Jacob was the most successful member of the family. Some sources record that he paid a "small weekly contribution" towards the children's food.[89] Yet what help he gave must have been modest. He had seven children of his own, and Bradlaugh's rivalry had reduced the earnings and funding available to him.

Both he and Bradlaugh were giving public talks, though Bradlaugh gave many more: as many as six in a typical week.[90] As this was not enough to live on, both men also solicited for donations.[91] At the suggestion of friends they merged their newspapers into a new title: the *National Reformer*.[92] Bradlaugh had editorial control, but at first agreed to pay Holyoake (and Holyoake's friends) £2 a week to write the first three pages. When this agreement broke down. Bradlaugh resigned as editor and called a general meeting of the governing National Reformer Company. Who should be editor in future? The directors favoured Holyoake but the shareholders voted 106 to 85 for Bradlaugh.[93]

Bradlaugh wanted the paper to agitate for atheism. Holyoake favoured his term secularism, which left the existence of God unclarified, focusing instead on the reduction of religious influence over society and the state. As he explained:

> The world... is our dwelling place. We know the laws of sanitation, economy, and equity, upon which health, wealth and security depend. All these things are quite independent of any knowledge of the origins of the universe or the owner of it.[94]

Many at the heart of these ideological wranglings saw no principled distinction between these two words, save that atheism had more negative associations than secularism. As Bradlaugh's daughter Hypatia explained, "Mr Holyoake... did not see that there was anything to be gained by the use of a name which had so undeservedly become a term of reproach; he preferred to find a new name and make a fresh start under new colours".[95]

Enough of the shareholders saw matters Bradlaugh's way for him to win the majority. But there was more going on here than Bradlaugh's greater fierceness against Christianity and Holyoake's reluctance to give his favoured term a more pointed substance. In his slower and less dynamic way, Holyoake was also still campaigning for the Owenite programme, in the shape of trade unions, workers' co-operatives, and the representation of labour in the House of Commons.[96] The promise of redistribution had been watered down, and a co-operative was often now little more than an alternative form of shop-keeping.[97] The communism was long gone – yet there was to Holyoake's politics a residual working-class appeal that continued to prevent Bradlaugh's victories over him from ever quite being decisive.

On both sides of the conflict, the antagonists were spending more than they could afford. Through 1863, they fought over the debts of *The National Reformer*. After arbitration, Bradlaugh had to pay Holyoake £81 and 18 shillings.[98] He sought to reinvent himself as a businessman, allied in the first instance with fellow free-thinker and reformer Montague Leverson,[99] the solicitor and coal importer, before striking out on his own when he came (correctly) to doubt Leverson's integrity.[100]

Iron and platinum had been discovered in a beach at Castellammare in Italy. The Naples Colour Company manufactured with these minerals a paint that (so it was claimed) was ideal for the protection of iron ships from rust. Taking the opportunity to extend his own political contacts with political supporters of Italian unification, Bradlaugh visited Italy at the company's behest – but the project, conducted in his name, failed to turn a profit. His daughter Hypatia would blame this on his lack of experience in the colour trade – while his being an infidel gave contractors an excuse to cancel their purchases.[101]

In 1863, Bradlaugh published an article: "Poverty: Its Effects on the Political Condition of the People". Why were workers poor? His answer was: because there were too many of them, a fact for which Holyoake's trade unions and co-operatives offered no solution. In a better world, the workers would pay fewer taxes – and reduce their own numbers by practising birth control. "It is with the problem of too many mouths for too little bread that the labourer has really to deal: if he must pray it should be for more bread and for fewer mouths".[102] We should ask what such politics offered Elizabeth Bottomley, as a widow with a young family. She could not reduce the number of mouths she had to feed.

In 1864, Elizabeth took ill, her doctors unable to diagnose that it was cancer until its final stages.[103] She died that same year, and is commemorated alongside parents and siblings by an austere white hexagon pillar at the family gravesite at Witton cemetery in Birmingham.

After the sky had fallen in

At first Horatio and Florence were sent to live with their uncle William at Hayter House on the Marylebone Road.[104] He was three years younger than his sister, an artist embarking on a successful career, and best known for his oil paintings of rural or religious scenes.[105] He was active in the Society of British Artists[106] and had already exhibited at the British Institution. But he had children of his own and was short of money.

George Jacob agreed to pay for their maintenance.[107] Florence was to be sent to live with family friends, an engineer and his family in Cheapside, who adopted her.[108] There she flourished. She was encouraged to write to her brother and to see him, which she did – but they would not take Horatio, so until 1869 he was housed with Mrs Wormley, a widow residing in Battersea.[109] Afterwards George Jacob made an unsuccessful application for him to be sent to the Orphan Working School and Alexandra Orphanage at Hampstead, as his sister and his uncle lived nearby, but they were told there was no vacancy.[110]

Bradlaugh was on the edge of bankruptcy after the "Black Friday" of May 1866. "I have great facilities for making money and great facilities for losing it", he admitted.[111] "People were much too good to do business with an Atheist", Hypatia would recall bitterly.[112]

In July a protest was to be held in London's Hyde Park, calling to further extend the franchise. As the Metropolitan Police had announced that it was to be banned, Bradlaugh was encouraging allies to attend.[113] He would be one of the main speakers. When the park gates were discovered shut, protesters pulled down several hundred yards of railings. The Liberal government's proposed Reform bill was defeated by the Conservatives, but in 1867 the government they then formed enacted the very reforms they had opposed. As an organiser of the Hyde Park protest, Bradlaugh's reputation was once more boosted among secularists and left-wing Liberals, and in 1868 he stood for election for the first time, winning over 1,000 votes as a Radical in Northampton. The two seats[114] would be taken by Liberals, but Bradlaugh had put down a marker. This campaign exacerbated tensions among the Holyoakes.[115] Austin organised Bradlaugh's election fund[116] while George Jacob declined his support.

Holyoake believed in elections. But, albeit in his now-familiar cautious way, he also continued to argue that the mere holding of Radical positions was inadequate. He wanted to see in Parliament not just people of left-wing views, but those who worked for a living, those who had known poverty. As he explained to one audience in Birmingham, "The House of Commons is a rich man's club, and at present it is meant to be so". However there was no other route towards democracy and equality save working-class representation. "Working men will have to create a great Political Fund, and contribute their share of all these costs, as a first step to representative action". Until that was done, "all sorts of inane, monotonous people, with money bags about them", would elbow the working man to the bottom of the poll.[117]

Looking to ground his address in local conditions, Holyoake ended with words of praise for the Nuneaton-born George Eliot and her novel, *Felix Holt, the Radical*. Holyoake praised Holt's "pride and simplicity... indomitableness and energy", dubbing Eliot as "the greatest [author] these Midland counties have nurtured, since the days of Shakespeare".[118]

In autumn 1869, Horatio was sent to Mason's Orphanage at Erdington in Birmingham, where he would remain for five years. This was a great, neo-classical building completed in July of that same year, with a central tower that stood over 200 feet high and statues of angels watching over the children at the four compass points of the roof. There were also 13 acres of playgrounds, fields and kitchen gardens, and it was large enough to house 230 pupils, boys and girls, to be educated in reading, writing, arithmetic, geography, and history, with additional household and domestic duties taught to the girls. There was no restriction whatever as to the locality, nationality or religious belief of the students, but it was a term of their admission that entrants be legitimate children.[119] The religious instruction was Christian, but not sectarian.

George Jacob sent Horatio's application off in November 1869. Victorian Britain was a society which repeatedly expected working-class people to plead for middle-class charity. To prosper, workers had to present themselves as respectable; as part of the so-called "deserving poor". As artisans rather than labourers, the Holyoakes had hoped all begging behind them. But in reality, the stain of poverty had returned. So we can imagine the frustration and even the bitterness as George Jacob solicited the votes and interests of the Governors on behalf of his nephew: Bottomley's father, he explained, "died in 1863, after recovery from an attack of mania, during which he was confined in the Bethlehem Hospital. The mother died suddenly in 1865, leaving two children of whom the above is the youngest".[120] For two years, his uncle explained, the family had been seeking to place Horatio with an orphanage, and the boy was "suffering morally for want of training". Holyoake described him as a "healthy, promising child, likely to turn out clever and, no doubt grateful".[121]

The founder of the orphanage was one Josiah Mason, a manufacturer of the metal hoops for key-rings known as split rings. Born in Kidderminster,[122] Mason had been the son of a weaver. He was 20 years Holyoake's senior, and from the 1820s had lived and worked in the same Birmingham streets, and had even been in the audience of some of Holyoake's socialist lectures.[123] His life's work, the promotion of education for the most vulnerable, was not so far from Holyoake's own Owenite belief in the virtue of education. And his gift to the orphanage was generous by any standards: besides the building itself, then valued at £60,000, he endowed 2,000 acres valued at £200,000 to pay for the college's annual expenses. To put this in context: the average annual salary in England at this time was still rather less than £100.

Holyoake was impressed. He noted the wooden baths and floors, intended to guard against the cold, and how the internal structures of the building – its roof-beams and gas and water pipes – had been left visible, for the teachers more to explain their workings.[124] Holyoake began a campaign for Mason to be knighted – as he was just a year later.[125]

Horatio was soon given an unpleasant reminder of the vulnerability of his new situation. On his first day the school was closed, for the burial of an orphan named Taylor.[126] Between 1871 and 1874[127] ten more pupils were buried at the Orphanage.

Adult visitors praised the institution. As a reporter for the *Birmingham Daily Post* noted: "Tender thoughtfulness and loving care is manifested in all respects for the comfort and happiness of the children. The Founder [Josiah Mason] knows all the children by name and is known and loved by them".[128] A second journalist, visiting not long before Horatio's arrival, was no less effusive about his meeting with the orphans: "Their writing is wonderfully neat, there is hardly a pin out of place in the whole school – and, as for blots – why they hardly know what they are!"[129] Others discerned a disciplinarian streak. Visiting in the 1870s a Birmingham educational officer saw that those whose handwriting was untidy were punished by having their knuckles rapped, and that canes and leather straps were used by the teachers.[130] In middle age, one of Bottomley's favourite sayings was, "I have learned to take my medicine".[131] The phrase has the ring of the institution at which he was educated.

Short for his age, with a heavy frame and a large head, he was a quiet boy, fond of reading. He had a quick superficial intelligence, but struggled to make friends. He enjoyed mathematics but not geography. He also liked athletics, including sprinting, winning (according to one account) "several prizes for the hundred yards".[132]

The children were allowed visitors on two days a year, one in January and the other in July, with visits requiring written permission in advance. There were other rules. A letter sent on Christmas Day from Bottomley to his uncle Jacob has survived: "You are allowed to send presents at any time, but they must be books, toys or fruit [but] nothing in the shape of pudding of any kind is allowed to come... I shall be very pleased with anything you can send".[133]

Another uncle, Walter Holyoake, lived with his wife Caroline in Birmingham, and they visited occasionally. Above all he wanted to see Florence, but London was too far away, and she did not once travel to the orphanage in all his time there.[134]

Nevertheless, his various families were thriving, in politics if not in business. Despite his caution, George Jacob had friends in France involved in attempts to bring down the dictatorship of Napoleon III, and he had gone so far as to test bombs intended for use in assassination attempts.[135] The news of the French defeat in the Franco-Prussian War and the abdication of Napoleon must have been a source of satisfaction.

If Bradlaugh also disliked the old regime, he disliked far more the press interest in the Commune. In a talk given at the Hall of Science in Old Street in 1871, he ignored the 20,000 Communards murdered by the new French government, instead criticising the uprising, with its demands for the "impossible", blaming them for the "violence". He criticised as malign the doctrine, which the Commune proposed, that nations were not a single body but an amalgam of hostile classes. He had read the "Address on the Civil War in France" delivered by a supporter, Karl Marx, and mangled it. Marx, he claimed, was in reality a supporter of the failed Bonaparte regime. As for Bradlaugh himself, he desired a republic in Britain and would work for it – but if there was no way to achieve it except via "bloody hands, fire and smoke and grim visage", he would rather turn away before it was too late.[136]

Meanwhile his attempts to make a living independent of journalism and politics were still unsuccessful: "After five years' severe struggle so severe as to repeatedly endanger my health – I find it utterly impossible to remain in business in the City in the face of the strong prejudice excited against me on political and religious grounds".[137]

By contrast, Horatio was starting to collect anecdotes in several of which he escaped from disasters of his own making. Age 13, so he would later claim, he had attempted to visit the girls' wing at night. The anecdote survives in the words of his later employee Henry Houston: "H. B. under cover of night left his own dormitory, accompanied by a friend and raided the girls' quarters by a circuitous route".[138] Horatio tried to escape through a window, dropping to the ground and hiding in a shrubbery. As the sun rose, Bottomley was dragged out. "He was given a severe thrashing, and sentenced to a week's bread and water in the clock tower of the orphanage, there to ruminate on the hazard of love".[139] Just 12 months after this incident is said to have occurred, a new wing was built at Mason's Orphanage, to separate male and female students.[140] Its construction suggests that some liaisons were indeed taking place.

For a child brought up in a city the size of London, free to travel wherever he was allowed, Bottomley's sense of incarceration within the orphanage must have been overpowering. He was required every day to remain within and never to walk beyond its bounds, and to be every hour in a set place. He had lost his parents; his home; and even the streets on which he had once walked.

On their 14th birthday, orphans were allowed to leave Mason's. Bottomley refused to wait. One winter day, long before 23 March came round, he slipped out of the building and ran away.[141] He made his way to his aunt Caroline's home. Long afterwards, he would recall this escape as one of the most glorious days of his life.[142]

His new family

Within a few weeks of this departure, on 10 April 1874, Bottomley's uncle Austin Holyoake died in London of tuberculosis. With mourners marching all the way from Holborn, he was buried at Highgate Cemetery. It was a secular service, written by Austin himself, the eulogy praising his adherence to "science and philosophy", rather than the fantasies of religion, but also stressing the inevitability of death ("all on earth must part"). Its conclusion: "The reward of a [good]… life is the conviction that our memory will be cherished. This is the only immortality of which we know".[143] Among the speakers was Charles Bradlaugh, declaring, "A quarter of a century's recollections, and 14 unbroken years of friendship, are now within that grave".[144] Horatio attended the funeral, and this was his first encounter with the man who would afterwards emerge as his "third father". On Bottomley's account, "I came up from school in connection with the funeral of one of Bradlaugh's most trusted and devoted allies, a relative of my own, Austin Holyoake, a younger brother of my distinguished uncle George Jacob Holyoake". There, Bradlaugh caught his eye. "I well remember how even in those early days I was impressed by the magnetic personality of the man; and how, as time went on, I fell more and more under his influence".[145] Bottomley grasped that – orphan though he was – he was connected, through his family, to figures of national importance. But why did Bottomley place all the significance of this realisation on Bradlaugh's shoulders rather than George Jacob Holyoake's, when the latter was his uncle and Bradlaugh had no direct connection to him?

At the time of this first encounter, Bradlaugh's name had been often in the press. He was president of London's Republican Club. He had stood a second time at Northampton, coming third with 1700 votes. In the public eye, though he disowned the red flag, rejected all talk of revolution, and used every opportunity to praise the intelligence of the Royal family,[146] Bradlaugh was the closest there was to an English Robespierre or Danton.

By 1874, Holyoake's reputation was still based on his imprisonment for blasphemy 30 years distant. He was just three years short of his 60th birthday. Bradlaugh was just 40, his involvement in the emerging social movements of the day both recent and obvious. It was a father that Horatio needed, and Bradlaugh seemed much better equipped to play this role. Bottomley was entranced by him. In the private museum of the artefacts of his triumphs that he kept in middle age were several portraits of himself and of Bradlaugh, interspersed like father and son, as if to prove their physical resemblance.[147] His need was so great that he would persuade himself that Bradlaugh really *was* his father, and that his parents had hidden this truth from him. When asked – for example by the journalist James Douglas – if he believed in life beyond the grave, this one-time product of a militant secularist home had a practised answer: "I am no religionist. You know that Bradlaugh was my father".[148]

So elaborate did the myth become that one version of it imagines a new mother also, the journalist Annie Besant: "If Charles Bradlaugh was my father and the lady you mention was my mother, I am more proud of my parents than ever".[149]

As an enduring controversy that dismayed Bradlaugh's children,[150] it is worth considering the arguments with care. Besant's role can be dealt with swiftly: she was 17 at the time of Horatio's birth, and would not meet Bradlaugh until after Austin Holyoake's funeral.

Why should Elizabeth Holyoake, the argument goes, have married William Bottomley, a lowly worker who was ill – unless she was concealing a relationship with a lover? In 1855 Bradlaugh had married Susannah Hooper, a brunette two years his senior. She became in middle age a chronic alcoholic and the marriage seems to have been unhappy.[151] Would two people both suffering in loveless relationships not seek mutual consolation? Horatio did not resemble his mother's brother George Jacob, nor it seemed her family – while he shared a high forehead and a large nose, lips and brow with Charles Bradlaugh.[152]

Although their respective faces in photographs do seem similar, the two men were different in other ways: Bradlaugh was over six foot,[153] while Bottomley was just five foot five.[154] No pictures survive of William, so we cannot say whether he and his son looked alike.

Even happy children sometime fantasise a concealed destiny. Horatio was orphaned, abandoned by his surviving family, placed in an institution that was locked at night, a kind of prison. At 13 he was released, then within weeks attended the funeral of an uncle. He discovered that within his family circle were people playing great roles in society. One leading figure was a charismatic and attractive public speaker, with all kinds of qualities lacking in the adults Horatio had known at the orphanage. How easy it was to conclude that Bradlaugh might have been, indeed must have been, his true father.

By imagining this secret paternity, Horatio Bottomley was beginning to create the conditions for his later advance. He was refusing to be cowed by his past, by his abandonment by his apparent parents and family – and by the shame of poverty. In place of death he was choosing life, and not just any life but in his uncle George Jacob Holyoake's life, as expanded by Charles Bradlaugh: the life of the writer and campaigner and figure of principle. But while it is one thing to tell oneself small and consoling lies, it is quite another to come to believe them, and to involve the whole world in them.

In identifying Bradlaugh as his father, Bottomley was doing something else as well: choosing from within the ideas around him. Mid-Victorian intellectual life was a sea of ebbs and flows, encompassing both Owenite rationalist socialism and his later spiritualism, communism, trade unionism, free-thought, republicanism, feminism, Liberal moderation and, on the right, imperialism, protectionism, and dreams of purging England of her Radical enemies. Of all these possible influences, Bottomley was choosing Bradlaugh's free-thought and republicanism. This decision would moor him. Yet that way of thinking was less generous than it first seemed. If, in the 1870s, Bradlaugh's social atheism was capable of becoming a majority view – the kindness of its age – the sense of possibility associated with that tradition would become ever less the longer Bottomley's life wore on.

Notes

1   By summer 2021, it had been renamed the Sly Old Fox.
2   G. J. Holyoake, *Sixty Years an Agitator's Life* (New York and London: Garland Publishing, 1984 edn), p. 15.
3   Holyoake, *Sixty Years*, p. 18.
4   Holyoake, *Sixty Years*, p. 19.
5   S. Pollard, 'The Decline of Shipbuilding on the Thames', *Economic History Review* 3/1 (1950), pp. 72–89. The shipowners responded to the strike by threatening a lockout. A. Aspinall, *The Early English Trade Unions* (London: Batchworth Press, 1949), p. 392.
6   E. P. Thompson, *The Making of the English Working Class* (London: Pelican, 1968), pp. 260–2.

7   'Ironfounders', *1835 Directory of Birmingham* (Birmingham: Wrightson and Webb, 1835).
8   L. E. Grugel, *George Jacob Holyoake: A Study in the Evolution of a Victorian Radical* (Philadelphia, PA: Porcupine Press, 1976), p. 1.
9   'Mr G. J. Holyoake', *Manchester Guardian*, 23 January 1906; Holyoake, *Sixty Years*, p. 19.
10 Holyoake, *Sixty Years*, pp. 13–15.
11 J. McCabe, *The Life and Letters of George Jacob Holyoake* (London: Watts & Co., 1906), pp. 10–11.
12 V. Skipp, *The Making of Victorian Birmingham* (Birmingham: Victor Skipp, 1983), pp. 128–9.
13 H. L. Beales, *The Early English Socialists* (London: Hamish Hamilton, 1933), pp. 62–7.
14 S. Pollard, 'Nineteenth-Century Co-operation: From Community Building to Shopkeeping', in A. Briggs and J. Saville (eds), *Essays in Labour History* (London: Macmillan, 1967), pp. 74–112, 105.
15 McCabe, *Life and Letters*, p. 15.
16 C. Howe, *George Jacob Holyoake's Journey of 1842* (Studley: History into Print, 2012), p. 9.
17 McCabe, *Life and Letters*, p. 24.
18 R. A. Davis and F. O'Hagan, *Robert Owen* (London: Bloomsbury, 2010), pp. 164–5.
19 McCabe, *Life and Letters*, p. 38.
20 Hollick emigrated to the United States (*Reasoner*, 3 June 1846), where he established a career as a "Medical Red Republican", publishing home health manuals which sold tens of thousands of copies. A. Haynes, 'The Trials of Frederick Hollis', *Journal of the History of Sexuality* 12/4 (2003), pp. 543–74.
21 Letter from F. Hollick, 5 February 1837. Holyoake papers, Bishopsgate Institute, Holyoake 1/1.
22 McCabe, *Life and Letters*, p. 41; D. Black and C. Ford, *1839: The Chartist Insurrection* (London: Unkant, 2012), pp. 94–6.
23 On 5 June 1839, a friend of Holyoake's family, John Watts, congratulated him on the marriage. "I see you seated beside your intellectual companion working a problem in mathematics…" Holyoake papers, Bishopsgate Institute, Holyoake 1/1.
24 Holyoake, *Sixty Years*, p. 71.
25 Letter from James Plant, 11 September 1840. Holyoake papers, Bishopsgate Institute, Holyoake 1/2.
26 Holyoake, *Sixty Years*, pp. 75–7.
27 McCabe, *Life and Letters*, p. 44.
28 Holyoake befriended the Sheffield poet and opponent of the Corn Laws, Ebenezer Elliott, who teased Holyoake, calling him a "Communist". Holyoake also wrote for the *Leeds Times*, edited by Samuel Smiles (later the author of *Self-Help*, a vastly successful guide to Victorian values of thrift and self-discipline). McCabe, *Life and Letters*, p. 51.
29 The Promoters of Freethought, *The History of the Fleet Street House* (London: The Promoters of Freethought, 1856), pp. 5–6.
30 Howe, *George Jacob*, p. 5.
31 Letter from William Galpin, 18 December 1841, Holyoake papers, Bishopsgate Institute, Holyoake 1/1.
32 Howe, *George Jacob*, pp. 1–2.
33 Howe, *George Jacob*, p. 62.
34 G. J. Holyoake, *The Last Trial for Atheism* (London: Trübner & Co., 1871), p. 13.
35 McCabe, *Life and Letters*, p. 63; Howe, *George Jacob*, p. 62.
36 McCabe, *Life and Letters*, p. 65.
37 Howe, *George Jacob*, p. 80.
38 McCabe, *Life and Letters*, p. 69.
39 Howe, *George Jacob*, p. 92; McCabe, *Life and Letters*, p. 72; *Reasoner*, 27 December 1848.
40 Howe, *George Jacob*, p. 103.
41 Howe, *George Jacob*, p. 112.

42 Howe, *George Jacob*, p. 109.

43 Holyoake, *Sixty Years*, p. 159.

44 McCabe, *Life and Letters*, p. 79.

45 McCabe, *Life and Letters*, p. 86.

46 McCabe, *Life and Letters*, pp. 181–3.

47 *Reasoner*, 3 June 1846.

48 *Reasoner*, 3 June 1846.

49 *Reasoner*, 24 June 1846.

50 McCabe, *Life and Letters*, p. 305. In 1846, Marx and Engels included Holyoake with Thomas More, the Levellers and Robert Owen in a list of the greatest "English communists". E. Hobsbawm, *How to Change the World* (London: Penguin, 2011), p. 421.

51 J. Saville, *1848: The British State and the Chartist Movement* (Cambridge: Cambridge University Press, 1987), p. 109.

52 London: Effingham Wilson, 1854; L. Barrow, *Independent Spirits: Spiritualism and English Plebeians, 1850–1910* (London: Routledge, 1986), p. 191.

53 "Secularism is the study of promoting human welfare by material means; measuring human welfare by the utilitarian rule, and making the service of others a duty of life", G. J. Holyoake, *The Principles of Secularism* (London: Austin & Co., 1871), p. 11.

54 Samuel William Bottomley, a boy living at Oxley-place, Bermondsey, was a prosecution witness at a theft trial in May 1839. Proceedings of the Central Criminal Court, 13 May 1839, p. 165. There are other fleeting press references to Bottomleys living in London in the 18th century, for example a William Bottomley, builder, of Bermondsey, who placed a notice in the *London Gazette* on 2 February 1793, p. 101.

55 Enumeration Schedule 48, Borough of Southwark, Township of Bermondsey, 1841 census.

56 Pollard, 'The Decline of Shipbuilding'.

57 C. Dickens, *Great Expectations* (London: Chapman and Hall, 1860), Chapter 19.

58 Hyman, *The Rise and Fall*, p. 120. Henry J. Houston, for many years Bottomley's confidant, recalls Bottomley telling him that his father had published a book full of diagrams, *Bottomley on Tailor's Cutting*. Houston, *The Real Horatio Bottomley*, p. 30. No copy of that manuscript has survived.

59 J. Maclochlainn, *The Victorian Tailor: Techniques and Patterns* (London: Batsford, 2011), p. 32.

60 A. Fried and R. M. Elman (eds), *Charles Booth's London* (London: Hutchinson, 1969), p. 101.

61 For an account of the Association's foundation, *Reynolds' Political Instructor*, 16 March 1850.

62 E. Jones (ed.), *Notes to the People 1851–2* (London: Merlin Press, 1967), p. 921.

63 Jones, *Notes to the People*, p. 746.

64 Horatio Holyoake to Catherine Holyoake, 22 April 1855 (but catalogued as 22 April 1885), National Library of Australia M392.

65 Today the site is occupied by the Imperial War Museum.

66 A. Godley, 'Singer in Britain: The Diffusion of Sewing Machine Technology and its Impact on the Clothing Industry in the United Kingdom 1860–1905', draft paper, Reading University, May 1995.

67 Such clothing might have been handed down between generations or purchased second-hand, perhaps at the markets on Petticoat or Rosemary Lane, at which shoes could be purchased for 2d in 1851, trousers from 6d and dress coats from around a shilling. *Mayhew's London: Being Selections from 'London Labour and the London Poor' by Henry Mahyew* (London: Spring Books, 1951), pp. 214–16.

68 Hyman, *The Rise and Fall*, p. 8.

69 D. Lavin, *Bradlaugh Contra Marx: Radicalism versus Socialism in the First International* (London: Socialist History Society, 2011), p. 4. Marx himself was less enthusiastic.

70 A. W. Besant, *Charles Bradlaugh: A Sketch of His Life and Work* (San Francisco, CA: Reader's Library, 1891), pp. 6–8; B. Niblett, *Dare to Stand Alone: The Story of Charles*

Bradlaugh (Oxford: Kramedart Press, 2010), pp. 8–9; H. Bonner, *Charles Bradlaugh: A Record of His Life and Work* (London: T. Fisher and Unwin, 1908), p. 22.

71   Niblett, *Dare to Stand Alone*, p. 22; Bonner, *Charles Bradlaugh*, p. 72.

72   "For many years the fault beset me of crowding too many objects on the canvas of my speeches". Holyoake, *Sixty Years*, p. 137.

73   A sign of the splits in the secularist movement was the publication of a pro-Holyoake pamphlet, J. Robertson, *Secularists and their Slanderers: or, the Investigator Examine* (London: J. B. Bebbington, 1858).

74   McCabe, *Life and Letters*, p. 301.

75   H. McCabe, *John Stuart Mill: Socialist* (Montreal: McGill-Queen's University Press, 2021).

76   As early as 1847, Mill had drafted a letter to Holyoake, with a view to publication in the *Reasoner*. T. Larsen, *John Stuart Mill: A Secular Life* (Oxford: Oxford University Press, 2018), p. 202.

77   F. E. Mineka and D. N. Lindley, *The Collected Works of John Stuart Mill, Volume XV – The Later Letters of John Stuart Mill 1849–1873* (London: Routledge and Kegan Paul, 1972), p. 132. Mill also corresponded with Bradlaugh. Bradlaugh papers, Bishopsgate Institute, Bradlaugh 201B.

78   Bradlaugh too was ill, complaining in spring and summer 1859 of rheumatic fever. Bonner, *Charles Bradlaugh*, p. 95.

79   Holyoake papers, Bishopsgate Institute, Holyoake 2/10 (1860).

80   As late as 1881, the proportion of London-born people in the population of Bethnal Green was higher than in any other London district. G. Stedman Jones, *Outcast London: A Study in the Relationship between Classes in Victorian Society* (London: Penguin, 1984 edn), p. 132.

81   A. Bloomfield, *Memoir of Charles James Bloomfield DD Bishop of London, with Selections from his Correspondence, volume 1* (London: John Murray, 1863), p. 244.

82   Hyman, *The Rise and Fall*, pp. 8–10. Symons, *Horatio Bottomley*, p. 11. There exists an 1889 photograph of Grace Madeline, taken at the Webster Bros photographic studio in Clapham Common and then sent by her to a cousin Eveline. Grace wears a dress, a white shirt with a neck-pin and has tight, curly, brown hair.

83   Julian Symons describes the cause of William Bottomley's death as tuberculosis. Symons, *Horatio Bottomley*, p. 11. However, the family's application to Mason's Orphanage, dated 30 November 1869, states that William died "after recovery from an attack of mania, during which he was confined in the Bethlehem Hospital". It is implausible that the family would have simply invented an episode that the governors of the orphanage would have considered a more demeaning cause of death. Houston, *The Real Horatio Bottomley*, p. 33; Hyman, *The Rise and Fall*, p. 11.

84   In the burial register, William's residence is given as Gilbert Cottage, Field Road, Forest Gate. Houston, *The Real Horatio Bottomley*, p. 31. Field Road is about a mile and a half to the northeast of Bethnal Green, and in the immediate vicinity of today's West Ham Cemetery which has been open since 1857.

85   Houston, *The Real Horatio Bottomley*, p. 32.

86   Houston, *The Real Horatio Bottomley*, p. 31.

87   'West Ham: Roman Catholicism, Nonconformity and Judaism', in W. R. Powell (ed.), *A History of the County of Essex: Volume 6* (London: Victoria County History, 1973), pp. 123–41.

88   Hyman, *The Rise and Fall*, p. 8; Houston, *The Real Horatio Bottomley*, p. 30.

89   Symons, *Horatio Bottomley*, p. 11.

90   Bonner, *Charles Bradlaugh*, p. 98.

91   Circular, April 1860. Bradlaugh papers, Bishopsgate Institute, Bradlaugh 78.

92   Niblett, *Dare to Stand Alone*, p. 34.

93   Niblett, *Dare to Stand Alone*, pp. 36–7.

94   G. J. Holyoake, *Sixty Years an Agitator's Life: Volume II* (London: Fisher Unwin, 1902), p. 294.

95 Bonner, *Charles Bradlaugh*, p. 333.

96 In 1868, Holyoake wrote of his own ineffective candidacy for Birmingham. "For 36 years the representation of Birmingham had been in the hands of the middle class and though the working class were twenty times more numerous than they, it had never occurred to the middle class that the industrious majority were entitled to any personal representation". Holyoake, *Sixty Years: Volume II*, p. 151. For all Bradlaugh's attacks on the institutions of the monarchy and the church, for all his insistence that he represented the interests of the poor, he was never as confident as Holyoake in appealing to the shared class experiences of his Radical audience.

97 R. Harrison, *Before the Socialists: Studies in Labour and Politics 1861–1881* (London: Routledge & Kegan Paul, 1965), p. 6.

98 Bonner, *Charles Bradlaugh*, p. 130. Bradlaugh papers, Bishopsgate Institute, Bradlaugh 140.

99 Some of Leverson's correspondence with John Stuart Mill appears in F. E. Mineka and D. N. Lindley (eds), *The Later Letters of John Stuart Mill 1849–1883: Vol. 3* (Toronto: University of Toronto Press, 1972).

100 Leverson fled the country four years later, to pre-empt a fraud trial for embezzling his own clients. Niblett, *Dare to Stand Alone*, p. 4; Lavin, *Bradlaugh Contra Marx*, p. 6.

101 Bonner, *Charles Bradlaugh*, pp. 100–1.

102 C. Bradlaugh, 'Poverty', *National Reformer*, 30 May 1863.

103 Symons gives the cause of Elizabeth's death as congestion of the brain. He does not provide a reference. Symons, *Horatio Bottomley*, p. 11. Houston, who knew Bottomley, states that the cause was cancer. Houston, *The Real Horatio Bottomley*, p. 30.

104 Hyman, *The Rise and Fall*, p. 10.

105 In 1874, a visitor to London's art galleries commended Walter Holyoake's painting 'Sanctuary', in the following terms: "A party of fugitives have taken refuge in a cathedral; their pursuers are at hand, but are stayed at the critical moment by a monk, who holds aloft the crucifix, and commands them in the name of Christ to halt. The grouping of the figures is effective, and the figure of a bending woman on the left is exceedingly graceful". *Western Mail*, 27 March 1874. Holyoake's 'In the Front Row at the Opera' focuses on three glamorous young women, two clutching fans and with a third showing a cross above her cleavage. It is reproduced in G. Reynolds (ed.), *Painters of the Victorian Scene* (London: R. T. Batsford, 1953), plate 79.

106 C. Wood, *The Dictionary of Victorian Painters* (Woodbridge: Antique Collectors' Club, 1978), p. 232.

107 Hyman, *The Rise and Fall*, p. 10.

108 Hyman, *The Rise and Fall*, pp. 10–11; Houston, *The Real Horatio Bottomley*, p. 32.

109 Hyman, *The Rise and Fall*, p. 11.

110 Symons, *Horatio Bottomley*, p. 11.

111 Niblett, *Dare to Stand Alone*, p. 47. In 1867, Bradlaugh was reduced to the humiliating expedient of having to borrow £150 from his father-in-law. Bradlaugh papers, Bishopsgate Institute, Bradlaugh 148.

112 Bonner, *Charles Bradlaugh*, p. 299.

113 Niblett, *Dare to Stand Alone*, p. 48; Bonner, *Charles Bradlaugh*, pp. 223–5.

114 Until the Redistribution of Seats Act 1885, certain constituencies elected up to four members of Parliament, with electors casting up to one fewer vote than the number of seats to be filled.

115 Among the letters in George Jacob Holyoake's archive is the following to Bradlaugh, dated 28 April 1871: "As my Brothers are known to the public in their own professions, it is my duty to them, as the Head of the Family, not to have imputed to me opinions I do not hold. This they desire. They have independence and prefer their own individuality, and because I respect it, I am sure my Brother Austin has not authorised you to insult me in his name". Holyoake papers, Bishopsgate Institute, Holyoake 1/4. Bradlaugh papers, Bishopsgate Institute, Bradlaugh 231.

116 Niblett, *Dare to Stand Alone*, p. 57.

117 G. J. Holyoake, *Working Class Representation: Its Conditions and Consequences* (Birmingham: Guest, 1868), p. 9.
118 H. Kingstone, 'The Two Felixes: Narrational Irony and the Question of Radicalism in Felix Holt and Address to Working Men, by Felix Holt', *George Eliot Review* (2013), pp. 629–640. Whether Eliot would have reciprocated Holyoake's praise is not at all clear; the Radicals in her fiction – not just Holt, but Ladislaw in *Middlemarch* – are permitted to win no more than partial victories, their young hopefulness "much checked" as they age. G. Eliot, *Middlemarch* (London: Wordsworth, 1987), p. 686.
119 *The Builder*, 18 September 1869, p. 744; Symons, *Horatio Bottomley*, pp. 12–3.
120 Hyman, *The Rise and Fall*, p. 11.
121 Symons, *Horatio Bottomley*, p. 12.
122 G. J. Limbrick, *Deeds of Love* (London: Word Works, 2013), pp. 10–16.
123 Holyoake, *Sixty Years: Volume II*, p. 295.
124 Holyoake, *Sixty Years: Volume II*, p. 296.
125 'Mr G. J. Holyoake', *Manchester Guardian*, 23 January 1906.
126 Houston, *The Real Horatio Bottomley*, p. 34, Symons, *Horatio Bottomley*, p. 12.
127 Limbrick, *Deeds of Love*, p. 62.
128 *Birmingham Daily Post*, 2 August 1869.
129 Hyman, *The Rise and Fall*, p. 13.
130 Hyman, *The Rise and Fall*, p. 13; Symons, *Horatio Bottomley*, p. 14.
131 Hyman, *The Rise and Fall*, p. 15.
132 Hyman, *The Rise and Fall*, p. 15.
133 Symons, *Horatio Bottomley*, p. 15.
134 Hyman, *The Rise and Fall*, p. 15.
135 J. Newsinger, *Fenianism in Mid-Victorian Britain* (London: Pluto, 1994), p. 49.
136 Lavin, *Bradlaugh Contra Marx*, pp. 8–9.
137 Niblett, *Dare to Stand Alone*, p. 63.
138 Houston, *The Real Horatio Bottomley*, p. 36.
139 Houston, *The Real Horatio Bottomley*, p. 36.
140 *The Builder*, 18 September 1869, p. 744.
141 Houston, *The Real Horatio Bottomley*, p. 36; Hyman, *The Rise and Fall*, p. 17.
142 Hyman, *The Rise and Fall*, p. 17.
143 Barrow, *Independent Spirits*, p. 234.
144 Niblett, *Dare to Stand Alone*, pp. 80–1.
145 Bottomley, *Bottomley's Book*, p. 165.
146 Niblett, *Dare to Stand Alone*, p. 69.
147 Felstead, *Horatio Bottomley*, p. 9.
148 Symons, *Horatio Bottomley*, p. 15.
149 Houston, *The Real Horatio Bottomley*, p. 29.
150 On 18 May 1915 one of Bradlaugh's friends Harry Lees Sumner wrote to Bradlaugh's daughter Hypatia Bradlaugh-Bonner to describe a chance meeting. "Today I met on a train a man who one would correctly call a gentleman". In the course of their conversation this gentleman remarked that Bottomley was Bradlaugh's illegitimate son. "I don't often swear", Sumner reported, "but I said, 'That's a damnable lie. Charles Bradlaugh was no more his father than I am yours. If you want evidence, I will give you Bradlaugh's gifted daughter's address'. He didn't need it, and as a gentleman, accepted my denial". Bradlaugh/3005, Bishopsgate Institute.
151 Susannah Hooper continued to live and sleep every night with Bradlaugh; they were not separated until 1870. Bonner, *Charles Bradlaugh*, pp. 50, 346.
152 The case for Bradlaugh as Bottomley's father is put in Hyman, *The Rise and Fall*, pp. 7–8. Though the argument for Bradlaugh's paternity seems speculative at best, often rooted in little more than a sexist disdain for Hooper's worth as a wife, the resemblance in photos is there.
153 Robertson, *Secularists*, p. 16.
154 Symons, *Horatio Bottomley*, p. 12.

3
FIRST STEPS IN BUSINESS AND POLITICS

Horatio lived for a short time in Edgbaston with his uncle and aunt Walter and Caroline, working as an office boy for a builder named Smith, with premises in Ryland Road, Birmingham.[1] He then stayed with relatives[2] in London. At the start of *Bottomley's Book* he says that these relatives – who must have included his artist uncle William[3] – put "much deliberation" into planning out an artistic career for him, but that after his "dismal" failure to justify their expectations, they accepted the need to find him a commercial apprenticeship.[4]

Before his 15th birthday he was working for a Parisian haberdasher with a Cheapside office to the east of St Paul's,[5] on Wood Street, pushing a barrow of fittings and trimmings round the City, while a more senior employee met from buyers from the great department stores to persuade them to order items. "Somehow or other", Bottomley recalled, "I could never grow enthusiastic over fringes and passementeries, and often, after a hard day's tramp, as I sat in the office and pondered over my lot, I felt that life itself was about as empty as many – or rather, most – of the cardboard boxes around me".[6]

Still despairing of his prospects, Bottomley met a "mysterious and impressive young gentleman" who worked in a solicitor's office, and invited Horatio to join him. "Even now I can clearly picture him proudly surveying me from the giddy height of the office stool, whilst I stood, spell-bound, listening to his startling revelations of the mysteries of the legal profession and its golden opportunities".[7] With reluctance, he declined the offer.

Soon afterwards the haberdasher told Bottomley that they were moving. He was to transport all their property in his barrow (or "truck") to their new premises. Left alone to this heavy work Horatio revolted: "Meditating mournfully upon the situation, I at length reached the corner of King Street where, in obedience to the policeman regulating the traffic, I brought my truck to a temporary

DOI: 10.4324/9781003306085-3

halt. I say 'temporary', because, when passing the spot some thousands of times since, I have noticed that the truck no longer stands there".[8]

Bottomley found a post with a solicitor's firm on Coleman Street in the City. This was not a large office; besides Horatio there was only the solicitor and his clerk[9] – but to the young office boy's vigorous imagination this must have seemed a complete transformation of his prospects. After months of menial work, he was a salaried professional. Before he could get comfortable, however, this business too suffered a crisis. The solicitor, says Bottomley, was a drunk while his clerk was a crook, writing to local businesses as if he had been appointed the representative of some department in local government, requiring them to pay rates on their property. If they declined, he sent across printed demands, followed by reminders and final notices. Some did indeed pay this fraudulent charge, but in the end "two gentlemen made their appearance upon the scene and requested our Managing Clerk to accompany them to the Guildhall". It was spring 1875, and Horatio was once more out of work.[10]

Bottomley worked for a time as an engraver for the *Illustrated London News* and *The Graphic*,[11] perhaps at his uncle William's recommendation. He lived for a time at Johnson's Court on Fleet Street with his uncle Austin's widow Alice, a singer and actress who would star in the first English language adaptation of Ibsen's play *Ghosts*[12] (she played Helene Alving, a philanthropist who praises the virtues of her dead alcoholic husband). Bottomley would remain an admirer of the theatre all the rest of his life.

Bradlaugh and the Holyoakes had by this time reconciled, Bradlaugh having circulated an appeal for funds for Austin's widow and children.[13] In 1875 he would donate £200 of his own money to a retirement fund for George Jacob.[14]

In 1876, Bottomley became ill and was sent in the autumn or winter of that year to convalesce for a short time in Brighton, where he worked in a jeweller's shop. In this era every self-respecting town had its own local debating society and many also had a local speaker's corner, where various denominations of Christians and sometimes free-thinkers would proselytise, with debates held between the political parties.[15] Horatio joined one such society and spoke one evening on the question: "Can anything justify a man in telling a lie?" He mugged up for his presentation by reading a paper, "What Is a Lie?",[16] delivered earlier that year in London by the barrister and colonial administrator Sir James Fitzjames Stephen.

No record of Bottomley's speech exists, but Stephen's – its model – is available. Considering Bottomley's growing fascination with his own paternity and his coming willingness to lie about it, it is worth exploring Stephen's argument. Here was a formidable figure, an Anglican and a Liberal who had in 1872 been handed the authority of Empire over the lives of millions, to draft India's laws of evidence and contract.

Stephen's best-known essay was a rejoinder to Mill's *On Liberty*, which criticised that pamphlet for its Radicalism and urged his assumed Liberal readers to reject it. "There are a vast number of matters", Stephen wrote, "in respect of which men ought not to be free; they are fundamentally unequal, and they are not brothers at all".[17]

So far, this book has taken care to explain the far-left of mid-Victorian politics, but there was a centre-left too. In contrast to the Chartists or Owenites, mainstream Liberalism was united by the belief that the balance of parliamentary reform in 1832 had been right. That argument appealed to the urban and industrial rich, who wanted the franchise, in order to advance their interests as against those of the landed aristocracy. It appealed to some newly enfranchised voters. It also appealed to former Whigs whose politics emphasised ideology not interest – i.e. support for Parliament over the Crown, for the rights of Nonconformist Christians. Mainstream Liberals may have despised the Conservatives and the class of rural aristocrats at that party's head, but they saw behind Chartism the threat that if workers were given the vote, their representatives would demand expensive reforms – pensions, health care, work for the unemployed. James Stephen was articulating a vision of England in which the propertied would continue to rule and the interests of the urban poor would go unacknowledged.

Stephen's paper on lies was written within that broad approach, and in a schoolmasterly style, at times arch, at times pedantic. Its author insisted that much of what we call lying does not deserve the name, let alone any reprimand. A lie is defined as an untruth told in order to deceive another. Therefore it is no real lie to tell a blatant falsehood when your opponent is on guard – as for example when a statesman seeks to persuade his country to go to war. Obviously, such a politician will lie; no one should believe anything they said. The opportunity for harm is therefore modest. Perhaps the most striking passage comes when Stephen speculates on the phenomenon of a child whose wealth is much less than his circumstances, for example a young boy asked to work in the garden of a rich person's townhouse. Suppose this boy declares, "All this belongs to me". This would be harmless, argues Stephen: the boy is doing nothing worse than "indulging in a delightful daydream".[18] Sometimes, a lie should be permitted.

Stephen's partial toleration of lying was not the whole of the Victorian attitude towards deceit. We can compare Melmotte, the anti-hero of Anthony Trollope's 1875 novel *The Way We Live Now*, a politician and a businessman who fraudulently invests a fortune supposedly given to his daughter in an attempt to save his business empire. To effect this transaction he forges various signatures, including those of his daughter and his clerk. Born poor, the son of a "noted coiner in the New York", Melmotte had chosen even to masquerade as a gentleman. Ruined and unmasked, he poisons himself. The moral of Trollope's book could hardly have been missed by its readers. Here the daydream – that a mere commoner might make himself rich – has become more than a passing fancy, but rather an incentive for someone to pretend to be something other than what he is.[19] Melmotte is denounced and humiliated. Readers would end his book with the reassurance that liars were punished.

At this time Bottomley's various relatives were all doing their best to keep him to a straight path. More than at any time afterwards he was in Bradlaugh's and Holyoake's care, and that of the wider secularist movement. Holyoake had always aimed his message at those self-taught workers who were coming to free thought by way of Nonconformist Christianity in its many forms. He expected his readers to be familiar with the works of the Liberal economists Adam Smith and David Ricardo, of the Liberal philosopher John Stuart Mill, and of Charles Darwin and his populariser Thomas Huxley.[20] Holyoake cast his nephew in the role of apprentice and expected him too to attend secularist lectures at the Hall of Science.[21]

Later in life Horatio would speak with some bitterness of all the improving books[22] he was made to read, including Mill and the biologist Herbert Spencer, another Darwinian populariser. To one journalist, he later claimed that J. R. Amberley's *An Analysis of Religious Belief*[23] was the only book from this time that he remembered. This was a comparative account of the various religions, and Amberley was a genealogist of beliefs, less interested in their truth or falsehood than categorising them according to such external phenomena as Religious Feeling, Adoration, Sacrifice, Festival and Rites at Puberty. Religious Feeling Amberley defined as the "desire felt by the human race in general to establish a relationship between itself and those superhuman or supernatural powers upon whose will it supposes the court of nature and the wellbeing of men to be dependent".[24] Examples were cited from South African villages, Jewish prophecies, Parsee rituals and Chinese customs (all as recorded by English visitors). The book was anthropological, encyclopaedic and wide-ranging, promising the quick accumulation of knowledge – which was perfect for this restless and imaginative young man.[25]

An unsigned review of Amberley's book, less than enthusiastic and in all likelihood written by Bradlaugh himself, had appeared in the *National Reformer*. That piece complained about the lack of footnotes and possible plagiarism, hinting that its treatment of the life of Jesus had been stolen from free-thinker works: "In many parts of the two volumes we recognise words extremely familiar to us, which have been adopted by the late author without any measure of acknowledgment of the sources from whence he drew".[26]

Later this same year a small number of articles appeared in the paper, under the initials "H. B." These were summaries of lectures delivered by the English positivist and recent supporter of the Paris Commune, Professor Edward Beesly. H. B. summarised the talks faithfully, noting Beesly's praise for the French philosopher Auguste Comte. The lectures, the author concluded, ought to be of particular interest to the wives and daughters of working men, but they "I am sorry to say, have been hitherto sadly in the minority".[27]

Annie Besant had come across the *National Reformer* at Edward Truelove's bookseller at 256 High Holborn,[28] and wrote to the journal saying she wished to join the National Secular Society. She heard Bradlaugh speak at the Hall of Science and was struck by his "stern, strong face, the massive head, the keen eyes". Warned to expect a "blatant agitator and ignorant demagogue", she was struck rather by his "sarcasm, pathos, passion".[29]

Besant was a young married woman separated from her husband, the Reverend Frank Besant, when she approached Bradlaugh. They met in his rooms, and

Bradlaugh told her, "You have thought yourself into atheism without knowing it".[30]

In late 1876, a bookseller named Henry Cook had been arrested and prosecuted for selling a pamphlet, *The Fruits of Philosophy*, written some 40 years before by the US physician Charles Knowlton, and sold in England ever since. It began with that familiar Victorian complaint (traceable back to the economist and philosopher Thomas Malthus) that there were too many people on the planet: "If population be not restrained by some great physical calamity, such as we have reason to hope will not hereafter be visited upon the children of men, or by some *moral restraint*, the time will come when the earth cannot support its inhabitants". The most controversial parts of the book were those in which were discussed methods of contraception, including "withdrawal", the condom, or as the pamphlet termed it the "baudruche" ("used to secure from syphilitic affections"), and the application of a contraceptive injection, with zinc sulphate "or any salt that acts chemically on the semen".[31]

The plates to this pamphlet were owned by the secularist printer Charles Watts, and the question therefore arose as to what stance the movement should take in response to the prosecution. Bradlaugh was happy to fight a free speech battle, though he admitted to disliking the pamphlet's "style" (he considered salacious its detailed discussion of bodies and sex). George Jacob Holyoake also warned against such a fight – in his case on the grounds that it had been written by a "quack".[32] But Besant urged the men to stand firm: "We did not like the pamphlet, but to stop it was to stop all".[33] She pointed out that leading secularists had long been Malthusians, including Bradlaugh himself. Birth control was their strategy against poverty. The secularist leaders had a duty to explain to the poor how to put their lives in order and to educate them; they had no choice but to defend the pamphlet.

When Bradlaugh and Besant re-published Knowlton's pamphlet,[34] they were arrested and prosecuted for publishing an obscene work, the trial starting on 18 June 1877.[35] Bradlaugh insisted the pamphlet was of the greatest interest to the poor: "I was born amongst them... I have had no University to polish my tongue... I plead her simply for the class to which I belong, and for the right to tell them what may redeem their poverty and alleviate their misery".[36] The jury's verdict was ambiguous: they found that the book had been published to deprave public morals, but that the defendants had had no corrupt motive. To the judge this meant guilty. He sentenced the defendants to six months imprisonment, offering a stay if they promised to cease publication pending an appeal – which they agreed to do.

The trial is often presented as a vindication of the secularists, and the decision not to jail them as a sign of the long ascent of Victorian liberalism, in parallel to the success of George Eliot's novels or of the philosophical works of Mill or Herbert Spencer. The latter's tract *The Morals of Trade* was being written as the trial began; it had as its subject the "illicit practices", the "venial deception" and the "lies acted or uttered" that were, he warned, the practical reality of commercial capitalism.

He called for a new standard of "civic distinction", a "purified public opinion", in which "industrial growth" was relegated and a "more moral public opinion cultivated". In such a different society, "the greatest homage" would "be given to those who concentrate their energies and their means to the noblest ends" – which meant Spencer's own ends, those of widespread education.[37] Surely, in such a society, Bradlaugh would have been well rewarded for a lifetime's promotion of ideas, undistracted by the need for fortune-seeking. In this very broad perspective at least, he and Besant were swimming with the most Liberal tide of the times, and towards first-wave feminism, even when the precise idea they were publicising (that the poor should be permitted to control their own fertility) was still too forward and too daring to escape censure and gain widespread acceptance.

There is however another way to read the trial – not from the viewpoint of the Radicals themselves, but from the perspective of today. For structured into the secularist defence of Knowlton were certain assumptions, including that the best way to deal with poverty was to preach sexual abstinence, since the inequality of the classes could be assumed into the indefinite future, as could the impossibility of decent wages or free health care, etc. From that perspective, the Knowlton trial becomes a story not of Besant or Bradlaugh's bravery, but of something else. Contrary to what Bradlaugh told the court, they were *for* not *of* the suffering poor, and they refused to imagine a future that would be more equal than their own times.

The trial did have the effect of increasing the audience for secularist and atheist ideas. Before the prosecution *The Fruits of Philosophy* was selling 700 copies a year. Between prosecution and trial, it sold 125,000.[38] The two had represented themselves, and the judge Lord Cockburn commended Bradlaugh for the "straightforward" way in which he had conducted his own case.[39] Yet the outcome was equivocal for them. They had exhausted themselves battling to defend a text that Bradlaugh was always dubious about. They were denounced in the press and smeared by hostile journalists.

Annie Besant felt the pain of the insults the most. In February 1878 her estranged husband Frank sued for custody of their children, Mabel and Digby. This time the trial judge, Sir George Jessel, was hostile throughout. His criticisms began at once, when she proposed once more to represent herself. Jessel denounced her refusal to instruct counsel as a "shocking waste of the time of the Court; it would be useless for the lady to attempt to argue the case, as it involves some very nice points of law".[40] He acknowledged Besant's love for her children, but explained in his decision that he must as a "man of the world" consider the stigma that must attach to Mabel, in having for a mother a woman such as Besant. *The Fruits of Philosophy*, he explained, had been an "immoral" book, and it was the court's duty to protect Mabel from such associations. The book had suggested that women might have sex without repercussions: it "would be subversive of all human civilised society", so Jessel held, "if the female population of our country were once imbued with the idea that they might safely indulge in unchaste intercourse without fear of any of the consequences such intercourse entails upon them".[41] Here was the voice of *The Times* and the *Telegraph*, indeed of all the great

newspapers of the day, and of significant blocks of middle-class opinion standing behind them. Custody was granted to Frank Besant – and this was not the
only harm that Jessel inflicted. He also refused permission for a divorce. Annie
remained married until Frank's death 40 years later.[42]

Bradlaugh and Besant submitted to the decision. Bradlaugh's wife Susannah
had died as the trial was prepared, but rather than re-marrying, he chose to
sustain with Besant an intense platonic friendship. They always slept in different
houses, but every day Bradlaugh would walk to Besant's home, where they studied together or played cards in the same room until late, when Bradlaugh walked
home. Chaperoned by Bradlaugh's daughters, they sometimes walked along the
Thames, or took trips to Windsor or Broxbourne. As close as Bradlaugh and
Besant were, they never allowed friendship to develop into romance.[43]

Bottomley's account of this period, written four decades later, captures the
emotions felt by Bradlaugh himself and by those around him. These were the
days of Bradlaugh's calumny and persecution, he recalled: "Respectable people
passed by him on the other side; the Press noticed him only to revile and libel
him; priests and politicians, if they mentioned his name at all, did so with a lie
upon their tongues". Only a small tribe of believers sustained him, "And yet
those of us who knew him – anticipating the verdict of history – felt that in him
we had found a great and wonderful man – a born leader of men".[44]

But how did Bradlaugh feel about young Bottomley? Bottomley never says –
which is, in its way, revealing. The whole history of the secularist movement was
one of intensity of friendships: George Jacob and Bradlaugh, Austin Holyoake
and Bradlaugh, Bradlaugh and Besant. And some were friendships between older
and younger people: Bradlaugh was just 17 when he first met George Jacob.
When Horatio sought him out, Bradlaugh was still in his early 40s, in between,
he had been both mentee and mentor. If the young secularist Bottomley had
shown the older some sign, however latent, of talent as journalist, where was the
patient encouragement? Instead what we have evidence for is of a somewhat less
equal relationship, of great longing met with by a complete absence of interest.

There is less suggestion still that Bradlaugh ever encouraged Horatio's conviction that Bradlaugh was his father. This impetuous and generous person was
more willing than most Victorians to defy convention. Had he believed that he
was in the presence of his son, he would have loved him – if not for the boy's
sake, then for the sake of Elizabeth (who must in this telling have been a lover)
or else for his former mentor George Jacob Holyoake's sake.

In the event, Charles Bradlaugh did little to encourage this ardent young dis-
ciple. Indeed, he rebuked him. We do not know why – but we do know what he
said, to George Jacob: "Young Bottomley will turn out a bad man".[45]

Stepping away from Bradlaugh's influence

Nevertheless, Bottomley was being shaped by the politics of his parents and
their friends. He inherited a party and a label ("Independent Liberal") as well as

certain cultural forms. He understood from a young age how to found a newspaper, how to write it and pay for it. He was equipped with a fascination for those popular institutions that imitated parliamentary democracy: speaker's corners, suburban parliaments. But there were also aspects of the secular Radical Liberal tradition that he was already beginning to resist, even as a teenager. His shaping heroes had been the authors of books as often as they were the editors of newspapers.[46] "My tastes", he would later boast, "have always been literary, journalistic, and political".[47] Journalistic he was and political, undoubtedly. But he was too impatient to read widely.

The milieu in which Bottomley was formed was one of working-class education, which emphasised the deferring of gratification. After all, to reject religion, you had to be able to read and to criticise it. You had to know the main authors and the defining theories of any tradition that you intended to debate. If you wanted to understand the Conservatives, then you must read Burke, Bulwer-Lytton, and Disraeli. Time spent on self-improvement was time well spent, a life thrown away on leisure activities was a life lost. The Holyoakes and the Bradlaughs spoke of time wasted with the same horror with which a religious person spoke of sin.

By contrast, from the mid-1870s onwards Bottomley was an avid follower of horse-racing, who also played billiards, attended the theatre and got drunk with friends. He did not cleave to the Chartist doctrine of "really useful knowledge" – which insisted that certain ideas would guide workers to the means of their liberation. Bottomley yearned to be rich. He could not fathom Bradlaugh's and Besant's innocent relationship, nor their interest in ideas. He had no intention of deferring his gratifications, whether of drink, food or sex.

Horatio next worked as an office boy and general clerk at an iron works, Messrs Leate, Edwards, and Norman of Euston Road.[48] From autumn 1878, he lived in Battersea.[49]

London at this time was expanding rapidly. A century before, Somers Town to the north of Kings Cross had been countryside.[50] Forty years before, trade unionists had met on Copenhagen Fields, the expansive meadow-land to the north and east of Euston Road, to march in support the Tolpuddle Martyrs. The Fields had been built over.

The London underground was more than a decade old, but it didn't yet pass under the Thames, so Bottomley had a commute of more than an hour by horse-drawn bus or tram from South London to Euston Road. His landlady, Mrs Hood, had a son Harry four years Horatio's junior. For now, Bradlaugh remained his model, and Bottomley prepared for the days of fame and vindication ahead by practising public speeches before the mirror, with Harry as prompter until the intended words and gestures[51] were memorised.

Mrs Hood and Horatio became friends. She is the first adult aside from family and family friends to have formed any recorded opinion of him. What she saw she liked. He was polite to her, even charming. When he was short of money[52] he admitted it cheerfully, and she supplied loans. He was also telling fantastic stories, for example of a rich married sister living in a large house on Clapham Common. He described her house in vivid detail: its servants, its horse and carriage. In truth, Florence lived in Cheapside, a very modest district, where she was being courted by a furrier's clerk, Charles Dollman.[53] But Horatio was claiming that he would inherit a fortune from a benefactor on his 21st birthday.[54]

Such brazen assertions of incipient wealth and good connections have strong echoes in Victorian fiction. We described Trabb the tailor in the last chapter, who guards the boundary in *Great Expectations* between Pip's humble start and his later wealth. For a guide to Bottomley's state of mind at this time, we can turn to another nearby character: Trabb's boy, the apprentice tailor. When Pip returns to the town he grew up in, the apprentice remembers Pip's origins and mocks and humiliates him as a parvenu, converting a blue bag into clothing that imitates Pip's great-coat: "Words cannot state the amount of aggravation and injury wreaked upon me by Trabb's boy, when, passing abreast of me, he pulled up his shirt-collar, twined his side-hair, stuck an arm akimbo, and smirked extravagantly". The apprentice accused Pip of having ghosted him: "Don't know yah, don't know yah, pon my soul don't know yah!" he then gathered together a gang who pursued Pip across the bridge, "culminat[ing] the disgrace with which I left the town, and was, so to speak, ejected by it into the open country".[55] Victorian society demanded both wealth and prestige, enforcing the harsh pretence that good money had always been passed down several generations. How vast the distance that lay ahead of Bottomley must have seemed. If he was set on being rich, he was no less set on being accepted. So many years of mockery lay ahead of him – and yet he was determined.

Somewhere, he had already learned the Pitman system of shorthand. Isaac Pitman's shorthand alphabet had been published when George Jacob Holyoake was still in Birmingham. The system (which Pitman termed Phonography) broke the English language into 36 typical sounds, so that consonants were "explodents", "continuants", "nasals" and so on. A p was written as a thin diagonal stroke from northwest to southeast, a b as a thicker stroke in the same direction.[56] This allowed for a transcription of speech up to speeds of 200 words per minute, with an accuracy impossible by earlier methods.

Horatio's own first business of sorts, already established before moving to Battersea, had been an evening and weekend school teaching shorthand. As he settled south of the river, he told his students that the school was moving with him and would not return. This was unpopular, as they had paid for their course in advance – but Harry, who was with him, saved him from a beating, his reward a meal in a restaurant on Fetter's Lane. Years later, at the age of 60, Hood recalled this feast: Bottomley had bought him an omelette.[57] He had never even heard of this dish before, still less tasted one. Around this time, Bottomley also gave Hood a copy of *Gulliver's Travels*, inscribed, "From his tormentor".[58]

In the later years of the 19th century there were 70 full-time professional shorthand-writers in England. Most were employed at the Royal Court of Justice on the Strand, in numbers enough to launch an Institute of their own.[59] Thanks to this skill, Bottomley could once again follow in Bradlaugh's footsteps to become a legal clerk: "The whole of my time was spent in the Court, recording the judgments and dicta of men like the late Sir George Jessel and Lord Justice James – the two greatest Equity Judges of our time".[60]

By 8 January 1879, Horatio was working for a solicitor, Best, Webb & Co at 6 Essex Street, just off the Strand.[61] For many years, the firm kept its one record of his time there, a deed on parchment, into which the word "share" had been inserted in Bottomley's hand.[62]

This same year he also made two friendships that were to last his whole life. The first was Alfred Locke ("Tommy") Cox, a medical student eight years his senior,[63] and the son of a barrister from Birmingham,[64] who for the next 40 years was the most consistent of his friends, his name appearing on countless documents, as agent in Bottomley's election campaigns and as director, secretary or treasurer of his companies.[65]

Horatio also met Eliza Norton, a dressmaker working at the corner of Lavender Hill and Queenstown, the daughter of Samuel Norton, a rent-collector for Sarson's vinegar brewery.[66] Previous biographers have tended to portray her as a vapid young woman whose sole redeeming quality was her pretty blond hair.[67] This is unfair. Eliza was loyal and loved her husband. She was calm where he was tempestuous. She also had something of his talent for winning friends by telling stories against herself. In one, she came home to find Horatio in possession of 50 sovereigns: "Visions of a feast worthy of Lucullus,[68] not to mention a much-needed dress or two, flashed before her eyes. But, alas, it was not to be". Bottomley laid out the 50 sovereigns on the table and proceeded to distribute them between absent shareholders. "Ten for Jim", he remarked, "Five for Bill, five for Ernie", and so it went on. "Oh Horace", Eliza wailed, "do give me some". At last, she had his attention:

> Ungraciously and unwillingly did her lord and master detach a couple of sovereigns from the pile and push them over. "Here you are", he grunted, "I don't know what the devil you do with all your money".[69]

To date Horatio was no richer than his parents had been. The furniture had been bought on down payment with instalments to come, including the one possession that Eliza requested and he had granted her: a piano. Bottomley found it hard not to spend the piano instalments on treats of his own. Saving what she could, fighting him when she had no choice, Eliza was just about able to keep up the payments.[70]

Even the date of the wedding was determined by Horatio's inability to live within his means. They had agreed to marry on Christmas Day 1879. Horatio was full of enthusiasm and insisted that his contribution would be to oversee the making of a great wedding cake. He washed the raisins and stoned the currants himself. When it was baked, Bottomley handed it over to a local baker for icing. On Christmas Eve he came to collect it. But the baker refused to release it without the 16 shillings owed him for decorating this masterpiece. Bottomley was unable to pay and a promise failed to appease. The next morning (after a large breakfast) Bottomley sent Harry Hood with a message that he was too ill to leave his bed and a request that the verger postpone the wedding without fee.

At last the money was found, and the couple were married, on 15 May 1880 at the New Wesleyan Chapel on London Road in Wandsworth.[71] Horatio gave his profession as shorthand writer. The form also required he set out his dead father's profession. Here Horatio becomes imprecise, describing William as a "clothier".[72] The two began wedded life in two rooms rented from a Mrs Foster of Eland Road, Battersea; Bottomley asking for credit (as he had with Mrs Hood) by hinting that a fortune was due to him on his 21st birthday. Mrs Foster sized up the husband's worn jacket and threadbare trousers, declined to lend him anything and insisted rather that the rent be paid a week in advance.[73]

In the same year, Bottomley joined a shorthand firm off the Strand,[74] Walpole's, and was enrolled as a Member of the Institute of Shorthand Writers Practising in the High Court, joining a caste he described as "men of education and ability... [having] as intelligent a knowledge of English law as the members of the Bar and quite as good an average income".[75] The Shorthand Writers were regulars in court and known by name to many barristers, who trusted them with the documents that set out their clients' cases.

Meanwhile Bradlaugh and Besant continued their ascent through the institutions. Besant for a time had a whim to become a lawyer, explaining in the *National Reformer* that she planned to make use of the opportunity now afforded to women to obtain degrees from the University of London. Matriculation required languages and science, and her tutor was Edward Aveling, four years Besant's junior, the son of a congregational minister.

Aveling contributed articles to the Secularist press: "On Educating Women" and "On Personal Influence".[76] Besant wrote about him in glowing terms: "His language is exquisitely chosen and is polished to the highest extent... to this artistic charm are added scholarship and wide knowledge". She invited her readers to "rejoice that Liberty has won this new Knight",[77] which perhaps charmed rank-and-file secularists but could not have pleased Bradlaugh.

In 1880, supported by Besant and Aveling, and with the backing of the Liberal Whips (who were looking for two candidates[78] to undo the split between the Liberal and Radical caucuses in that town), the secularist leader stood once again in Northampton. The election delivered a considerable swing, and a majority of 39 to the Liberals, alongside the 61 Irish Home Rulers who could be expected to vote with them in the House of Commons. Bradlaugh was elected, alongside Henry Labouchere, a Liberal at the leftmost edge of that party's support. Bradlaugh promised that he and Labouchere would be the government's loyal rebels, the people to keep the party on a principled track.

First though they had to deal with the Conservatives, and Bradlaugh's open atheism and republicanism. Before taking his seat, he wrote to Sir Henry Brand, the Speaker, and to Sir Erskine May, the Clerk of the House of Commons. Since his atheism would render worthless the swearing an oath of allegiance to the Crown, might he not rather be permitted to affirm? This, he proposed, would be consistent with the Evidence Acts (which permitted witnesses to affirm in court rather than have to swear on a Bible) and with the Parliamentary Oaths Act (which allowed "Quakers, and every other person for the time being permitted to make solemn Affirmation or Declaration", to affirm their loyalty and in that way take their seat in Parliament). Neither May nor Brand accepted that the Evidence Acts were relevant, and nor (more to the point) did the Conservatives. Opposition to Bradlaugh was led by Randolph Churchill, who linked Bradlaugh's election to the *Fruits of Philosophy* trial. The atheists, insisted Churchill, were the "residuum, the rabble and the scum of the population; the bulk of them persons to whom all restraint – religious, moral or legal – is odious and intolerable".[79] The question of whether to allow Bradlaugh to sit was referred to a Select Committee and then to a vote of the House. The Conservatives persuaded enough Liberals – and almost the entire bloc of (Catholic) Irish Home Rulers – that Bradlaugh should not be permitted to take his seat.

Here, we see one of the issues which would split the Liberal coalition over the next 30 years. The presence of an Irish bloc in Parliament was seen by the Liberals at first as a distraction and later as an opportunity. If their party agreed to an amount of devolution ("Home Rule") they could expect 60 additional votes in the Commons. For that reason, under Gladstone, they accepted the principle of self-government. But that choice also shrank the Liberal coalition, breaking up a hegemony which had been based on new voters' gratitude for the enfranchisement going back to 1832. Alliance with the Irish tended to antagonise other groups of Liberal voters, including those who saw themselves as English patriots who were switching to the Conservatives in significant numbers; as well as other parts of the Liberal coalition such as Nonconformists and in this instance Radicals, who could not get what they wanted (i.e. Bradlaugh in Parliament) without defying the Irish MPs.

Over the next three years, Bradlaugh was front-page news. Ordered to withdraw following a vote of his fellow parliamentarians, he refused – and was imprisoned in the Clock Tower. Re-elected to the Commons in 1881, albeit with a majority reduced from 675 to 132, he was yet again not permitted to take his seat. Knowing he was not permitted to affirm, Bradlaugh attempted to give the oath of allegiance, but this was refused. He was permitted to take his seat on sufferance, it being understood that the courts would have to determine the matter. A private prosecution was initiated against him.

Bradlaugh turned to the people, speaking at public meetings five nights a week, with thousands attending. Among the crowds following every step in his career was a Coventry-born engineer, four years Bottomley's senior, Tom Mann. Mann described Bradlaugh as the "foremost platform man in Britain", as the inspiration to a generation of young workers, with a "command of language and power of denunciation superior to any other man of his time... He was a thorough-going Republican... the iconoclast, the breaker of images".[80]

This legal struggle was to be the model for Horatio Bottomley's own subsequent dealings with the law. The case was first heard in March 1881: Henry Lewis Clarke has charged that Bradlaugh (yet again representing himself) had taken his seat in Parliament without swearing an oath to the sovereign. For this there was a fixed penalty of £500 for every time he had voted without giving the oath. Bradlaugh lost at first instance, Mr Justice Matthew finding in the High Court that he had indeed breached the statute. He appealed, first to the Court of Appeal and then to the House of Lords.

Bradlaugh failed with arguments that the Evidence Acts provided a general entitlement to affirm, or that the prosecution, begun before he had cast any votes, was defective. One exchange gave him heart. Mr Justice Grove asked Bradlaugh if he had had brought a prosecution for "maintenance" against Charles Newdegate, Conservative MP for North Warwickshire, and the man funding Clarke's litigation. Bradlaugh had the good sense to hear this question, to reflect and to act. He then sued Newdegate for maintenance, and this delivered victory, with the House of Lords dismissing Clarke's action.[81] Bradlaugh had many reasons for gratitude. Had he not succeeded on appeal, then he would have had to pay Clarke's costs as well as the statutory fine, which stood, after many votes in the House of Commons, at around £350,000. No mass movement could have paid such a sum.[82]

When Bradlaugh stood again at Northampton, and won for the second time, he had been prosecuted for blasphemy. His victory in the Clarke case allowed him to be elected at Northampton at last, with a majority of 368, the third time he stood. In this long struggle[83] between the constitution and the people, Bradlaugh showed that he had the support of the latter.

Yet all this time Bradlaugh was expending just as much energy denouncing those on his left as he was campaigning to reform Victorian society. 1881 had seen the launch of a Democratic Federation, Britain's first socialist party since the collapse of the Owenites. This would become the Social Democratic Federation, one of whose offspring was the Independent Labour Party, the parent of today's Labour Party.[84]

Bradlaugh had played no part in this launch. But several people involved in its inception had been close allies, including Joseph Cowen, one of a handful of Radical MPs alongside Bradlaugh. At the Federation's first meeting, Joseph Cowen was invited to join, and he presided at its second meeting. Delegates came from a large number of local organisations, including the Marylebone Radical Club, the Land Nationalisation Society, the London Society of Compositors, the Tower Hamlets Radical Club, the King's Cross Radical Club, the Social Democratic Club, the Lambeth Democratic Association, and the Battersea Liberal Club.[85] So far, it was a coalition of London's Radicals. But now, at its third meeting, the chair would be H. M. Hyndman, the son of a barrister (and the grandson of a slaver). Hyndman had been a Radical and Republican and an admirer of Mill and Spencer at Cambridge; he later read Karl Marx's *Capital* and announced his conversion to socialism. Self-satisfied, bombastic, seen in public always in a stockbroker's tail coat, Hyndman repelled as much as he appealed. He became the Federation's leader, moulding it into a Social Democratic party in the image of the German socialists who had seen 13 of their members elected to the Reichstag in 1881, and were on their way to recruiting hundreds of thousands of supporters. From the first signs of Hyndman's ascent, Bradlaugh treated the existence of the Federation as a personal insult.

Bottomley, meanwhile, had been offered a partnership at Walpole's.[86] He and Eliza moved to Clapham, sharing rooms for a while with his sister Florence, and with their own daughter, Florence Grace. Money was short but prospects were good. Just as his mentor so often had, Bottomley was convinced that he stood on the verge of a great breakthrough.

The *Hackney Hansard*

The parliamentary reforms of 1832 had enfranchised the middle classes, but the decision not to extend the vote wider led to a great swell of anger within the working class, and to the Chartist movement of the 1840s. Although this movement had been defeated by 1848, other campaigns followed, including those led by Holyoake and Bradlaugh. Thanks to further protest and the passage of the Second Reform Act of 1867, all male householders had the vote. This doubled the total number of the enfranchised, from one to two million. The sons of the artisans of the Owenite period (though not yet their daughters) had been recognised as citizens.

From here, Bottomley's success would be shaped by such changes. The deeper the franchise went down into society, the more people expected of it and demanded of it. Its expansion encouraged a desire for local participation. New voters refused to limit themselves to demonstrating their approval for candidates once every seven years, the potential interval between elections. They wanted to participate in the life of these parties, and local "parliaments" sprang up, debating societies modelled on Westminster, complete with caucuses, locally appointed ministers,[87] programmes for legislation, and prime minister's questions. Most were hobbyists with no real powers, even over the local party, but many future councillors and mayors also found a kind of training in this milieu, all of which expanded the horizons of the workers. A significant number of working-class people were taking part in these activities, some (such as Ramsay MacDonald and John Hodge) finding seats in the Commons 20 years later and crediting it all for teaching them the essentials of procedure.[88]

From Battersea, Bottomley was drawn to one of the most dynamic of the local parliaments, in Hackney. This claimed some 983 participants: 449 Liberals, 443 Conservatives, 32 Independents and 9 supporters of Irish Home Rule.[89] Setting up an office on Chancery Lane, Bottomley launched the *Hackney Hansard* in 1882 to report on proceedings.[90]

Before this, the local parliaments relied on the local press to publicise them. In a typical issue of the *Hackney and Kingsland Gazette* you might find an announcement that the debating society would meet the next day, and a summary of its planned debate: for example, whether the government had been wise to spend two million pounds on sending troops to Egypt. But this coverage was limited, buried deep among pages of advertisements.[91] Bottomley was proposing to raise the profile of the movement.

He invited other publications to publish reports of this new movement, and one of them, *The Freemason*, obliged. It began its October 1882 report by commending the local parliaments: "They educate debaters in the fair and temperate discussion of subjects, excluding and forbidding the angry and general attack, which in tavern societies of the same kind disgrace and deform the speakers". The report explained that the *Hackney Hansard* would have joint owners, Bottomley and the shorthand firm Walpole's, Bottomley's existing employers. The journal was commended for the accuracy of its note-keeping, and its technical quality, "The typography is perfect, and the work produced in a form which, when bound up, will make a good library volume".[92] This was modest praise but nonetheless welcome.

By October 1883, the Hackney parliament meetings had grown so large that it was becoming hard to find buildings of sufficient size to host them. Membership had to be limited to 1000 people.[93] Speeches by participants were taken down verbatim. Advertisements hymned the merits of worm tablets, cough lozenges and Dr Scott's Electric Hairbrush, to "cure nervous headache in five minutes... [and] prevent falling hair and baldness".[94]

A fictional portrayal of Horatio Bottomley's milieu can be found in George Gissing's *New Grub Street*, whose anti-hero Jasper Milvain is a "young man of five-and-twenty, well built". His clothes were of an "expensive material, but had seen a good deal of service". Part of the insecure middle class, Milvain has tastes his current employment is unable to supply, such as a "really fresh egg... very excellent buttered toast... coffee as good as can be reasonably expected in this part of the world". In his daytime job, "Jasper of the facile pen" is a journalist, albeit a cynical one: "Literary production", he insists, must be a "paying business", while he jokes at the expense of the "conscientious" people around him. He starts writing for a magazine, *The Current*, whose "tone is to be up to date, and the articles are to be short; no padding". Its owner's genius was to imagine a paper consisting of no more than sketches "of typical readers of each of the principal daily and weekly papers".[95] All of which resembles, in other words, *The Hackney Hansard*, as it offered its readers the chance to see themselves in print.

Bottomley's paper sold well, and within weeks he had launched a sister edition, the *Battersea Hansard*, to report on the parliament closest to his home. This second paper lost money, however. Unsure he could sustain both, Bottomley produced a prospectus suggesting that they were profitable, and approached friends to invest. Such conversion of adversity into opportunity would become a theme in his later business career, and a method. When one company was in trouble, he would set up a new one, merge the two and close the old. When contractors demanded payment, he insisted that the original was no more.

So the *Hackney* and *Battersea Hansards* were merged and closed, and Bottomley founded a third newspaper, the *Debater*, to be the national publication of the entire movement. This combined sketches of the parliaments in Hackney, Lambeth, Battersea, Highbury, Tower Hamlets, Sydenham and Forest Hill, Portsmouth, Manchester, and Leicester,[96] with features that offered hints and tips to debaters. Some of the societies, Bottomley acknowledged, sent donations to the *Debater*, "receiving in return special attention from our reporting staff"[97] (the staff at this time consisting of one shorthand writer plus Bottomley as the proprietor).

If, as Bottomley would often later claim, he was a Radical, there was little sign of this in the *Debater*, which presented itself as the non-partisan organ of an entire milieu, that of the local parliament movement, dominated as this then was by Britain's two main parties, the Liberals and the Conservatives. His paper published reports of Charles Bradlaugh's speeches,[98] advertisements for Henry George's *The Land Question* and *Progress and Poverty*, and books appealing to supporters of the Liberal party and those to their left. But alongside these were lectures on elocution and the tracts of the Marriage Law Defence Union – with titles such as *What the Bishop of Lincoln Says*, or, *What the Table of Affinity Says, Compared with Leviticus*.[99] You could be an Anglican minister and read the *Debater*. You could be a Conservative and still feel that the newspaper was yours.

Soon it was also publishing opinion pieces. When senior politicians were in 1884 once more proposing the extension of the franchise,[100] Bottomley invited "Cygnus" to comment. The author poured scorn on the philosophical underpinnings of both the moderate traditions of Liberalism and of their left-wing critics, the Chartists. "Any public appreciation", Cygnus began, of the need to extend the franchise "has been enslaved, so to speak, by enthusiasm for democratic change, and people have been taught to suppose that if there is anything visibly wrong about Parliament the only thing to be done is pour in more of the stock remedy, popular voting".[101] There followed a brief and unsympathetic account of the main programmes for parliamentary reform, including Home Rule in Ireland, each being dismissed as unworkable.

Bottomley's hunch had been that a paper covering the local parliaments might prove a success. He had learned other things, as well. The first was personal. Bottomley had grasped that he had a talent to talk himself out of disadvantage. As we saw in his relationship with Mrs Hood, his opening gambit was often to acknowledge fault in himself. He realised that the most effective way of persuading her to bail him out was to admit a problem, to appeal to her better instincts, to play the part of the sinner seeking forgiveness. To prosper as an independent businessman with no capital of his own, Bottomley had to go beyond placating his creditors, but via flights of eloquence to transform them into his regular patrons.

His next insight built on the first. The *Hackney Hansard* had seemed conceived, at first, as a Walpole and Bottomley business. Yet within just a few weeks the name of Bottomley's former employer had quite disappeared. It is impossible to reconstruct how this decision was taken, or by whom. Was Horatio Bottomley dismissed, or did he resign? One suggestion is that Walpole was committed to the *Hackney Hansard* and had made it profitable, while Bottomley, set on emulating this success in Battersea, had failed.[102] But however the decision was made to break this alliance, it was never reversed. Bottomley was convinced that he would survive as a proprietor. He preferred to fix his own hours, and work for no one but himself. He was convinced that he had what it took, whether skills, contacts, talent or luck, and that he would be able to maintain his own business no matter what bad news came his way.

The third insight was this; society's sanctions to punish personal or corporate indebtedness were less draconian than they had been. Following the passage of the Debtors' Act of 1869, the earlier system of debtors' prisons, had been abolished. A person could not be imprisoned for debt unless the sum owed was greater than £50 and if the debtor, having the apparent means to do so, had failed to pay.[103] In the absence of more punitive sanctions, a self-acknowledged serial debtor was best advised to accumulate further debts with all possible haste. While the lowliest debtors in late-Victorian England still spent their days in workhouses and prisons, the greatest shone in the House of Commons. Bottomley wanted to be rich, he needed to be successful and he was desperate to be loved. He was determined to match and overreach both halves of Bradlaugh's career, his political success but also his business failures – in which Bottomley could spy a route to a different kind of success.

Notes

1 One source suggests that Bottomley was with the builder's firm for 18 months, that is, from around March 1874 (his 14th birthday) to the autumn of 1875. Tenax, *The Rise and Fall*, p. 12. Yet in Bottomley's own memoir, the young boy was back in London and working for a solicitor before the end of 1874. Bottomley, *Bottomley's Book*, p. 1.
2 Symons, *Horatio Bottomley*, p. 13. Houston suggests that Bottomley was back for a while with Mrs Wormley, *The Real Horatio Bottomley*, p. 36.
3 William Holyoake would have more success with his son Rowland Holyoake (1880–1907) who became a painter of genre, portraits, landscapes and interiors. Wood, *The Dictionary of Victorian Painters*, p. 232.
4 Bottomley, *Bottomley's Book*, p. 1.
5 Bottomley says that the haberdasher was at King Street in Cheapside. Bottomley, *Bottomley's Book*, p. 1. Tenax gives the location of the haberdashery as Wood Street, that is, about a third of the way from St Paul's to Bank. *The Rise and Fall*, p. 12.
6 Bottomley, *Bottomley's Book*, p. 1.
7 Bottomley, *Bottomley's Book*, pp. 1–2.
8 Bottomley, *Bottomley's Book*, pp. 2–3.
9 Bottomley, *Bottomley's Book*, p. 4.
10 Bottomley, *Bottomley's Book*, p. 6. Symons, drawing on Bottomley's memoir, suggests that Bottomley moved straight from this fraudulent solicitor's office to a more reputable solicitor's firm. *Horatio Bottomley*, p. 14. While it is true that Bottomley suggests as much by placing the first occupation directly before the second in his memoir, there was in fact a four-year gap (1875 to 1879) between these two positions.

11 Bottomley, *Bottomley's Book*, p. 90.

12 Hyman, *The Rise and Fall*, p. 21; Symons, *Horatio Bottomley*, p. 13. Bottomley's aunt performed under the stage name of Alice Austin or sometimes Alice Austin Wright. The first performance of *Ghosts* was at the Royalty Theatre in London in March 1891. H. Ellis (ed), *The Pillars of Society, And Other Plays. By Henrik Ibsen* (London: Walter Scott, 1888).

13 Circular, 16 April 1874. Bradlaugh papers, Bishopsgate Institute, Bradlaugh 378.

14 Cheque, 7 June 1875. Bradlaugh papers, Bishopsgate Institute, Bradlaugh 423.

15 This culture continued into the late 1940s and early 1950s; for a description of it in South Hackney, see D. Renton, *Fascism, Anti-Fascism, and Britain in the 1940s* (London: Palgrave, 1999).

16 Houston, *The Real Horatio Bottomley*, p. 39.

17 J. F. Stephen, *Liberty, Equality, Fraternity* (New York: Holt & Williams, 1878), p. 319.

18 J. Stephen, 'What is a Lie', paper given to the Metaphysical Society, 11 July 1876, p. 1.

19 A. Trollope, *The Way We Live Now* (London: Humphrey Milford, 1941), pp. 31, 675.

20 Symons, *Horatio Bottomley*, p. 16.

21 R. Blathwayt, *Horatio Bottomley: The Man as He Is* (London: Odhams, 2016), p. 15; A.-M. Kilday and D. S. Nash, *Shame and Modernity in Britain: 1890 to the Present* (London: Macmillan, 2017), p. 66.

22 Symons, *Horatio Bottomley*, p. 16.

23 London: Trubner & Co., 1876, 2 vols.

24 Vol. 1, p. 13.

25 Vol. 1, pp. 19, 30, 49, 67.

26 *National Reformer*, 30 July 1876.

27 *National Reformer*, 29 October 1876. Bottomley means that the audiences were mostly male, and is being either gallant about the young women he would have liked to see – or (depending on how you take it) seedy.

28 Later the correspondence address of the General Council of the International Working Men's Association (the First International).

29 Niblett, *Dare to Stand Alone*, pp. 81–3.

30 Niblett, *Dare to Stand Alone*, p. 83.

31 C. Knowlton, *The Fruits of Philosophy: An Essay on the Population Question* (London: R. Forder, 1894 edn), pp. 7, 40–1.

32 A. Taylor, *Annie Besant: A Biography* (Oxford: Oxford University Press, 1992), p. 109.

33 Besant, *Charles Bradlaugh*, p. 38.

34 Their preface to the pamphlet was reprinted in the *National Reformer*, 21 March 1877.

35 J. Larkman, London Necropolis Company, to Charles Bradlaugh, 29 May 1877. Bradlaugh papers, Bishopsgate Institute, Bradlaugh 502(a)

36 Niblett, *Dare to Stand Alone*, p. 118.

37 H. Spencer, *The Morals of Trade* (London: Taylor and Co., 1887), pp. 30, 79, 81, 82, 84, 85.

38 D. Rubinstein, 'Besant, Annie', in J. M. Bellamy and J. Saville (eds), *Dictionary of Labour Biography, Volume IV* (London: Macmillan, 1977), pp. 21–31, 22.

39 Niblett, *Dare to Stand Alone*, p. 122.

40 M. Sreenivas, 'Birth Control in the Shadow of Empire: The Trials of Annie Besant, 1877–1878', *Feminist Studies* 41/3 (2015), pp. 509–37.

41 Niblett, *Dare to Stand Alone*, pp. 128–9; R. Manvell, *The Trial of Annie Besant and Charles Bradlaugh* (London: Elek Books, 1976), pp. 159–61.

42 Niblett, *Dare to Stand Alone*, p. 130.

43 Niblett, *Dare to Stand Alone*, pp. 132–3.

44 Bottomley, *Bottomley's Book*, p. 166.

45 Houston, *The Real Horatio Bottomley*, p. 29.

46 Houston describes Bottomley as owning a book about secularism, signed on its fly-lead by William Holyoake (although it is more likely that it would have been signed

by William's brother George). He also saw a copy of *Gulliver's Travels*– as given by Bottomley to Harry Hood in 1879. Houston, *The Real Horatio Bottomley*, pp. 33, 41.

47 Bottomley, *Bottomley's Book*, p. 90.
48 Houston, *The Real Horatio Bottomley*, p. 39. He may possibly have been living with his uncle William again at this point, whose home was but a short distance away.
49 Houston, *The Real Horatio Bottomley*, p. 39.
50 E. Walford, 'Somers Town and Euston Square', *Old and New London: Volume 5* (London: Cassell, Petter, Galpin and Co., 1878), pp. 340–55.
51 Symons, *Horatio Bottomley*, p. 23.
52 Alan Hyman writes that Bottomley had already acquired a gambling habit. Hyman, *The Rise and Fall*, p. 22.
53 Symons, *Horatio Bottomley*, p. 22.
54 Houston, *The Real Horatio Bottomley*, p. 40.
55 Dickens, *Great Expectations*, Chapter 30.
56 *Manual of Phonography: Pitman's Shorthand Manual* (London: Sir Isaac Pitman & Sons, 1894).
57 Houston, *The Real Horatio Bottomley*, p. 41. Hood later worked in the City as a stockbroker for the Union Discount Company before emigrating to Canada.
58 Houston, *The Real Horatio Bottomley*, p. 41.
59 Which they did in 1885. Hyman, *The Rise and Fall*, p. 21; M. Levy, *Shorthand: Its History and its Prospects* (London: Institute of Shorthand Writers, 1885).
60 Bottomley, *Bottomley's Book*, p. 7. Jessel was the judge who had ruled against Besant.
61 Tenax, *The Rise and Fall*, p. 12. Bottomley's name is noted as an employee in an advertisement in *The Standard*, 14 June 1879.
62 Tenax, *The Rise and Fall*, p. 12.
63 Cox had passed his Preliminary Examination for Membership of the Royal College of Surgeons in 1873, *Calendar of the Royal College of Surgeons of England* (London: Royal College, 1874), pp. 285–9.
64 Tenax, *The Rise and Fall*, p. 14.
65 Tenax, *The Rise and Fall*, p. 14.
66 Hyman, *The Rise and Fall*, p. 23; Symons, *Horatio Bottomley*, p 23.
67 "The people in Bottomley's circle – businessmen, racing men, barristers, bookies, theatre people and hangers on – found her dull and rather stupid". Hyman, *The Rise and Fall*, p. 59. In a similar vein, see Felstead, *Horatio Bottomley*, p. 13; and Symons, *Horatio Bottomley*, p. 17. With a little more sympathy, Tenax notes that in the 1880s, William Holyoake auctioned a portrait of Eliza. *The Rise and Fall*, p. 14.
68 A general of the Roman Republic, who was said to have returned to Rome with so much captured booty that the whole treasure was beyond any counting.
69 Felstead, *Horatio Bottomley*, pp. 12–13.
70 Hyman, *The Rise and Fall*, p. 28.
71 Symons, *Horatio Bottomley*, p. 14; Houston, *The Real Horatio Bottomley*, pp. 42–3.
72 Houston, *The Real Horatio Bottomley*, pp. 42–3.
73 Symons, *Horatio Bottomley*, p. 26.
74 That Bottomley worked there is attested by multiple sources; although no such firm is recorded in either the main *Post Office London Directory 1880*, or its legal sub-directory.
75 Bottomley, *Bottomley's Book*, p. 6.
76 Niblett, *Dare to Stand Alone*, p. 137.
77 Y. Kapp, *Eleanor Marx: Volume 1: Family Life 1855–1883* (London: Virago, 1972), p. 269.
78 See earlier note: this was a constituency in which two candidates were to be elected.
79 F. Mount, 'Get off Your Knees', *London Review of Books*, 30 June 2011.
80 D. Torr, *Tom Mann and His Times* (London: Lawrence and Wishart, 1956), p. 47.
81 A maintenance is a wrong which, if provable, means that the underlying action is unlawful. The basic idea is this: if person A sues person B and A is a proxy standing

in for the real interests of person C, then A's action is illegal and cannot succeed. The difficulty is usually evidential: that of proving A is a sham litigator put up by C.

82 Niblett, *Dare to Stand Alone*, pp. 181–4, 191–5, 223–4, 240–2.

83 This back-and-forth of actions consisted of some seven years (1880–87) of overlapping political, legal and judicial actions, and until Clarke lost his case, Bradlaugh kept being denied his election wins, until his final victory. Told in full, the story would swamp Bottomley's own at this point, since the latter was only a bystander.

84 Torr, *Tom Mann and His Times*, pp. 186–8; E. P. Thompson, *William Morris: Romantic to Revolutionary* (London: Merlin, 1955), pp. 344–5.

85 M. S. Wilkins, 'The Non-Socialist Origins of England's First Important Socialist Organisation', *International Review of Social History* 4 (1959), pp. 199–207.

86 G. Rawling, 'Swindler of the Century', *History Today* 43, July 1993; G. S. Messinger, *British Propaganda and the State in the First World War* (Manchester: Manchester University Press, 1992), p. 203.

87 Bottomley claims that by 1887 he was serving as Prime Minister in two local parliaments. Bottomley, *Bottomley's Book*, p. 51.

88 R. McKibbin, *The Ideologies of Class: Social Relations in Britain 1880–1950* (Oxford: Oxford University Press, 1991), pp. 22–3.

89 *Hackney and Kingsland Gazette*, 27 October 1882.

90 'The "Hackney Hansard"', *Freemason*, 28 October 1882.

91 *Hackney and Kingsland Gazette*, 25 October 1882.

92 'The "Hackney Hansard"', *The Freemason*, 28 October 1882.

93 'Odds and Ends', *The Debater*, 11 October 1883.

94 *The Debater*, 11 October 1883.

95 G. Gissing, *New Grub Street* (London: [Smith, Elder & Co., 1891), Chapters 1 and 6.

96 *The Debater*, 11 October 1883.

97 Symons, *Horatio Bottomley*, p. 18.

98 *The Debater*, 5 January 1884.

99 *The Debater*, 15 March 1884.

100 The vote was essentially now to be extended to all middle-class and a significant minority of working-class adult men: the artisans mentioned earlier. The registered electorate after 1884 was 5.7 million people (after 1918 it would be 21 million people, including women over 30).

101 'The real problem of reform', *The Debater*, 15 March 1884.

102 Tenax, *The Rise and Fall*, p. 13.

103 Section 5, Debtors Act 1869; W. R. Cornish and G. de N. Clark, *Law and Society in England 1750–1950* (London: Sweet and Maxwell, 1989), p. 230.

4

PROPRIETOR, POLITICIAN, DEFENDANT

Bradlaugh had won election in Northampton in 1880, but as of April 1884 the question of whether he would be allowed to remain in Parliament was unsettled. He was under enormous pressure to court respectable opinion. The MP made himself the greatest public critic of the socialists, beginning with a debate with their leader H. M. Hyndman, where Bradlaugh delivered one of his most famous speeches. He began by emphasising that there was much on which both he and the socialists agreed:

> We [i.e. both Hyndman and Bradlaugh] recognise the most serious evils, and especially in large centres of population; arising out of the poverty already existing, aggravating and intensifying the crime, disease, and misery developed from it...

Bradlaugh, however, insisted that positive change could come about only by rising up the poor, not by tearing down those above them. "I want to remedy the evil, attacking it in detail by the action of the individuals most affected by it... Social reform is one thing because it is reform; Socialism is the opposite because it is revolution". Hyndman was wrong, Bradlaugh insisted, because his vision of society required violence:

> Socialism would require a physical-force revolution, because you would want that physical force to make all the present property-owners who are unwilling, surrender their private property to the common fund.[1]

In his response Hyndman insisted that the revolutionary transformation intended by the socialists was, above all, a change of ideas, with great economic and social forces powering it: "Electricity is supplanting steam, and steam is supplanting

DOI: 10.4324/9781003306085-4

in other directions the old mechanical powers; and that constant competition of machinery with the skilled working man is producing a revolution in his lot".[2] A revolution need not require force, provided that the majority of the people were persuaded of the need for change:

> I say that two or three years ago it would have been impossible to have had this hall crowded by an audience perhaps evenly divided between those who agree with Socialism and those who are opposed to it.[3]

The very fact that these two speakers could stand in the same hall debating Socialism, organised revolutionary Socialism, was itself a sign of the coming revolution.

It would be wrong to see the clash between Bradlaugh and Hyndman as just two leaders, both from middle-class backgrounds, motivated by hostility to one another. There was also a disagreement between them as to what the audience was for change. As he had aged, Bradlaugh's audience had become more respectable. The London Radicals of the 1880s were older than their Socialist counterparts, unwilling to organise among the poor, less interested in two key socialist constituencies, Irish workers and the unemployed.

This animosity between Bradlaugh and the socialists became further heated as Annie Besant was estranged from Edward Aveling. Aveling had taught her and she had brought him into the leadership of the secularist movement. But within weeks of the Bradlaugh–Hyndman debate, he had joined the Social Democratic Federation. By June 1884, he was living with Karl Marx's daughter Eleanor,[4] the change in their relationship manifested when Eleanor adopted, in defiance of Victorian morality, the surname Marx-Aveling. Aveling still had a wife, Isabel – but as Eleanor explained to her friend the children's author and Fabian Edith Nesbit: "We are going to be together – true husband and true wife".[5]

Several pioneering English socialists were shocked by Eleanor Marx's willingness to live with a man to whom she was not married. Recording their meeting, another Fabian, Beatrice Webb, the future historian of trade unions, social investigator and eugenicist, [6] seems to allow hostile judgment to colour her portrait: "In person [Marx] is comely, dressed in a slovenly picturesque way, with curly black hair flying about in all directions. Fine eyes full of life and sympathy, otherwise ugly features and expression and complexion showing the signs of an unhealthy excited life, kept up with stimulants and tempered by narcotics".[7]

Besant was furious at Aveling's political conversion, accusing him of having stolen from the secularists and claiming that Eleanor had libelled her. Aveling told readers of the socialist newspaper *Justice* that "all monies... have been fully accounted for". Bradlaugh took Besant's side and supported a motion for consideration by the next meeting of the National Secular Society, which demanded Aveling resign from all positions.[8]

Secularist accounts of this controversy tend to emphasise Bradlaugh's truthfulness, and his good faith when it came to allegations of financial impropriety.

Socialist accounts seek to exculpate Marx, noting that her father and Bradlaugh had long been at odds, going back to their reactions to the Paris Commune. Both sides prefer to skip over the inflamed feelings at the heart of the conflict, those of the polyamorous Aveling and his betrayed companion Besant.

Besant had attended the Bradlaugh–Hyndman debate, applauding as Bradlaugh declared, "Class war is murder, class war is fratricide, class war is suicide".[9] Sedley Taylor was a Cambridge lecturer long in pursuit of Eleanor's father in the pages of the *Times*, where he had accused the old agitator of having misquoted Gladstone in *Capital*.[10] Besant wrote to Taylor requesting his help in challenging Marx's "literary and political honesty".[11]

Taylor could not assist with the kind of documentation Besant wanted, but she was undaunted. Reviewing a copy of the first issue of the socialist newspaper *Justice*, Besant told the readers of the *National Reformer* that England had no need for redistribution. It was a country with "free press and free platform for political and social agitation", and the demand for socialism was "the worst enemy of social progress".[12] Her contempt was unrestrained.

Members of the Dialectical Society had invited another convert from secularism to socialism, the young Fabian playwright and novelist George Bernard Shaw, to address them in January 1885. They warned him that they felt obliged, for the sake of balance, to invite Besant also, expecting her to disagree with Shaw. To their surprise and his, [13] Besant refused to speak when prompted but remained seated. When another speaker attacked Shaw, she rose to denounce this critic and later invited Shaw to dinner.[14] This was the start of another intense platonic friendship.[15] Soon after, Besant announced that she had become a socialist. She acknowledged the debt she owed Bradlaugh but insisted that secularism was no longer enough: "The cry of starving children was ever in my ears, the sobs of women poisoned in lead works, exhausted in nail works, driven to prostitution by starvation, made old and haggard by ceaseless work". The misery of the working-class majority, she now argued, was:

> inseparable from private ownership of the instruments of wealth production [and] that while the worker was himself but an instrument, selling his labour under the law of supply and demand, he must remain helpless in the grip of the employing classes.[16]

Bradlaugh tolerated Besant's decision and she continued to write for the *National Reformer*, "but he never again felt the same confidence in my judgment as he felt before, nor did he any more consult me on his own policy, as he had done ever since we first clasped hands".[17]

Youth

By 1884 enthusiasm for the local parliament movement was showing signs of a downturn. Bottomley was reliant on this income, and though the *Debater* continued to publish for two more years, he needed to found other papers to thrive. Looking towards new writing and editing projects, he was facing his first real tests as an editor. He had filled the *Debater* with advertising and verbatim reports of meetings. He began to turn to pre-established audiences and perhaps better recognised models for a newspaper.

Over the next few years, Bottomley was buying and selling titles at a furious rate. The *Municipal Review*, [18] for example, was the monthly paper of the town councils and local board. Its model, as Bottomley grasped it, was an even more blatant form of self-advertising, this time by local politicians, than he had refined at the *Debater*. One of the magazine's principal sources of revenue was the publication of notices commending various mayors, usually accompanied by portraits of them in their municipal regalia:

> The portraits and notices were usually supplied by the subjects themselves; the only conditions of their publication being a well-implied contract to take a large quantity of the journal for distribution amongst the various burgesses.[19]

With around 300 new mayors elected every year, and a publication cycle no busier than weekly, Bottomley was confident that the paper could break even.

The most ambitious of these acquisitions was a penny weekly, *Youth*.[20] It had been published for several years, carrying reports from various schools, but dominated by long extracts from boys' fiction, some stories running over 20 or even 30 successive issues of the magazine. As Bottomley told it, his "sub-editor" on *Youth* was a "pale-faced, thoughtful-looking young man", one Alfred Harmsworth.[21] Harmsworth's barrister father had paid for his son's apprenticeship with £150, a sum Bottomley later described as his "first big touch".[22] Harmsworth senior, also named Alfred, was a lawyer and also a writer, a regular contributor to the *Dublin Review*, who had passed his taste for journalism on to his son.[23] Aged 20, the younger Harmsworth had been a distinguished school sportsman and captain of his day-school cricket and football teams. But he had also messed up his exams, failing to secure a university place. Among the titles he wrote for were the *Hampstead and Highgate Express*, *Cyclist and Wheeling*, the *Globe*, the *Morning Post* and the *St James' Gazette*.

As Harmsworth himself told it, he had applied for the post of assistant editor at *Youth* before Bottomley was even on the scene, explaining to them that he had founded a school newspaper: "There were no mysteries of type and proof for me".[24] Soon afterwards he found himself editor, [25] but was dismissed within the year, the victim of an elaborate prank conceived by Eton schoolboys. They had informed Harmsworth of a craze in which the school's pupils took mint dishes ("slunch") and ran with them around the school paddocks.[26] Between late 1883 and June the following year Harmsworth had run two dozen Eton stories, including a fictitious list of school worthies ("Captain of the Curling Club, T. T. Vator..."), [27] a report of an imaginary hockey match between two school teams (the Field Mice and the Jolly Boys), and a version of the "far-famed" school song, "Pulcra Etona".[28]

His dismissal, however, seems to have been followed by his re-engagement at Bottomley's hands, as a freelance contributor – suggesting that the £150 was less an apprenticeship fee (as Bottomley had characterised it) than the price of a promise from Horatio that no mention would be made of his predecessor's embarrassment.[29]

In July, *Youth* was relaunched in a smaller format. A short story by Harmsworth appeared on the first page of the first number of the new series ("Reginald Oliver was 18, and he had moped away 12 long weary months since he left school"). In the back were advertisements for tricycles and bicycles (a hang-over from the Harmsworth days) as well as a new suggestion: "Readers of *Youth* should secure copies of the *Debater*".[30]

Another of Bottomley's modest innovations was the publication of columns of replies to readers' correspondence – though not the original letters to which the answers were addressed. So, in one issue, three answers were published as follows:

R. A. Neville Lynn – Received with thanks.
Edward Butler – We shall announce full particulars in our next.
A. J. P. – Thanks for further contributions, all of which we hope to use.[31]

This of course gave the editor an excuse not to respond; the most important letters, they could say, would be answered in due course. And since one of Bottomley's most common answers was to say, in effect, *Thank you for writing, I have no time to respond now but I promise to reply in the paper next week*, it gave the paper a pleasing and gentle sense of mystery for readers, and a reason to return. There was a further advantage. No one other than Bottomley knew whether there was a real "R. A. Neville Lynn"[32] or "Edward Butler".[33] The technique enabled him to pretend that he had a vast network of informants to draw on, each equipped with an insider's knowledge of any possible topic.[34]

Another contributor was John Jennings Giles, a former Captain in the British Army. "He one day submitted to me, for the delectation of my youthful readers, a long and learned article on the subject of 'Parasites in Mackerel'".[35] A third handed in detailed accounts of life spent in America and Australia, all very thrilling and vivid and – despite Bottomley's doubts – quite believable. Until the day that the subject of these vivid experiences made the mistake of writing his own by-line. It began "author of", and then four of his memoirs were listed, but it ended "and other stories". After this damning phrase, his editor was never able to take him seriously. "If you want to meet queer people", Bottomley concluded, "become a journalist".[36]

Other acquisitions followed. The *British Mail* specialised in biographies of successful men,[37] and the *Mercantile Shipping Register*[38] is self-explanatory, but turning a profit with the *Daily Recorder of Commerce* as a business paper was beyond

Bottomley's talents. Its readers were interested in all business, not in one isolated sector, and Bottomley struggled to keep up with the paper's wide demands. He found a purchaser: Harry Marks, also a journalist, who had just returned to London after a decade working in the United States.[39]

Despite this busy rate of purchase, the core of Bottomley's business should not be considered steady or successful. He remained short of funds and was looking to load debts onto businesses which could then be sold or declared insolvent.

Bottomley announced in 1887 that *Youth* was to be relaunched with great reserves of capital (£10,000). A board was set up, combining worthies (the honorary secretary of the Recreative Evening Schools Association) and those with hidden links to Bottomley (including his uncle William, described as Master of the Schools of Painting, Royal Academy).[40] Some money came in from this appeal, but not enough for Bottomley's purposes.

Defeat in victory

Meanwhile Bradlaugh's last great battle – over the right to affirm – was reaching its conclusion. After two select committees, multiple parliamentary debates, four speeches at the Bar, repeated Northampton by-elections, and a general election placing the Conservative Party in power, the politicians blocking him from taking his seat determined to fight him no further. In 1887, the Speaker permitted him to affirm. He and the Speaker shook hands. A great battle had been concluded, and Bradlaugh's victory was unconditional.

What would the great Radical achieve in power? In another speech, Bradlaugh mocked the "few poets and a few idiots" who claimed "that socialism was gaining ground in this country. It was not".[41] He had good reason to fear the growth of a new left. It was reducing the base of his own support. In October 1887, he wrote to the *National Reformer* noting with regret Annie Besant's resignation as the paper's joint editor.[42]

Bottomley remained a supporter of the Liberal Party. He was looking for a suitable constituency. In the same month as Besant's resignation, he received a letter from the late Mr Carvell Williams of the Liberation Society, inviting him to stand in a by-election as Hornsey Liberal Association's candidate. In that contest,[43] Bottomley praised Liberal leader William Gladstone's policy of Home Rule for Ireland,[44] and led a procession of 1500 people through the streets of the constituency.[45] He lost by two thousand votes, to the Conservative Henry Charles Stephens, the owner of Stephens Ink.[46]

As a reward for this fight, Bottomley was selected as the Liberal candidate for North Islington, a Nonconformist and left-wing constituency with a much narrower Conservative majority, of just 600.[47] The sitting Conservative MP, G. C. T. Bartley, was characterised by Bottomley as a "redoubtable electioneerer, a democratic, go-as-you-please sort of Tory, and a stupendous believer in the apostolic injunction to be 'all things to all men'". Yet there were other features of the constituency that made it attractive to him: part of the borough had been in Finsbury, an old Radical stronghold. And the Liberal Club on the Holloway Road offered the chance to smoke, to read and to play billiards.[48] No election would take place for several years, and Bottomley spent the time wooing Nonconformist voters, speaking on Ireland in favour of Home Rule,[49] and taking the temperance pledge. Among the speakers who accompanied him was a young Welsh firebrand, David Lloyd George.[50]

The socialists of the 1840s had sought to root themselves in particular forms of working-class organisation: principally, the workers' co-operative. Their counterparts in the 1880s attempted to organise a different category of worker, the unemployed. Between spring 1886 and autumn 1887, a series of protests were held, with out-of-work builders and dockers demanding relief works for the unemployed. In November 1887, a great protest of socialists, unemployed workers and Irish Nationalists marched from East London to Trafalgar Square. Among the speakers were Annie Besant and the artist and poet William Morris, at the time a prominent partisan of H. M. Hyndman's Social Democratic Federation. The demonstrators were attacked, their banners torn out of their hands, and their poles broken. In Morris's words, "The police struck right and left like what they were, soldiers attacking an enemy".[51]

Three protesters were killed: John Dimmock, William Curner and Alfred Linnell.[52] Curner was a follower of Bradlaugh, and Besant spoke at his graveside. But this was no longer a sign of Radical influence over the emerging movement; rather, for the first time in years Bradlaugh's authority over popular movements was in decline. As the 22-year-old future novelist H. G. Wells wrote to an acquaintance Elizabeth Healey around this time: "I am very sorry indeed that you are a Radical". To illustrate the differences between Socialism and Radicalism, he listed all the great ideas of the age, from Communists at one end through Democratic Socialists, Social Democrats, Liberals, Tories, Reactionaries and Extreme Individualists. The Radicals he placed next to Liberals, at the centre of British politics, where that centre encountered the left. He described himself as a Revolutionary, and promised: "The Commune which sank at Paris will rise next in London".[53]

New beginnings

In late 1887, fearing that his nascent press empire was already in danger of collapse, Bottomley approached the financier Henry Osborne O'Hagan for help. O'Hagan was a much richer man than Bottomley, and had been as a company promoter for 20 years. Having started work as a clerk to a tramway manager, he had survived a prosecution for fraud in his 20s before going on to make a fortune. He owned breweries, railroads and cement companies. He would invest money in emerging businesses and insure them against the risk of failure.[54] Within the City, he had a reputation as a man of integrity.[55] At key points in his ascent, Bottomley benefitted from association with men of such standing.

O'Hagan at first declined to provide funding: Bottomley's project seemed too small to be worth his interest. He had no need for a newspaper, let alone a whole portfolio of them. But he had wanted for some time to own a printing business and asked Bottomley if he had any ambition to found one. Encouraged, Bottomley returned a few days later. He proposed that his existing newspapers (Catherine Street Publishing) be merged with a printing firm owned by one Douglas MacRae: the resulting newspaper publisher, Curtice and Co. Savings, would then print the Catherine Street and Curtice newspapers on MacRae's machines. Responding to O'Hagan's words at their earlier meeting, Bottomley assured O'Hagan that MacRae's current printing machines were working under capacity; there was no reason O'Hagan should not use them too. O'Hagan agreed to underwrite half the shares of the new company.[56] Bottomley founded MacRae, Curtice and Co., announcing that it was backed by capital of £120,000.[57] By the end of the year, he had access to more funds than ever.

Chairing the *Financial Times*

On 13 February 1888, the Sheridan brothers had founded the *Financial Times*, taking as their inspiration an existing paper, the *Financial News*, [58] which specialised in stock market listings and financial scandals. The *News* was owned by Bottomley's old associate Harry Marks, and was then at the peak of its influence, having broken the news of corruption at the Metropolitan Board of Works. Marks gives a flavour of the financial press prior to the launch of these papers: "Investors had great difficulty in obtaining trustworthy information about the securities in which their money was embarked". Traders were manipulating stocks, but none of their knowledge escaped beyond "the inner rings of Stock Exchange speculators". Shareholders had "to wait for news from their proprietors until it suited the directors, in their own good time, to communicate so much of the intelligence to hand as they saw fit to publish".[59]

What this account fails to convey is how Marks combined a few genuine scoops with mere advertising for companies that he knew to be worthless – for example by encouraging his readers to buy shares in the Rae Gold Mining Company, even though he knew it was collapsing, in order to dump his own holdings in the business.[60]

The *Financial Times* mimicked the *News* model down to the size of the newspaper (broadsheet), the length of the paper (four pages), its price (one penny), its publication schedule (daily), [61] the layout of the text, and the location of share prices (some on the front page, others on pages two and three). Perhaps because it was so similar, it struggled to sell enough copies to pay for its printing bills, and the Sheridans were looking for a buyer. On 10 March 1888, Bottomley became a director of the Financial Times Ltd, and chairman four months later.

His influence can be seen straight away. The paper begins to print brief summaries of stories already covered in other newspapers, [62] as well as answers to unpublished correspondence ("W. R. (East Moulsey) – No. We advise you to sell Russians"), [63] short single-sentence reports, [64] parliamentary sketches, [65] and notes on trials past[66] and forthcoming.[67] None of these features came from the *Financial News* – and none would be part of its future. All were typical of Bottomley's journalism.

Under his chairmanship, the paper reported the opinions of Charles Brad-laugh, for example covering a speech he gave in Northampton deprecating the finances of British rule in India.[68] It also published several articles promising great wealth waiting to be found, for example in Australia. One noted that the manager of an Australian pearling fleet had received a telegram from one of his boats: "Gold discovered – good prospects".[69] This would not be the last time that Bottomley would announce huge wealth to be found in Australia.

As so often with his journalism, Bottomley's *Financial Times* blurred the distinc-tion between news and comment. In June 1888, for example, he reported in a tone of ironic exasperation the gossip that Sir Edward Watkin, the Liberal-supporting Chairman of the South-Eastern Railway Company, was urging ministers to in-vest in a rail tunnel to France: "Are we to have again the old wearisome discussion over the Channel Tunnel scheme?" an unsigned piece began, "What with the everlasting Irish Question, the perplexing Local Government Bill, and the new Stamp Act muddle, the average mortal has not had a very happy time of it. It might be thought that Sir Edward Watkin had enough on his hands".[70]

As late as Christmas 1888, the paper was still publishing Bottomley-esque an-swers to correspondence: "Victor – (1) A very good property, and well-managed. You could not find a safer mining investment. (2) We are very doubtful as to the result. (3) Sell by all means".[71]

O'Hagan explains his mentee's departure from the newspaper: "A company of £120,000 was small fry to a man of Bottomley's ambition; he figured on manag-ing a concern with £500,000 or £1,000,000 capital". Bottomley tried to interest O'Hagan in a scheme but was unsuccessful. He went about exploring options on printing and publishing companies: "Bottomley again tried to interest me, but failed, so took his goods elsewhere. Douglas MacRae liked not the venture any more than I did, and he retired from the combination, taking with him the *Financial Times*".[72] Under MacRae's stewardship the *Financial Times* would at last mark itself as something quite different from the *Financial News*, including by adopting the famous salmon-pink paper[73] that it still uses to this day.

Still Bradlaugh's disciple

As Bottomley's ambitions grew, he remained on the lookout for ever grander business opportunities. *Hansard*, the journal of parliamentary proceedings, took its name from T. C. Hansard, who had purchased the journal from the Radical William Cobbett 70 years before. Its reports were well edited, and it received a grant for publishing them. Hansard's son sold the company to Bottomley, [74] who in turn sold it soon after acquiring it. Bottomley used the name thereafter as one of the trading names for his business: the Hansard Union.

In January 1889, the rumour surfaced (no doubt with Bottomley's encour-agement) that the Conservative MP for Islington North George Bartley was considering resignation.[75] In the event, however, Bartley held his nerve – and was still in office 17 years later.

Bottomley was forever looking for other ways to keep his name in the news. In October 1889, he gave ten guineas to the tram-drivers' strike fund.[76] In light of Bottomley's later politics, this modest gift deserves a little context.

The end of the 1880s is often recalled as a breakthrough period in the history of labour. The year before, Annie Besant's paper *The Link* had published an account of the women employed at the Bryant and May factory, which was about two miles east of Bottomley's birthplace. The women worked for poverty wages; 1400 of them were on strike. The match-girls walked all the way to meet Besant in her Fleet Street headquarters, [77] just a quarter of a mile from Bottomley's offices on Chancery Lane.

Besant noted that the Fabian Society had passed a motion that its members refuse to purchase Bryant and May matches, as the women were paid just two pennies and a farthing for every 144 boxes they made, while the company was paying a huge dividend to its shareholders, £20 per year for every £100 of shares they owned. The hours were punishing: "The hour for commencing work is 6.30 in summer and 8 in winter; work concludes at 6 p.m. Half-an-hour is allowed for breakfast and an hour for dinner. This long day of work is performed by young girls, who have to stand the whole of the time". (The word "girls" was misleading: although many of the workers were young, a number were married women in their 30s and older.)

Managers were permitted to fine workers for slow or inadequate labour. Besant also described the workers' righteous anger at the factory owner Mr Bryant, and his visible support for key Liberal causes, which included stopping a shilling from each girl's wages so that he might build a statue for the party leader William Gladstone.[78]

A new spirit could be seen in all the great cities. In the words of the Irish playwright Oscar Wilde: "We are often told that the poor are grateful for charity... They are ungrateful, discontented, disobedient, and rebellious. They are quite right to be so".[79]

In 1889 gas workers at Beckton had recruited 3,000 members to a new, general union for unskilled labour, whose principal demand was the eight-hour day. By August, dockers were on strike, calling a London-wide general strike on 28 August. Although the call for a general strike was rescinded, the message had been received. Those who participated in it included 6,000 Jewish tailoring workers. That autumn in central and east London there were around 50 strikes, many of them small and localised but the majority victorious.[80]

We can perhaps begin to understand why the tram workers struck, and also why Bottomley might have seen their protest as in line with his politics, and why he wanted to be seen to support them. He was not a socialist, no natural friend of trade unions, and not of strikes. Calculated or not, Besant's mention of the Gladstone statue in the Bryant and May story must have irritated this aspiring young

Liberal politician. Yet these leftward-moving workers were also the potential audience for Bottomley's preferred project.

An old theme of George Jacob Holyoake's politics was coming back into fashion: the demand for labour representation in Parliament. So were other old ideas from the socialist programme of decades before, including the trade unions once championed by Robert Owen, so many of whose members were on strike. To an ambitious young left-Liberal candidate, it was too soon to know whether or not these forces could still be accommodated within his camp, as they had been for most of the past 40 years. The wisest thing was to say little and to keep friends in both the Radical and Socialist camps.

His greatest chance to contribute was not the donation of modest sums to strikes but through reporting the protests in his newspapers. Bryant and May already appeared in the *Financial Times*, as a company whose stock prices were quoted daily. Two weeks after Besant's first article, the *Financial Times* reported the fact of the match workers' strike. But where Besant showed them to be the victims of low wages and unsafe conditions – including the phosphorous poisoning that led to deformed "fossy" jaw – the story of the dispute as Bottomley told it was of a virtuous British company trying its best to pay a living wage, and being sabotaged by the reality of foreign competition.

Good working conditions had long been widespread throughout the British industry, or so Bottomley assured his readers. Those conditions were being "pushed aside by the much cheaper productions of Sweden where the whole conditions of labour are much inferior to this country". Warming to his theme, he continued: "The huge trade in small Swedish safety matches that has sprung up within the last few years must have attracted the attention of all our readers, and this trade is yet in its infancy". While the Scandinavian businesses had the benefit of access to cheap timber, the English manufacturers were "large importers", and were "helpless" to provide their workers with safe working conditions. "We have one large Company (the Swedish Match Company) employing about 3,000 hands at six factories in Sweden, who are pouring their goods into this country in competition with native labour". It was the Swedish company's access to timber and the finest machinery in the world which ensured the "unfortunate" conditions of the match-makers of East London.[81]

Had the owners of Bryant and May been paying Bottomley for his services,[82] he could have done little more to excuse their workers' conditions.

Bottomley's swindle

By 1889, Bottomley had already sold Hansard, but, retaining the association with its name, he launched the Hansard Publishing Union Ltd. He asked O'Hagan to back the proposal but O'Hagan declined. Directors recruited in his place including Sir Henry Isaacs (a recent Lord Mayor of London) and his brother Mr Joseph Isaacs.[83] Bottomley wooed Sir Henry with a generous signing-on fee of £2,000.

Others brought in included the publisher[84] C. Kegan Paul and Sir Roper Lethbridge, a Conservative MP.[85]

Bottomley delegated the task of identifying possible directors to another journalist, Frank Harris, former editor of the *London Evening News* and current editor of the *Fortnight Review*, for which George Bernard Shaw and Max Beerbohm also wrote. A cynic, a blackmailer and an adventurer,[86] Harris persuaded the banker Coleridge Kennard to finance Bottomley's company in return for his own personal cut, a commission of £10,000.[87]

The idea behind the scheme remained the same. Bottomley was desperate to increase the size of his business. The Hansard Union was intended to be a giant corporation combining printing and publishing. In the City, seasoned financiers were already dubbing it "Bottomley's swindle".[88] It all seemed to be too good to be true: a huge business growing from nowhere, with a young owner no longer supported by his previous patron (O'Hagan). Within a week of Hansard's launch, a small news story broke which should have given any prospective shareholder reason to pause. Bottomley was bringing a High Court case against his own stockbrokers Vigne & Co, complaining that they had prematurely sold shares in a company called Primitive Nitrates. Had they delayed for a week, the stocks if sold could have realised a profit of £1,000. The stockbrokers' said that when they realised that Bottomley did not have the funds to pay for the shares, they had no choice but to sell. Bottomley lost the case.[89]

In December, Hansard Union purchased *Galignani's Messenger*, an English-language newspaper for expatriates living in France. Bottomley was also discussing with friends the possibility of a new and suggestive title for it: *International Times*.[90] Bottomley had arranged for James Phillips, a junior clerk, to purchase Bottomley's papers from MacRae, Curtice.[91] In essence a dummy purchaser, Phillips paid £238,000 for them and then sold them to the Hansard Union, the directors making payments of £340,000 altogether. The difference between these two sums, or £102,000, went to Bottomley.[92]

The young plutocrat then suggested that still more printing capacity needed to be purchased. By seeming coincidence, a certain Charles Dollman had written soon afterwards to the directors, offering to sell them two printing mills in Devon for £105,000: the Cullompton mills and the Athenaeum works at Redhill.[93] Bottomley instructed his accountant Dalton Easum to value the mills at this amount,[94] and encouraged his fellow directors to accept the offer. But Dollman was Bottomley's sister Florence's[95] husband, playing a role he'd been assigned by Bottomley. Indeed, he'd earlier purchased the mills, with Bottomley's assistance, for just £15,000.[96] Scrutinising the acquisition, an industry publication, *The Paper Record*, suggested that the price paid for the mills had been exaggerated.[97]

In summer 1890, Bottomley obtained a court order preventing yet another paper, *The Vanguard*, from reporting on Hansard's various difficulties.[98]

The Hansard Union was still losing money. Its proprietor's answer was more acquisitions. Horatio announced that he would tour Austria, purchasing still further mills to solve his continued lack of printing capacity. But the mission was quixotic. Bottomley spoke no German, and knew but a single person in Vienna, a retired patent officer. What he did have was Bradlaugh's legacy – whose commercial visits had taken him to Italy. If his mentor found success overseas, then the younger man should follow him.

The patent officer prepared for Bottomley's arrival by insisting he was travelling as the agent of the Lord Mayor of London, Sir Henry Isaacs. Bottomley was met at the station and driven to the Grand Hotel. The entire staff had been assembled, and he was conducted to the Prince of Wales's personal suite.[99] He found an anglophile lawyer, Dr Ludwig Kunwald, to carry out negotiations with the printers, and agreed to acquire their businesses for £75,000.[100] He established another company, the Anglo Austrian Printing and Publishing Union Limited, to administer business – though the intended purchase was never in fact completed.[101]

Meanwhile other events were tending to suggest that the new rise of the general trade unions had already been halted. After two years in which seemingly every union recruitment drive and every strike had been successful, defeats were beginning to be reported. One of the most important was the silk weavers' strike at Manningham Mill in Bradford in winter 1890–91. Mill owner Samuel Lister had boasted that his plant was a model factory, ideal for sober, Methodist workers, but in December 1890 he had cut wages by a third. The weavers struck for five months, but were forced to return to work with the pay cut still in place. When conditions were favourable for strikes, the dockers' leader Ben Tillett had called the idea of expecting reforms, such as works for the unemployed, from Parliament "absurd".[102] But as the Manningham Mill strike went down to defeat, Tillett was forced to reconsider, and many drew the same lesson.

As Bottomley was fighting keep his business alive, Annie Besant was embarked on her most dramatic intellectual conversion – to Theosophy, a movement founded in America a quarter of a century before by a Russian immigrant Helena Blavatsky, which emphasised the supernatural and the esoteric. It had taken Blavatsky to India, where for years she had a headquarters in Tamil Nadu. By the time of Bottomley's victory over *The Vanguard*, Blavatsky was in London, ill, and looking for a successor.[103] As the workers' movement retreated, Besant followed her, just as after 1848 Robert Owen had swapped socialism for spiritualism.

On 30 January 1891 Charles Bradlaugh, while speaking on a public platform, caught a severe chill and died. Besant was the sole mourner to wear black. Others paying their respects at the graveside included 17 MPs, the artist Walter Sickert, George Jacob Holyoake, and even the future Mahatma Gandhi, then still a young law student. The Catholic monarchist G. K. Chesterton recalled his adversary's "gigantic stature, his warm temperament, his good health and good humour, his bull-necked obstinacy, his generous and open temper".[104] Henry Labouchere published an obituary in his newspaper *Truth*: "Mr Bradlaugh was a man of herculean physical strength, but of great nervous susceptibility. I believe that he never entirely recovered from the rough usage which he met when he sought to force his way into the House of Commons". Bradlaugh's critics, he explained, had profoundly misunderstood him, in treating him as a leveller and a democrat. "Never was a man less understood. I never knew anyone with a stronger sense of public decorum or with a deeper respect for the law".[105]

Bottomley was still pre-occupied with keeping his business afloat, and had to make his way in life without a father-figure. The Debenture Asset Corporation lent him £50,000. But the loans never came fast enough to cover the debts. In March, a committee of the shareholders of the Anglo Austrian Printing and Publishing Union produced a damning report: "The result of our investigations as to the conditions and prospects of the company is to show that its condition is insolvent... The company has acquired no business in Vienna or elsewhere, has no property whatsoever, and its whole capital appears to be lost". The only hope of saving anything lay in expelling the present board, including Bottomley, from their posts.[106]

In light of this report, the Attorney General was asked in the House of Commons in April 1891 whether he had any plans to prosecute Bottomley. He answered no; others were better placed to investigate.[107] The Hansard Union went into liquidation[108] and on 1 May Bottomley was declared bankrupt. His debts were estimated at £265,000, the largest being £150,000 owed to the Hansard Union – and £75,000 for the expenses of the trip to Austria.[109]

His insolvency brought his hopes of a political career to an abrupt halt, since a bankrupt may not stand for Parliament. Rival candidates put themselves forwards, including the Fabian socialist Sidney Webb. This must have been a disappointment to Bottomley, but it was not his most immediate concern – the seat in question was after all still held by the Conservatives.[110] The more immediate threat was the likelihood of criminal charges, carrying the risk of imprisonment. The facts against him seemed overwhelming.

Hansard Union: reckoning and vindication

The collapse of the Hansard Union left a large number of aggrieved creditors. A meeting of its shareholders called for a proper investigation of the books: "Mr Horatio Bottomley's name was repeatedly mentioned in very uncomplimentary terms, being received with hisses and other signs of indignation".[111] The shareholders had invested in a company which on dissolution seemed to have few assets and debts in the tens of thousands. Several institutions had been persuaded to loan the company money, including the Debenture Corporation. The collapse gave every impression of fraud. Bottomley, his directors Joseph and Sir Henry Isaacs, and Charles Dollman, were charged with conspiring to obtain £30,000 from the shareholders of the Hansard Union and of Anglo Austrian Printing and Publishing.[112]

For three weeks between 30 January and 25 April 1893, the case of *R v Bottomley* was heard before Mr Justice Hawkins and a special jury in the High Court.

As it opened, a conviction must have seemed a formality – yet the prosecution was soon in difficulty. At the start of the case, Henry Isaacs had instructed Sir Charles Russell to act as his barrister, a choice that may well have appealed to Bottomley, since Russell was a Liberal.[113] He was also an avid sportsman on the verge of being elected president of the Pegasus Club, [114] which organised annual point-to-point races for barristers. And he was the sitting MP for Hackney South, just two miles from the Islington North seat that Bottomley was still cultivating.

A previous chapter described how the mainstream Liberalism of the 1870s sought to balance social interests, looking for a middle way between the Conservatives who had the support of the rural rich, and such movements as Chartism who looked to the urban poor. By the 1890s, these debates were entwined with arguments about the Empire. The Conservatives were no longer a party of mere rejection (*against* 1789, *against* 1832) but had since the mid-1870s[115] become the party of the expansion of British military power. The Liberals, too, were for Empire, but of a fairer sort. Russell incarnated these politics, being the son of a County Down brewer, and Catholic, who had moved to London in the 1850s, and become a successful barrister. While voting with the Home Rule party on Irish issues, he was elected to Parliament on a Liberal ticket, and was one of the leaders of that party.

As it happened, Russell was unable to take up Isaacs' instructions. In autumn 1892, the Liberals had appointed Russell Attorney General, meaning that one of his first duties in the post was to take over the prosecution of his own former client.

Bottomley announced that he would represent himself, declaring that his model in this was once more Charles Bradlaugh, who had so often done so, with such repeated success.

The defendants were lucky in the Crown charge of conspiracy, which was an overreach. It is one thing to prove that a director has benefited from a failed business but it is always more difficult to prove that a director has conspired with others. Bottomley was also fortunate in the judge, Mr Justice Hawkins. Known as "hanging Hawkins", [116] he had a reputation for toughness but few things pleased him more than a celebrated barrister being teased by a confident defendant. As a barrister he had also worked with Bradlaugh some 30 years before, defending Bradlaugh's friend Simon Bernard when he was accused of conspiring to kill Napoleon III.[117]

Hawkins showed Bottomley considerable indulgence. Bottomley spoke constantly, joking, interrupting his opponents' speeches, and so confusing the proceedings that the allegations faded from memory. All that remained was his performance. At the start of the hearing, he remarked that while not yet 33, he was supposed to have committed 21 pages of crime. Hawkins replied "That is nothing. I can remember an indictment with 99 counts". Continuing the joke, Bottomley answered, "That must have been for some older criminal".[118] All this was bad law but terrific theatre. As Bottomley's friend Frank Harris wrote, "I was never more amused in my life, or more interested".[119]

Before the case ended, Russell was replaced as leading counsel for the prosecution by the Solicitor-General, Sir John Rigby, who was incapable of restraining so determined a courtroom troublemaker. Bottomley treated Rigby dismissively: "After the dreary legal arguments to which they have listened, it will be the duty of the jury and I almost said their pleasure to hear what the defendants have to say in their defence". He went on, "The Crown has had unqualified access to all documents of mine and to every scrap of paper, however private. I will satisfy the jury that the Hansard Union was no fraud, and I am no criminal".[120]

As to the allegations of conspiracy, Bottomley had a defence of sorts. It was not unusual, he maintained, for company directors to employ agents as purchasers of property. If he had made a profit on the purchase of the Devon mills, this was of no consequence: the mills had been worth the money paid for them. In short, the effect of the prosecution was to destroy a good company on the verge of greatness: "The Hansard Union was from beginning to end an honest, a sound and a prosperous undertaking". It had been brought low by the timidity of institutional shareholders, "these Moneylenders with their 20 percent in their pockets".[121]

On 19 April, still confident he could secure a conviction, Sir John Rigby began his closing speech. His set out how the defendants had conspired to purchase a paper mill at an inflated value, thus committing a fraud against their own shareholders.[122] Mr Justice Hawkins asked him for some compelling evidence of the correct value. Rigby said that Dollman had bought them for £15,000. This, Hawkins answered, was insufficient to prove that they were worth less than the £105,000 that Hansard paid for them. He went on to direct that the charges against Henry and Joseph Isaacs be dropped.[123]

Bottomley's closing speech represented all charges against him not as a punishment for anything done in business but as the work of a Conservative government and its Official Receiver, punishing him for failing to go along with them. Yes, the Hansard Union had purchased the mills for more than they were worth, but they were bought because they "were the only suitable ones of which particulars reached the company. It was a matter of complete indifference to me as to whether the Hansard Union purchased or not".[124] (In fact, far from being a matter of complete indifference, even on Bottomley's own version of events the translation had earned him a windfall profit of more than £50,000.)

The company, he insisted, had been a success right until up its end: "The Hansard business never failed – it was wrecked! Its business is still flourishing. I refused to be a party to the wrecking and therefore been singled out by the prosecution".[125] This, too, was rather less than the full truth. The business had exhausted its capital and its income. It could not even pay the interest on its debts. But the story was put bravely and with confidence, and the prosecutors were unable to dispel the good effect of Bottomley's words.

Mr Justice Hawkins told the jury that the directors had been careless and neglectful, but this was not enough to constitute conspiracy. He criticised the prosecution and said that the Official Receiver had been animated by personal dislike.[126] As for Bottomley, Mr Justice Hawkins advised, "A man ought not to be told by the jury, 'We are not satisfied of the evidence; therefore we are giving you the benefit of the doubt'. He has a right to say, 'I claim the right to be acquitted if you are satisfied'. That is the right every Englishman has".[127]

No defendant could have asked for a more favourable jury direction. After just 25 minutes of deliberation the jurors acquitted Bottomley. They then lined up to shake his hand and congratulate him as he left the court.

Just like his hero, Charles Bradlaugh, Bottomley was both editor and candidate. He had founded a company and unlike Bradlaugh had kept it going – until it was worth hundreds of thousands. Like Bradlaugh he had been tested in court, and had won. Unlike Bradlaugh, he had shown it was possible to be both at once a successful businessman and a campaigner.

Notes

1 Niblett, *Dare to Stand Alone*, pp. 266–7.
2 H. M. Hyndman, *Will Socialism Benefit the English People?* (London: Freethought Publishing Company, 1884).
3 Hyndman, *Will Socialism*; H. M. Hyndman, *Record of an Adventurous Life* (London: Macmillan, 1911), pp. 311–2.
4 Aveling to Bradlaugh, 29 July 1884, Bradlaugh papers, Bishopsgate Institute, Bradlaugh 1128.
5 Y. Kapp, *Eleanor Marx: Volume 2: The Crowded Years 1844–1898* (London: Lawrence and Wishart, 1976), p. 17; P. Brent, *The Edwardians* (London: British Broadcasting Corporation, 1972), pp. 141–70.
6 C. Shaw, 'Eliminating the Yahoo Eugenics, Social Darwinism and Five Fabians', *History of Political Thought* 8/3 (1987), pp. 521–44.
7 B. Webb, *My Apprenticeship* (London: Penguin, 1938), p. 349.
8 Kapp, *Eleanor Marx*, Vol. 2, pp. 36–7.
9 Taylor, *Annie Besant*, p. 164.
10 Kapp, *Eleanor Marx*, Vol. 2, pp. 725–30.
11 Taylor, *Annie Besant*, p. 163.
12 Taylor, *Annie Besant*, p. 163.
13 M. Holroyd, *Bernard Shaw* (London: Chatto & Windus, 1997), p. 99.
14 Niblett, *Dare to Stand Alone*, p. 280.
15 In his diary for 1887, Shaw noted that their intimacy had reached "a point at which it threatened to become a vulgar intrigue, chiefly through my fault. But I roused myself in time and avoided this". Holroyd, *Bernard Shaw*, p. 99.
16 Taylor, *Annie Besant*, p. 175.
17 Taylor, *Annie Besant*, p. 176.
18 The price was 4d.
19 Bottomley, *Bottomley's Book*, p. 93.
20 This was bought by Bottomley in c1882. Its previous title had been *Boy's Newspaper*.
21 Bottomley, *Bottomley's Book*, p. 92.
22 Houston, *The Real Horatio Bottomley*, p. 171.
23 In a nice parallel with Bottomley's career, Harmsworth reports that his father regarded his career in journalism as a waste of time and "urged that I should abandon the Street of Adventure for Pump Court" [i.e. to become a barrister]. A. C. W. Harmsworth (Lord Northcliffe), *The Rise of the Daily Mail* (London: Carmelite House, 1916), p. 6.
24 R. M. Wilson, *Lord Northcliffe* (London: J. B. Lippincott, 1927), pp. 49–50.

25 Wilson, *Lord Northcliffe*, pp. 50, 52.

26 *Youth*, 5 December 1883.

27 *Youth*, 5 March 1884.

28 P. Ferris, *The House of Northcliffe* (London: Weidenfeld & Nicolson, 1971), p. 24; R. Bourne, *Lords of Fleet Street: The Harmsworth Dynasty* (London: Unwin, Hyman 1990), p. 10; J. Goodwin, *Eton as She Is Not* (London: R. Ingalton Drake, 1884).

29 It's perhaps worth saying that Bottomley and Harmsworth each told a different version of this story to their respective biographers – and both versions are inaccurate.

30 *Youth*, 30 July 1884.

31 *Youth*, 14 January 1885. The *Debater* had also published similar replies to correspondents, see for example, *The Debater*, 18 October 1883. In an earlier period, Holyoake's papers had done similar, for example, *The Secular World*, 1 August 1863. As had Bradlaugh's, for example, *National Reformer*, 16 July 1876.

32 A person of that name, living in the Regent's Park district of central London, was a Vice-President of the Youth Scientific and Literary Society of London. 'Out Scientific Directory', *Hardwicke's Science Gossip: Volume XXII* (London: Chatto and Windus, 1886), p. 65.

33 An Edward Butler designed one of the world's first motorised tricycles in 1888. G. N. Georgano, *Cars: Early and Vintage 1886–1930* (London: Grange-Universal, 1990), p. 22.

34 It may be that Harmsworth was taken with this innovation. His career as a publisher would begin in 1888 with the publication of a journal of his own, *Answers to Correspondents*. Its selling point was the supposed employment of experts in medicine, law, employment, household matters, etc., who would then answer readers' questions on a range of topics. *Answers to Correspondents*, 2 June 1888.

35 Bottomley, *Bottomley's Book*, p. 92.

36 Bottomley, *Bottomley's Book*, p. 92.

37 The price was 1 shilling; there were special editions for the colonies and abroad. *May's British and Irish Press Guide* (London: May & Co, 1885).

38 The price was 21 shillings.

39 Bottomley, *Bottomley's Book*, p. 92.

40 Prospectus, 1887. Bottomley's scheme received favourable comment in the *York Herald*, 23 February 1887.

41 Niblett, *Dare to Stand Alone*, p. 297.

42 Niblett, *Dare to Stand Alone*, p. 300.

43 Bottomley, *Bottomley's Book*, p. 51; *Daily News*, 2 July 1887; *The Standard*, 2 July 1887.

44 *Daily News*, 6 July 1887.

45 *The Standard*, 18 July 1887.

46 *North-Eastern Daily Gazette*, 20 July 1887.

47 *Daily News*, 29 August 1887; *The Standard*, 25 October 1887. One of the topics on which Bottomley chose to address the Islington voters was the abolition of the House of Lords. *Daily News*, 13 December 1887. The present-day MP for the constituency is Jeremy Corbyn.

48 Bottomley, *Bottomley's Book*, p. 55.

49 'Political items', *Reynolds's Newspaper*, 3 November 1889.

50 Bottomley to Lloyd George, undated but 1923 or 1924, Parliamentary archives, LG/G30/2/62.

51 E. P. Thompson, *William Morris: Romantic to Revolutionary* (London: Merlin Press, 1996 edn), p. 489.

52 Thompson, *William Morris*, pp. 492–6.

53 D. C. Smith (ed), *The Correspondence of H. G. Wells* (London: Pickering & Chatto, 1998), Vol. 1, pp. 95–6.

54 R. Davenport-Hines, 'O'Hagan Henry', *Dictionary of National Biography* (Oxford: Oxford University Press, 2004), Vol. 41, p. 619.

55 O'Hagan claimed never to invest in a business except after having made close investigation of the terms under which it was being sold. One of his rules of thumb was that whenever a company sought a public sale, the previous managers should remain with it and continue to have a financial interest in the business even after the transfer. P. L. Cottrell, *Industrial Finance 1830–1914* (London: Routledge, 2005), pp. 185–6.

56 Symons, *Horatio Bottomley*, p. 2.

57 The company's launch was reported in *Leeds Mercury*, 23 November 1887. The details of its dissolution, two years later, are set out in Tenax, *The Rise and Fall*, p. 287.

58 Originally this was titled the *Financial and Mining News*. Despite competition from the *Financial Times*, it remained into the 20th century the best-selling financial paper in England.

59 *Financial News*, 23 January 1904.

60 G. Robb, *White-Collar Crime in Modern England: Financial Fraud and Business Morality 1845–1929* (Cambridge: Cambridge University Press, 1992), p. 116.

61 The *Guide* originally appeared on Mondays, Wednesdays and Fridays. Its successor the *Financial Times* was daily from its inception.

62 *Financial Times*, 5 March 1888. Bottomley would later run a similar column in *John Bull*.

63 *Financial Times*, 6 March 1888. Bottomley would later an almost identical "service" in *John Bull*.

64 For example, "Foreign Industries and Mines: The Oregon Wheat Crop Promises a Bountiful Harvest". *Financial Times*, 7 March 1888. Bottomley employed a similar format of very brief stories at *John Bull*.

65 *Financial Times*, 24 April 1888.

66 'Bankruptcy court', *Financial Times*, 8 March 1888.

67 *Financial Times*, 7 March 1888.

68 *Financial Times*, 23 August 1888.

69 *Financial Times*, 13 March 1888.

70 *Financial Times*, 28 June 1888.

71 *Financial Times*, 25 December 1888.

72 D. Kynaston, *The Financial Times: A Centenary History* (London: Viking, 1988), p. 21.

73 MacRae was able to keep the paper going only by generous subsidies from O'Hagan.

74 W. P. Hall, 'Printer to the House', *American Historical Review* 59/3 (1954), pp. 612–13.

75 'The Representation of North Islington', *Aberdeen Weekly Journal*, 31 January 1889.

76 'A London Tramway Strike', *Freeman's Journal*, 14 October 1889.

77 J. Charlton, *"It Just Went Like Tinder": The Mass Movement and New Unionism in Britain 1889* (London: Redwords, 2009), p. 15.

78 'White Slavery in London', *The Link*, 23 June 1888.

79 O. Wilde, *The Soul of Man and Prison Writings* (Oxford: Oxford University Press, 1962), p. 4.

80 Charlton, *"It Just Went Like Tinder"*, pp. 95–7.

81 *Financial Times*, 10 July 1888.

82 Besant's biographer Anne Taylor reports that Bryant and May's Managing Director G. P. Bartholomew had resorted to precisely this ruse; putting in advance orders for thousands of copies of newspapers on the day that they might be expected to print the Company's annual report, then, when any negative coverage of the company appeared in their columns (as it did, for example, in the *Daily Telegraph*) refusing to pay the bill. Taylor, *Annie Besant*, p. 209.

83 Felstead, *Horatio Bottomley*, p. 19.

84 The Kegan Paul business amalgamated with Routledge in 1912.

85 Hyman, *The Rise and Fall*, p. 31.

86 Among the many scandals in which Frank Harris played a part was assisting the Marxist propagandist and former mistress of King Edward VII, Daisy Warwick, in her proposal that the royal family should purchase her memoirs for £100,000 to avoid press coverage of their affair. Brent, *The Edwardians*, p. 213.

87 Symons, *Horatio Bottomley*, p. 31.

88 A. J. A. Morris, 'Bottomley, Horatio', *Dictionary of National Biography* (Oxford: Oxford University Press, 2004), Vol. 6, p. 770.

89 'Law Intelligence', *Morning Post*, 11 April 1889.

90 'The English Press on the Continent', *Daily News*, 14 December 1889.

91 Symons, *Horatio Bottomley*, p. 29.

92 The Annual General Meeting of the company took place just as this issue was being fought through the board. 'Joint Stock Companies', *Morning Post*, 21 January 1890.

93 That is, as far away from proper scrutiny as Bottomley could reasonably travel.

94 Hyman, *The Rise and Fall*, p. 42.

95 Florence died in 1909. On her anniversary, Horatio always went to Highgate Cemetery to leave flowers on her grave. Hyman, *The Rise and Fall*, p. 132.

96 Symons, *Horatio Bottomley*, p. 31; Hyman, *The Rise and Fall*, p. 37. Of this £15,000, only £2,500 was actually paid.

97 Bottomley accused the paper's editor John Strachan Smith of raising these matters maliciously, to blackmail him, after which Smith sued Bottomley for libel, and was awarded £100 damages. Bottomley applied for but was refused an order delaying payment. 'The Affairs of the Hansard Union', *Pall Mall Gazette*, 13 April 1891; 'London', *Daily News*, 16 April 1891.

98 'Law Intelligence', *Morning Post*, 28 August 1890.

99 The Prince was away from Vienna at the time.

100 Bottomley, *Bottomley's Book*, pp. 159–64; 'English Enterprise in Vienna', *Morning Post*, 11 February 1890.

101 One major investor in this company was the Conservative MP for Cheltenham, Sir James Tync Agg-Gardner, who lost £15,000 on the company, and retired from public life soon after.

102 D. Renton, 'Class Consciousness and the Origins of Labour', *International Socialism Journal* 88 (2000), pp. 143–8.

103 G. Stedman Jones, 'The Flight of a Clergyman's Wife', *London Review of Books*, 27 May 1993.

104 Mount, 'Get off Your Knees'.

105 A. L. Thorold, *The Life of Henry Labouchere* (London: Constable and Company, 1913), p. 146.

106 Hyman, *The Rise and Fall*, p. 34.

107 'Parliamentary Notes', *Birmingham Daily Post*, 14 April 1891.

108 'The Affairs of the Hansard Publishing Union Limited', *Manchester Guardian*, 22 July 1891; Tenax, *The Rise and Fall*, p. 287.

109 'Horatio Bottomley's Enormous Liabilities', *Blackburn Standard and Weekly Express*, 13 June 1891.

110 'Mr Bottomley and North Islington', *Pall Mall Gazette*, 15 May 1891. George Bartley held Islington North for the Conservatives until 1906.

111 'The Hansard Publishing Union', *Birmingham Daily Post*, 5 May 1891.

112 'The Hansard Union', *Western Mail*, 23 February 1892.

113 Russell's best-known client was Charles Parnell, the leader of the Home Rule party in the Commons. R. B. O'Brien, *The Life of Lord Russell of Killowen* (London: Smith, Elder & Co., 1901), pp. 208–58.

114 C. P. Hawkes, *Bench and Bar in the Saddle* (London: Eveleigh Nash and Grayson, 1928), p. 224.

115 That is, since Disraeli's decision to have Queen Victoria proclaimed Empress of India in 1877.

116 Hyman, *The Rise and Fall*, p. 36. In the same way judges today might be known as "Custody Clark" or "Custody Cooper", the nicknames owe as much to alliteration as to the judges' personality in court.

117 Lavin, *Bradlaugh Contra Marx*, pp. 44–5.

118 Symons, *Horatio Bottomley*, p. 31.

119 Hyman, *The Rise and Fall*, p. 37; Symons, *Horatio Bottomley*, p. 31.

120 Hyman, *The Rise and Fall*, p. 39.

121 Tenax, *The Rise and Fall*, p. 30.

122 Hyman, *The Rise and Fall*, p. 41.

123 Symons, *Horatio Bottomley*, p. 33; Tenax, *The Rise and Fall*, pp. 30–1.

124 Hyman, *The Rise and Fall*, p. 45.

125 Hyman, *The Rise and Fall*, p. 46.

126 Symons, *Horatio Bottomley*, p. 34.

127 Tenax, *The Rise and Fall*, pp. 30–1.

5
COMPANY PROMOTER, BUCKET-SHOP KEEPER

Bottomley had to find new employment. His first offer, or so he claimed, came from within the legal system, when he was invited to Mr Justice Hawkins' chambers at the end of the trial. Hawkins complimented him and encouraged him to train as a barrister. The solicitor Edward Bell writes that Bottomley considered qualifying and even applied to an Inn to see if a place might be found for him: "An intimation, however, was conveyed to him, that it would be a wise decision if he withdrew".[1] In his Pall Mall mansion he would afterwards display a judge's wig and a notebook containing notes of the trial, telling guests that Hawkins had given them to him. Theodore Felstead, who knew Bottomley and is less reverential than other biographers, doubts this, terming it a "very strange thing for a cynical old gentleman like Hawkins to do". He notes that Bottomley did not reveal the wig until after the judge had died.[2]

The real decision facing Bottomley was not of course between the law and commerce, but instead how to re-establish himself in the business world. Or to put it differently, when he returned to finance, how would he approach this? The events that had led the trial were all to his discredit: he had built a business larger than he had the talent to control; he had channelled its funds into his own pockets. He had taken other people's money; he had done so through deceit. Another person might have reigned in their ambition before it was too late, or perhaps even dispensed with the habit of lying. This would have been the perfect time to have quit company promotion and re-establish contact with his parents' friends, including his uncle George Jacob Holyoake, who was still alive. Bottomley could have re-immersed himself in this world and learned some humility before building himself up again.

But if he even considered such a return, he must have known that left–Liberal politics were fracturing and recombining in ways very alien to him. With

DOI: 10.4324/9781003306085-5

Madame Blavatsky dead, Annie Besant had assumed leadership of the Theo-sophical Society, her recent socialism forgotten. The defeat of the silk weavers at Manningham Mill had convinced many trade unionists of the merits of Holy-oake's old cause: the need for labour representation in Parliament. Three months after the end of Bottomley's trial, Ben Tillett, now a member of the Parlia-mentary Committee of the TUC, stood in Bradford West as a "Labour Union" candidate, securing an impressive 2,700 votes, which was 30 percent of the poll. Following this strong performance, an Independent Labour Party held its first conference in Bradford in January 1893, with one of its speakers, Keir Hardie, declaring that the "aim of the Labour movement is to direct the attention of the workers [to] the one problem of how to restore to the working classes of the community the capital and the land without which they cannot carry on their industrial operations". The history of this notion within the workers' move-ment, of acquiring ownership of capital and land, was as old as the Owenites. Nevertheless, this rebirth of some of these demands had its critics. In particular the *Manchester Guardian* wanted its readers to know that, while it had always been on the side of the workers, they should never be so reckless as to consider splitting the existing left vote, from which no one save for the most vehement anti-Labourites (i.e. the Conservatives) could benefit: "There is a great deal to be done by... insisting on a plentiful direct representation of Labour; but there is nothing to be done by embarrassing Liberalism to the sole profit of the one anti-Labour party in the State".[3]

Rather than follow Holyoake's path, Bottomley chose instead to return to finance and the Hansard Union, to rebuild his career without a pause, and to do so using the same techniques that had almost brought him low. Still protected by his reputation as a Radical, Bottomley found himself in demand for interviews. He was approached by the *Pall Mall Gazette*, the forerunner of today's *Evening Standard*. The *Gazette's* editor William Thomas Stead had campaigned against child prostitution, writing a series of articles in 1885 under the title of "The Maiden Tribute of Modern Babylon". To prove the widespread availability of prostituted children in London, Stead had paid £5 to buy 13-year-old "Lily" (Eliza Armstrong) from her parents. The campaign was popular: the government responded with a Criminal Law Amendment Act making it a crime to abduct a girl for sex (meanwhile section 11 of the same act, passed on the motion of Henry Labouchere, criminalised all homosexual acts between men, even in private). But Stead's purchase of Lily had also led to his own prosecution for child abduction, and he had been jailed for three months.[4]

Eight years after these events, Stead's paper was still recovering from their taint. In his account of Bottomley's trials and vindication, the *Gazette's* journalist seemed star-struck: "We believe that Mr Bottomley is the only man who has had practical experience of every possible application of the Companies Acts; he has been chairman, managing director, and ordinary director of several important companies". In court he had been victorious:

> He has had over two years' personal experience of the Bankruptcy Court, fighting bitter and powerful opponents… reducing half a million of claims to a few thousands, and finally obtaining from the court a vindication of his commercial integrity.[5]

The reporting of the trial itself was no less breathless:

> For nearly 40 days he fought a most vigorously conducted Treasury prosecution… securing in the end not only an unqualified acquittal upon every charge, but also a great judicial tribute to himself from Mr Justice Hawkins.[6]

We can see in this passage the beginnings of a potent myth. Bottomley could be trusted as an investor, and should indeed be seen as a financial genius. The proof of his greatness was that he had been forced to justify himself and had vanquished his enemies in court.

Yet despite the acquittal Bottomley's company was still insolvent and he had personal debts of just under £100,000.[7] Three months later he was back before the courts, as his finances were examined following bankruptcy. He proposed to return to Austria to reclaim debts owed there. Justice Vaughan Williams agreed to this proposal, against the objections of the Official Receiver, who complained that Bottomley had been guilty of a gross, if not perhaps a criminal breach of trust, and was continuing to run his affairs recklessly.[8] Discharged from bankruptcy Bottomley did travel to Austria, but returned to London with no new funds.[9]

O'Hagan loaned him a vital £2,000 which was just about enough to set Bottomley up in business again.[10] In December 1893, Bottomley announced the launch of a Joint Stock Institute with a capital of £500,[11] to promote other people's companies. Compared with the £120,000 Bottomley had claimed to control when he launched Catherine Street publishing, this was a clear reduction of personal ambition.

However, Bottomley soon hit on a new scheme to create something from nothing. He proposed that his creditors should accept shares in a number of West Australian gold mines. Once again, we can discern the influence of his family. Forty years before, his uncle Horatio Holyoake had written to relatives in England about the gold trade: "I have been almost as many trades as I have been weeks in the colony. Now I think I have turned the last trade I shall be and that is Digger and I am only sorry I did not come to digging on my first onset in the colony".[12] Holyoake had warned that conditions in Australia were harder than they seemed because of competition from Chinese rivals, about whom he warned in lurid terms: "Shiploads of Chinese have been landed and as they can live upon one meal a day and that meal consists of one rat and a pound of bad rice".[13] But the gamble on gold was worth taking: "There is plenty of gold for digging for, and I shall get my share".[14] Some creditors may have been taken in by these promises, of wealth waiting under the ground. Others no doubt accepted out of desperation; if they wanted to be paid, what else could they do?

When he was living in Battersea, Bottomley had invented affluent relatives, any one of whom was likely, at any moment, to rescue him from poverty. Who was better placed to do this than this pan-handling uncle?[15] There is a wider salience to Bottomley's fantasies within the economic history of this moment. In 1860, considered as a nation, Britain already accounted for a staggering 19.9 percent of the world manufacturing output. By 1880, this share had risen to an even more impressive 22.9 percent. The figure would fall again over ensuing decades – but in 1893 the country remained the greatest manufacturing power the world had ever seen.[16] A close friend of George Jacob Holyoake's, the Liberal economist J. A. Hobson,[17] was a keen observer of the country's boom, speaking of "banking, broking, bill discounting, loan floating [and] company promoting", which, so he warned, were resulting in a troubling process of territorial expansion and threats of war.[18]

Australia and its gold industry were very relevant to the analysis. Settlement, wrote Hobson, "has commonly implied the extermination of the lower races, either by war or by private slaughter, as in the case of Australian Bushmen".[19] There was no expansion of the British colonies without the genocide of indigenous people, and however offensively the term "lower races" reads to us today, this was a declaration of opposition to the killings and to the economic processes driving them. But Hobson went on to warn of the risk of quitting the imperial territories: "If organised Governments of civilised Powers refused the task, they would let loose a horde of private adventurers, slavers, piratical traders, treasure hunters, concession mongers, who, animated by mere greed of gold or power, would set about the work of exploitation under no public control and with no regard to the future".[20]

Treasure hunters: here was the category that Bottomley aspired to join. The global advance of British industry and its subsequent relative decline were opening doors for him. The growth produced a large class of people made wealthy by the export of manufacture: the owners of industrial businesses, their suppliers, the sellers of manufactured goods. And the decline would require them to reinvest their surplus in new vehicles for profit-making. At a point when British industrial capacity was perhaps reaching a limit, Bottomley's shares offered a quick fix and might even seem like a wise investment.

Through the 1890s, British economic development saw financial as much as industrial expansion, as funds from financial services, insurance and shipping all passed through the City of London, which was beginning to dominate our economic life. The financier Sir Ernest Cassell described the transformation taking place: "When I was young, people called me a gambler. As the scale of my operations increased, I became known as a speculator. Now I am called a banker. But I have been doing the same thing all the time".[21]

The risks of exposure

Through the spring and summer of 1895, Horatio Bottomley could also observe what happened to anyone who offended Victorian standards of morality, in this case the Irish dramatist and socialist Oscar Wilde. In February the Marquess of

Queensbury, the father of Wilde's beloved Lord Alfred Douglas, had left a card at Wilde's club: "To Oscar Wilde posing Somdomite" [sic].[22] Acting on the advice of Travers Humphreys, a young and ambitious barrister, Wilde brought a private prosecution for criminal libel. When he approached Frank Harris – who was lunching at the Café Royal with Shaw – and asked him to be a witness, Harris warned Wilde that he would lose and urged him to drop the case: "You haven't a dog's chance, and the English despise the beaten".[23] As Shaw recalled, Wilde left enraged: "Oscar finally rose with a mixture of impatience and his grand air, and walked out with the remark that he had now found out who were his real friends".[24] But Harris was right. Marshalled by the barrister and politician Edward Carson, Queensbury's team announced it would be calling some of the male prostitutes Wilde had hired. Wilde withdrew the prosecution, but found himself being prosecuted in turn, for sodomy and gross indecency, as set out in section 11 of the Criminal Law Amendment Act. In May he was sentenced to two years hard labour. His final question, "May I say nothing, my Lord?" was drowned out by cries of disgust from the public gallery.

The Radical editor W. T. Stead had employed Wilde as a reviewer at the *Pall Mall Gazette*,[25] and had criticised the sentence as too severe but, now at the *Review of Reviews*, refused to publish defences of homosexuality, even when oblique or coded.[26] Outside England, socialists were defending Wilde and noting that homosexuality had existed throughout history; but in Britain the left joined in with the denunciations. The Independent Labour Party's paper *Labour Leader* claimed that the trial had revealed the "uncleanness" of the idle rich, with their lives of "filthy abomination". The SDF's *Justice* promised that the "addiction" of homosexuality would not survive socialism.[27]

Nugget in hand

Gold-mining in Australia had been a significant industry since the 1850s, the time of Horatio Holyoake's settling there. In the 1890s,[28] Arthur Bayley, a butcher's son, headed a team of prospectors from the nearby town of Southern Cross, a town of "white shacks… stars of the constellation on a dark night". A new boom began: "The first bar of gold smelted in the blacksmith's forge raised hopes sky high, although that bar of gold disappeared mysteriously".[29] With Bayley's renewed discovery of gold, the "town went mad… Every man who could stand brought stores, tried to beg, borrow, steal horses, a buggy or spring cart, and packed his tools and camping gear".[30] Prospectors arrived in their thousands. At first the miners owned what they dug. But as the boom continued, larger companies followed in their wake, buying the best mines, hiring the miners as cheap labour. The profits from the richest leases circulated upwards, enriching shareholders in London.

Gold exports from Western Australia reached £750,000 in 1895, rising by half again in 1896, then further doubling the following year.[31] Most diggers were British expatriates, who would return home telling of the treasures beneath the ground. To those who listened, gold seemed the ideal investment. The spread of the railways made it easier to transport workers to the sites where gold had been discovered and then to bring the gold home. The range of alternative investments had been narrowed by financial crises in Argentina and in North America, while the British government was scaling back its borrowing.[32]

From Bottomley's perspective, there were several advantages to this turn to mining. The first was this: a gold mine was by its very nature speculative, since no one knew until it had been dug whether there would be sufficient quantity to justify the digging. And at its start a mine always sucked up capital. If a seam proved rich its profits might cover the outlay, sometimes a decade or more after these costs had been incurred. Second, the speculators in London were 10,000 miles from the mines on which their hopes were pinned. Bottomley could promise the world to prospective buyers with little risk of being proved wrong. If enough people bought his shares their value would rise, and the initial purchasers could sell at a profit. They were trading on futures, and Bottomley excelled at selling hope.

Launched in winter 1894–95, Bottomley's first mining company was West Australian Loan and General Finance Corporation Limited, with a paper value of £50,000. It was followed by Associated Gold Mines of West Australia Limited, with a paper value of £375,000. Prospects were good, Bottomley insisted: "[In] a total area of between 10,000 and 12,000 square miles, there was a phenomenally rich gold bearing formation, which had hitherto been worked in a spasmodic and unscientific manner, chiefly by Chinese labour". The replacement of Chinese workers with men of European origins would guarantee the cultivation of a vast wealth: "the returns were of such a character that, having verified their genuineness by a reference to Government records and other official sources, your Directors lost no time in securing options upon nearly all of the best developed properties".[33]

"We own no mines", Bottomley said, "we do not go mining, and speaking for myself personally I do not profess to understand very much about mining".[34] Bottomley offered his services as a promoter. Capital for the development of mines was to be raised by the selling of shares to the general public; and Bottomley had an undoubted talent as a salesman.

At the end of the 1890s, Bottomley wrote back to his stockbroker, looking back on ruses they had worked together in the middle years of the decade: "What on earth have you done with our nugget – the one we used to show to shareholders in the old days? I've got hold of a promising client; all he wants is sight of the stuff".[35]

Beginning in 1894 and for the next six years, Bottomley, with offices in Broad Street Avenue[36] near Liverpool Street, founded 37 companies, with a combined paper value in excess of £15 million.[37] To put such figures in perspective, this is more than the annual spending by the government on welfare (£14 million at the end of this period).

Yet Bottomley was not operating on quite so grand a scale as this suggests. The 37 companies were in fact just one business: the Hansard Union, in a state of constant restructuring. Bottomley had made such a good job of settling this firm's debts that he did it twice. The first time was after his acquittal in 1893, when he persuaded those owed £30,000 or more to exchange their debts for mining shares. Four years later came the second settlement, when to cheers Bottomley announced that he was giving £250,000 to those who had lost from the Hansard crash.[38] He read out a letter from his accountant Dalston Easum, certifying that Bottomley had handed over to him disbursements amounting to £32,470.[39] "Hansard is dead", the press enthused, "but the calumniators of Mr Bottomley are themselves *Hansard* now".[40]

The money invested by former Hansard shareholders helped Bottomley to found a new company, the West Australian and New Zeeland Market Trust Limited. On its foundation in July 1897 it was worth £2.5 million. It went into voluntary liquidation just a year later.[41]

The millionaire

A novel that conveys the spirit of the times is H. G. Wells' *The Invisible Man*. Born six years after Bottomley, Wells had also experienced poverty as a boy. He too had run away from school and worked as a draper's assistant; he too had renounced that role[42] in favour of journalism. Published in 1897, *The Invisible Man* tells the tale of Griffin, a scientist and inventor who altered the pigmentation of his body to make himself invisible. Yet with this achievement comes no wisdom. To pay for his rooms, Griffin steals £2 10s in half-sovereigns from a small-town vicarage: witnesses see a "fist full of money" travelling through the air. Charged later with explaining his invention and his ill-fortune, Griffin blames a former mentor: a "scientific bounder, a journalist by instincts, a thief of ideas", who had threatened to plagiarise his student's discoveries. Griffin steals from his father, who then shoots himself. This is not to say that Griffin is Bottomley – or that Wells' book was influenced by Bottomley or even by Bottomley's craft of company promotion. But the novel does capture a late Victorian sense that wealth is created by theft upon theft, with each one the consequence of one earlier.[43]

The world economy was changing, and our present financial system was born. Unprecedented sums of capital were in circulation. In 1897 Bottomley would feature as one of a dozen magnates dubbed by the *Financial Times* "men of millions". Another was Barney Barnato, a South African diamond- and gold-mine owner who that June drowned in mysterious circumstances off the island of Madeira. The following year Barnato's heir Woolf Joel was murdered in his office, and his killer acquitted after claiming that Joel had been involved in a plot to kidnap the President of the Transvaal Boer Republic. A third was Whitaker Wright, a printer-turned-coal-millionaire who committed suicide after being convicted of fraud.[44]

In his memoirs, Bottomley insisted that "at heart" he had never "been a City man". Instead, he insisted, he had always been a political person, indeed a Radical:

> If I were asked to describe the square mile which constitutes the City, I should say that it represents that portion of the earth upon which are daily

gathered together all the worst types of the human race from a physical, moral and intellectual standpoint.[45]

We do not need to trust the author unduly here to acknowledge nevertheless that he saw himself as an outsider in the square mile – since others there had been born into far greater wealth or status. Compared to them, Bottomley looked on his surroundings with a sceptical eye.

Bottomley also offered a taxonomy of the various classes of investors attending the meetings of his companies (held by tradition at the Cannon Street Hotel, just south of the Bank of England). Among them was the anti-Board shareholder, who would "pester the Secretary with endless correspondence... seek interviews with the Directors, circularise the members, and at every meeting of the Company give vent to his dissatisfaction with the administration"; the pro-Board shareholder, a "benign old gentleman... usually a retired officer"; the accountant shareholder, "who tells the meeting he has made a study of figures all his life"; the legal shareholder, "he prefaces most of his sentences with the phrase 'Speaking as a lawyer'"; the facetious shareholder, whose function was to "keep everyone in good humour"; and the professional shareholder: "His remarks will invariably take the form of qualified hostility towards whomsoever he represents, and at the right moment he will if necessary get up and demand numerous explanations in the interests of the shareholders, who, little suspecting his real designs, will applaud him to the echo". But these demands were never sincere, since "eventually he will advise his co-proprietors not to press matters further".[46]

None of these were Bottomley's invention, but this last type does seem to reflect the growing number of individuals on Bottomley's personal payroll.[47] One such may have been the unnamed shareholder whose interventions are recorded at a Cannon Street meeting of Northern Territories Goldfields Ltd, asking the chairman Mr Smith if there was, as promised, £4 million of gold to be dug from the company's mine at Howley:

> Chairman: I think if you want to get a direct answer –
> Shareholder: Where is it?
> Chairman: Ask Mr Bottomley.
> Shareholder: Mr Bottomley is not here. I cannot ask him.[48]

Minutes later, Bottomley appeared at the back of the room. There were cries from the audience to let him speak, and he repeated his belief that there were indeed £4 million to be had. The chairman then spoke, repudiating these remarks. Mr Bottomley might have such a report, he said, but the company did not. Viewed in the round, the total scene seems a well-scripted piece of public theatre. Those who doubted the value of their shares could feel their voices had been heard. Those who trusted Bottomley could leave the room in a spirit of optimism. As for those looking in a more scrupulous fashion for a detailed analysis, they had been given nothing. Nobody could later have sued the company for any recklessness in its statements.

Eight days after the Northern Territories meeting, Bottomley received a letter from a Dr Alexander of Putney, who had set himself up as the champion of the shareholders in two of Bottomley's businesses, the Westralian Market Trust and the Joint Stock Trust. Alexander complained that the "continual fall in the price of shares must have some definite cause" – beyond the general depression of the sector, that is. In these circumstances, Alexander asked, would Bottomley agree to meet him and allow him to look into the books? Before agreeing to the request, Bottomley played for time: "I am sure the boards of both companies would require more definite information as to the character and extent of the representative authority which you claim". Alexander pressed him and Bottomley wrote back, asking that Alexander not get involved in any "internal agitation", but promising that if he supplied the names of any disaffected shareholders, Bottomley would approach them directly. Alexander delivered the names of many hundreds of shareholders in person to Bottomley's office. Again Bottomley promised to investigate; again he did nothing.[49]

Before his 40th birthday, Bottomley had already learned one of the most important skills for those who seek to prosper from other people's misery: the art of drowning any criticism beneath a weight of scorn. If people asked where the money had gone, Bottomley laughed at them. He insisted that it was ridiculous for anyone to doubt his word.

Bottomley addressed the shareholders of the Westralian Market Trust, saying the company had assets of £3 million. A member of the audience pointed out that the company had published no accounts, and that the sums quoted to shareholders were £700,000 less than Bottomley had promised. Bottomley replied that he had been asked "where the £700,000 had gone. He could only say, in all sincerity and honesty, he had not the remotest idea".[50]

In 1900, Bottomley wrote to one J. K. Peachey, who had bought shares in his Joint Stock Institute. "Perhaps you would like to run down and see me... I am naturally desirous of doing my best to prevent you from ultimately losing over the transaction".[51]

This same year Bottomley received a stark warning that his present business model could not continue. Over the past decade, another company promoter had been occupying very similar territory, with similar success: Whitaker Wright. Just like Bottomley, Wright had in 1897 been described by the *Financial Times* as a man of millions. He had specialised in Australian and South African mining companies, including one titled (Bottomley-style) the West Australian Exploring Corporation. To inflate their balance sheets, Wright's companies would trade assets and liabilities between themselves. But increased scrutiny of his South African activities, coinciding with the Boer War, had caused them to fail. Everything about Wright was swagger, *Blackwood's* wrote: "Swagger directors, swagger officers, swagger bankers, a swagger house at the West End, a swagger palace down at Surrey, a swagger yacht at Cowes".[52] Wright fled to the US. He was extradited, but swallowed cyanide in the Royal Courts of Justice rather than serve a seven-year jail term.

Back before the courts

During 1900, Bottomley was pursued by a creditor named Taylor, whose pamphlet *Horatio Bottomley, Politician, Philanthropist, Financier and Labour Candidate* accused him of packing shareholder meetings with his hangers-on and using them to put forward bogus resolutions. Bottomley brought a libel action, at which point Taylor announced himself satisfied by the receipts of the Hansard Union Relief Fund and withdrew the pamphlet.[53] But the episode encouraged a second sceptic into print, Henry Hess, the publisher of a rival paper, *The Critic*. On 22 September 1900, Hess claimed that the libel had been bogus, that Bottomley had deployed Taylor as a fake critic.[54] Bottomley was a rogue, Hess insisted. "Since the day when this barefaced swindler had the luck to escape conviction over the Hansard Company's frauds, he has engineered one imposition after another upon the credulous public". Over the past decade, fraud had succeeded fraud, "His West Australian Market Trust (reconstructed twice), his Howley, his Northern territories, his Joint Stock Institute, and his Associated Finance Corporation, have been deliberately planned schemes to rob the public". Bottomley's victims were "in the workhouse", while the thief was standing for Parliament. "His place is at the Old Bailey, not at Westminster", Hess concluded.[55]

Hess ran the piece in *The Critic* and then reproduced it as a pamphlet. Bottomley sued for libel.[56] All through his career, Bottomley liked to boast of himself as the finest lay lawyer in the kingdom – and most biographers take this claim at face value, citing his success as an unrepresented litigant.[57] But in this case against Hess, Bottomley called on the assistance of no fewer than three barristers, R. A. Jermaine, Redwood Davies and W. M. Thompson,[58] representing Associated Finance, North Western Associated Claims Western Australia, and the Liberal Party of South Hackney, the new constituency he was courting. If each was in theory independent of Bottomley, he was in reality paying their fees.[59]

Bottomley was an experienced courtroom performer. One observer noticed how Bottomley's voice rose or fell to punctuate his disapproval with Hess, "The voice is one of singular charm and power. Low, melodious, strong, it is an admirable instrument for an advocate". As for his face, "It is the face of a strong, determined man. It is capable of softness and tenderness to friends and relatives; it is the face of a man with an active conscience; but it can also be stark and stern and even pitiless at times". The author concluded that "Mr Bottomley represents the solid stuff out of which England's greatness has been woven".[60]

Cross-examined by a Mr McCall, who was investigating Hess's claim that Bottomley had been lucky to evade prosecution in the Hansard case, Bottomley refused to answer. The jurors asked to see evidence of fraud. Mr Justice Grantham explained to them that when Hess had sought the disclosure of the Hansard books, Bottomley had refused him permission to see them.[61] The reports in the press suggest that Bottomley withstood the inquisition:

"Presently Mr Bottomley got on Mr McCall's nerves. Papers were mislaid, references got lost, important dates could not be fixed. Long pauses ensued while counsel consulted with his colleagues, or listened to the eager advice of Mr Hess". While McCall moved about the room, anxiously, Bottomley held himself quite still: "Mr Bottomley stood calm and imperturbable in the box, rarely glancing at a note, relying almost entirely on a marvellously exact memory".[62]

The Taylor previously sued by Bottomley for libel then gave evidence, insisting that Bottomley had been blameless. Another witness was Sir Charles Turner, a trustee of the Hansard Relief Fund. Turner praised Bottomley for his generosity to his creditors.[63]

Henry Hess testified. Mr Justice Grantham complained that he spoke with a strong foreign accent (he had until recently lived in Johannesburg).[64] As Bottomley concluded his cross-examination of Hess, he was watching the jury:

> Bottomley: Now, Mr Hess, do you still persist, after all you have learnt in the course of this trial, in these charges against me?
> Hess: Yes, in all of them.
> Bottomley: And you say you are worth £7,500.[65]

This sum, he was implying, would be a fair sum for the damages owed to him.

Mr. Justice Grantham summed up for Bottomley. He had been acquitted in the Hansard Union trial; and Hess had no right to say that the acquittal had been fortunate.[66] The jury returned after just 25 minutes. Bottomley was awarded £1,000 in damages.

For years afterwards, Bottomley relied on this victory over Hess to warn off potential antagonists and to demonstrate the risk to them should they criticise him. For, as unsuccessful as he had proved in this case, Hess was a significant opponent. In his subsequent career as a journalist he would bring many low. One was to be Bradlaugh's former colleague at the Northampton hustings, the Liberal parliamentarian Henry Labouchere. In 1905, Hess would publish an exposé which showed that Labouchere had used his newspaper *Truth* to promote the interests of companies in which he was a shareholder. Faced with the choice of fighting Hess or running from his accusations, Labouchere adopted prudence. He told friends the allegations were true, and that he would stand down from Parliament at the next election.[67]

From public company to private theft

After 1905, Bottomley's tools and tactics would change. Previously, there had always been a vestigial relationship between real economic activity and the shares Bottomley was trading. If an Australian region contained gold deposits in its soil, the value of the company's shares would in all likelihood rise. When none of Bottomley's promises made good, the price would fall. But now the relationship between business and production was to be sundered, and he came to rely far more on private and individual fraud. He was almost as likely to issue a shareholder with a duplicate certificate as a real one, and to trade in fake companies as often as those genuinely floated on the stock exchange.

The new approach was risky. Before, a typical customer was someone who had seen Bottomley's shares advertised in the press. His typical client was now a private person buying shares from Bottomley himself. They had met him and knew the inside of his offices. Wine and a fine meal were part of the performance. He (it was almost always a he) was parted from his money after being told that here, for the first time in this person's life, was a true bargain that had to be seized immediately. This way of making money had shed much of the trappings of commerce. These customers had greater wealth than their predecessors and their losses were greater. This gave them greater incentive to sue, and many did.

To take money from large crowds of investors, Bottomley had needed a showman's talents, the ability to put together a bona fide-seeming organisation, the talent to manipulate a meeting and work a crowd. To trick individuals, different skills were required: the talent to charm, the ability to ignore any amount of unwelcome correspondence.

We can date this change in approach with precision to 1905 because this is the year that Bottomley met fellow speculator Ernest Torah Hooley.[68] Born in Nottingham in 1859, Hooley had also had a provincial family but not the youthful poverty. Hooley's father was a substantial East Midlands businessman. Hooley had joined the family business and by 30 was rich enough to buy Risley Hall in Derbyshire, an 11th century country house with 16 bedrooms. Quitting the family business, he then worked as a company promoter in Nottingham, before heading to London with (on his own account) £100,000 in the bank: which was already a fortune, but nothing compared to what he would soon possess.

As a stockbroker and company promoter Hooley had bought into some of the best-known brands in Victorian and Edwardian England, including Raleigh, Schweppes and Bovril, before selling them at a profit. In his first coup, which is also his most famous, he had hired a floor of the Midland Grand Hotel at St Pancras, and entertained lavishly. An unnamed earl was short of money and Hooley invited him to join the board of his business, asking him to recruit more aristocrats: "I'll give you £10,000 for a duke, and £5,000 a piece for a couple of ordinary peers".[69] Soon the board was groaning with ennobled peers, or as Hooley termed them, "front-pagers" and "guinea pigs": the Earl De La Warr, the Duke of Somerset, Lord Albermale, Lord Warwick and Lord Norbury.[70] Offered the Dunlop Tyre Company for £3 million, Hooley first told the world that rubber tyres would transform cycling, and then re-floated the company for a staggering £5 million.[71]

Hooley used his wealth to purchase two estates and acquire the trappings of social status: first he became High Sheriff of Cambridgeshire and a Lieutenant of the City of London, then Conservative candidate for Ilkeston.[72] His exploits were well known, discussed sometimes with fury but often celebrated, as one music hall song suggests:

> He works into the Stock Exchange, and everybody there
> Cries: "Look out! Here comes Hooley, the famous millionaire!"
> He can buy a share for tuppence and sell it for a pound
> When he's bought St. Paul's Cathedral, he'll buy the Underground.[73]

When he purchased a company, Hooley did not change its basic structure: the managers remained. Rather, he tacked on ornamental directors and re-advertised it, insisting that the business had become a much more valuable asset, and leaving the company with the tricky task of paying the dividends this new proclaimed price required – a task made all the harder since Hooley had stripped it of cash reserves. Hooley bribed financial journalists to write puff pieces about the company's fine health, or else to suppress unfavourable stories[74] (£2,000 each, for example, to the *Pall Mall Gazette* and the *Financial Post*). On another occasion he paid Harry Marks £17,000 to publish a positive report of a failing bicycle business.[75]

In Hooley's words: "I bought a business as cheaply as I could and sold it again for the biggest price it would bring. Some people might say that by this method I robbed the public of millions of pounds, but nevertheless I did not do anything against the law".[76] Fraudulent or not, his millions were dissipated, and when he met Bottomley, he was an undischarged bankrupt, living in his old Derbyshire and Cambridge estates, now transferred to his wife.[77]

One encounter between the two concerned Bottomley's company West Australian Trusts. Hooley had the idea of buying up all two million of its shares. When his brokers instructed him that they had completed this task, he discovered that Bottomley had sent them not two million but four million shares. Hooley grasped at once that the paper was worthless, and the recognition must have been mutual, because Bottomley denied nothing: "My dear Ernest, I've been selling those shares for 17 years and now you of all men want to stop me?"[78]

A friend of Hooley's, William Carter, bought the canal in Basingstoke for £10,000. Worldlier than Carter, Hooley explained that the income to be gained from a canal was far less than the cost of maintaining it. Carter sold the duff asset to Bottomley, who with Hooley's assistance identified two buyers: Reginald and Vincent Eyre, both in their 20s. Bottomley sold to them for £100,000: this was their life savings.[79]

Around this time, Seymour Hicks, a junior court reporter, was invited by mutual friends to dinner with Bottomley. Much wine was drunk, and the two men shared various anecdotes. Towards the end of the meal, Bottomley turned to Hicks and confided in him that he had spare shares to sell in a company, Northern Territories: "They stand at 2½ [pence]. Sell them when they go up to 5½, which they will do in a fortnight, and you will be better by £1,000". Profuse with gratitude, Hicks "left the restaurant treading on air and proclaimed to the world that Bottomley was the jolliest and biggest-hearted man in London". Had a bystander not intervened, grabbing him before he left the building with Bottomley, Hicks might have handed Bottomley every penny in his bank accounts, suffering the same fate as the Eyres.[80]

Word was passing among Bottomley's victims that a solicitor, one Edward Bell, was interested in representing them. Bell would be Bottomley's Javert – except that, unlike his fictional counterpart, very little is known about him. Biographers have described him as "tall", "gaunt", and "with a love of lost causes exemplified by his enthusiastic Jacobitism".[81] Years later, to write about Bottomley's affairs, Bell would permit himself the aptronym "Tenax", and this conveys something of the spirit in which he pursued Bottomley, collecting every detail he could of his opponent's wrong-doings, waiting for the moment to attack.

One of Bell's clients told how Hooley and Bottomley collaborated to steal from him. Hooley had met the hopeful purchaser, conveying him to Bottomley's mansion in Pall Mall. The door was opened, and the man was ushered into a sort of tent of red cloth, with a light outside. Inside was a brazier and the victim was invited to compose himself. Hooley described the difficulties he had gone to in setting up this introduction and hinted that Bottomley might be too busy to be seen. The purchaser waited, desperate to meet the great man.

Eventually, a servant dressed in the plumes of an exotic bird opened the curtain of the tent and Bottomley could be seen beneath a red light. He told the investor that he had torn himself away from business of national importance but could spare five minutes. Hooley introduced the victim, who was taken into a drawing room with blue and gold furniture and asked to sit in a large armchair.[82] A dreamy sort of music was playing in the background, perhaps on a phonograph, at the time a luxury item. Canaries twittered all about. Champagne flowed. All this convinced the victim that the shares he was being induced to buy were worth a fortune. It would be a mere trifle to sell them for profit beyond dreams.[83]

Clients taken in this way might well turn against Bottomley; the magnate had to dodge many threats. One disgruntled former investor broke into his Pall Mall flat, bearing a pistol. He approached Bottomley, demanding immediate payment. Bottomley promised to satisfy him: "Just wait a minute while I get my cheque book. In the meantime, we'll have a bottle". The visitor left Bottomley's flat the next morning unrepaid, having spent a further £10,000 of his own money on Bottomley's worthless shares.[84]

The office in Long Acre, near Covent Garden, was structured with exposure in mind. His room was decorated in oak and green leathers, with a large bust of Bradlaugh and the walls and mantelpieces covered with cartoons of Bottomley. A visitor leaving might notice that there were two doors out. The main one (through which visitors entered) took one back to the offices. The other led out onto Anne Street. Faced with bailiffs, Bottomley could run into the street and hide.[85] His creditors might seek him out but when they arrived – just like Macavity in T. S. Eliot's poem[86] of the same name – Bottomley wasn't there.

Notes

1 Tenax, *The Rise and Fall*, p. 31.
2 Felstead, *Horatio Bottomley*, p. 29. A postcard from this period shows a notepad, open with a handwritten list of the parties from the first day of Bottomley's trial, and a judge's wig, photographed from behind. The contents of the notepad are what you would expect of a judge or a counsel's note. But the document could have been produced by any of the legal representatives in court, including any of the six counsel who appeared for Bottomley's co-defendants. The wig in the image is indeed a judge's wig, but it is in suspiciously good condition; the tassels are good as new. By the time of Bottomley's trial Hawkins had been a High Court Judge for 17 years, and this wig is supposed to have been given to Bottomley on his retirement a further five years' later. If it had been the genuine article, you would expect to see more signs of wear.
3 *Guardian*, 14 January 1893.
4 L. Brake, E. King, R. Luckhurst and J. Mussell (eds), *W. T. Stead: Newspaper Revolutionary* (London: British Library, 2012), p. 167.
5 'Horatio Bottomley's Institute', *Pall Mall Gazette*, 1 December 1893.
6 'Horatio Bottomley's Institute'.
7 'Mr Horatio Bottomley's Affairs', *Manchester Guardian*, 20 May 1893; Felstead, *Horatio Bottomley*, pp. 33.
8 Symons, *Horatio Bottomley*, p. 48.
9 Felstead, *Horatio Bottomley*, pp. 32–5.
10 Symons, *Horatio Bottomley*, p. 50.
11 The Institute existed from 1894 until the early years of the new century mainly serving to give Bottomley a certain formal distance from his interest in Australian gold. Its success was far from complete: in July 1895 for example it was sued by a disgruntled investor Pilling, who claimed to have given Bottomley a cheque for £1000 to fund a railway in Damascus. Pilling was suing for the return of the money, with Bottomley counterclaiming for debts which he claimed were owed to him of £10,000. Pilling's claim succeeded in full; Bottomley's counterclaim failed entirely. 'The Railway to Damascus', *The Standard*, 31 July 1895.
12 Horatio Holyoake to Catherine Holyoake, 22 April 1855 (but catalogued as 22 April 1885), National Library of Australia M392.
13 Holyoake, 22 April 1855.
14 Holyoake, 22 April 1855.
15 Another uncle, Henry Holyoake, had settled in Melbourne, where he worked, less helpfully, as a saddler: Horatio Holyoake to George Jacob Holyoake, September 1881, National Library of Australia M392.
16 P. Bairoch, 'International Industrialization Levels from 1750 to 1980', *Journal of European Economic History* 11 (1982), pp. 296–304. In 2009, by contrast, China accounted for 21.4% of world industrial output, the US 18.6% and the UK 2.3%. 'International Comparisons of Manufacturing Output', House of Commons Library SN/EP/5809, 15 February 2011.
17 Hobson conducted George Jacob Holyoake's memorial service in 1906. *The Times*, 23 Jan 1906.
18 J. A. Hobson, *Imperialism: A Study* (New York: James Pott & Co., 1938 edn), pp. 56–7, 88. Hobson's interest in the growing power of finance helped him to see developments which other economists missed; it had the significant weakness however that it caused him to exaggerate the part played in the Edwardian banking system by Jews. D. Feldman, 'Jeremy Corbyn, "Imperialism", and Labour's Antisemitism Problem', *History Workshop*, 12 June 2019.
19 J. A. Hobson, 'Imperialism a Study', *Marxists.org*, Chapter 4.
20 Hobson, 'Imperialism a Study', Chapter 4.

21 E. Chancellor, *Devil Takes the Hindmost: A History of Financial Speculation* (London: Farrar, Straus & Giroux, 1999), p. ix.

22 'Letters', *London Review of Books*, 4 January 2018.

23 R. Ellmann, *The Trial of Oscar Wilde* (London: Penguin Books, 1996), pp. 16–18.

24 F. O'Toole, *Judging Shaw: The Radicalism of GBS* (Dublin: Prism, 2017), p. 84.

25 D. Barleben, *Staging the Trials of Modernism: Testimony and the British Modern Literary Consciousness* (Toronto: University of Toronto Press, 2017), p. 23.

26 S. Rowbotham, *Edward Carpenter: A Life of Liberty and Love* (London: Verso, 2008), p. 194.

27 Rowbotham, *Edward Carpenter*, pp. 194–5.

28 The story is told from the prospectors' view in J. Marshall, *Battling for Gold: Stirring Incidents of Goldfield Life in West Australia* (Melbourne: E. W. Cole, 1903).

29 K. S. Prichard, *The Roaring Nineties* (London: Virago, 1986 edn), pp. 4–6.

30 Prichard, *The Roaring Nineties*, p. 7.

31 Tenax, *The Rise and Fall*, pp. 41–2.

32 R. C. Michie, *Guilty Money: The City of London in Victorian and Edwardian Culture* (London: Pickering & Chatto, 2009), p. 131.

33 'The West Australian Joint Stock Trust and Finance Corporation Ltd', *Dundee Courier and Argus*, 17 September 1896.

34 Symons, *Horatio Bottomley*, p. 53; Houston, *The Real Horatio Bottomley*, p. 46.

35 Hyman, *The Rise and Fall*, p. 69.

36 Felstead, *Horatio Bottomley*, p. 35

37 Tenax, *The Rise and Fall*, pp. 287–8.

38 'Mr Bottomley and the Hansard Shareholders', *Reynolds's Newspaper*, 2 May 1897.

39 Tenax, *The Rise and Fall*, p. 36.

40 *Fun*, 4 May 1897. Though it's hard to spot even by cryptic Victorian standards, this seems to be a pun – with "*Hansard*" a contraction of "hoist on their own petard".

41 Tenax, *The Rise and Fall*, p. 288.

42 In one novel, Wells gives his own version of Bottomley's abandoned wheelbarrow story. "Parsons" (i.e. Wells) is dismissed from his work as a draper after he is given the plum job of window-dresser and uses it to build an asymmetrical display, illuminated by electric light, advertising the shop's goods. As familiar as that sort of display might be today, this part of the novel is set in the early 1880s, and the idea antagonises his senior managers, leading to a fist-fight and Parsons's prosecution. He is bound over to keep the peace and leaves for London. H. G. Wells, *The History of Mr Polly* (London: Pan Books, 1910), pp. 36–44.

43 H. G. Wells, *The Invisible Man* (London: Penguin, 2005), pp. 69, 87, 93.

44 Morris, 'Bottomley, Horatio', *Dictionary of National Biography*. Another named in the same piece was Ernest Torah Hooley, of whom more shortly.

45 Bottomley, *Bottomley's Book*, p. 131.

46 Bottomley, *Bottomley's Book*, pp. 136–9.

47 There were references to the entourage in the evidence given against Bottomley by a former employee in 1909, 'The Bottomley Case: A Confidential Clerk's Evidence', *Manchester Guardian*, 8 January 1909.

48 Symons, *Horatio Bottomley*, pp. 53–4; Tenax, *The Rise and Fall*, pp. 47–8.

49 Hyman, *The Rise and Fall*, pp. 67–9.

50 Tenax, *The Rise and Fall*, p. 53.

51 Bottomley to Peachey, 26 January 1900, London Metropolitan Archives F/PEY/35.

52 Robb, *White-Collar*, pp. 108–9.

53 Felstead, *Horatio Bottomley*, p. 64; Symons, *Horatio Bottomley*, p. 60.

54 The details of the conflict with Taylor are now obscure, but on other occasions, Bottomley *did* employ people to publish fake libels about him. The prime example is the Midlands printer John Greaney, who was engaged by Bottomley to libel him in 1918, see Chapter 9, below.

55 Tenax, *The Rise and Fall*, pp. 55–8.

56 Felstead, *Horatio Bottomley*, p. 67.

57 Symons, *Horatio Bottomley*, p. 27; also Hyman, *The Rise and Fall*, p. 36; and Houston, *The Real Horatio Bottomley*, p. 136.

58 Thompson had represented Britain's best-known Marxist Henry Hyndman of the Social Democratic Federation in charges of sedition brought in 1886 following the so-called "West End" riots of that year. See Hyndman, *The Record of an Adventurous Life*, Chapter 24.

59 Tenax, *The Rise and Fall*, p. 56.

60 Symons, *Horatio Bottomley*, p. 28; Hyman, *The Rise and Fall*, p. 73; Felstead, *Horatio Bottomley*, pp. 66–7.

61 Tenax, *The Rise and Fall*, p. 56.

62 Hyman, *The Rise and Fall*, p. 73

63 The monthly payments never in fact materialised.

64 *South African Review*, 7 March 1902.

65 Symons, *Horatio Bottomley*, p. 61.

66 Hyman, *The Rise and Fall*, pp. 74–5; 'The Financial Libel Case', *Manchester Guardian*, 10 March 1902.

67 G. R. Searle, *Corruption in British Politics 1895–1910* (Oxford: Clarendon, 1987), pp. 37–8.

68 E. T. Hooley, *Hooley's Confessions* (London: Simpkin, Marshall & Co, 1925).

69 Hooley, *Hooley's Confessions*, p. 13.

70 *The Hooley Book* (London: John Dicks, 1904), pp. 34–6.

71 Hooley likely never had the money in hand to actually buy the company, but was able to sell it (for more money) before payment fell due, so the shortfall was obscured.

72 A safe Liberal seat. It may be that Hooley was more concerned to prove his loyalty to that party – and entitlement to honours – than actually win it. Searle, *Corruption*, p. 41.

73 Robb, *White-Collar*, p. 115.

74 J. Nye, 'Business, Bribery and the Broadsheets: Researching Companies and Industry with the *Daily Telegraph*', *The Telegraph Historical Archive*, 2016.

75 Robb, *White-Collar*, p. 104.

76 Robb, *White-Collar*, pp. 104–7.

77 K. and M. Richardson, "Hooley, Ernest Terah", *Dictionary of Business Biography* (London: Butterworths, 1985), Vol. 3, pp. 326–32.

78 Felstead, *Horatio Bottomley*, pp. 44–5.

79 Symons, *Horatio Bottomley*, p. 122.

80 S. Hicks, *Not Guilty M'Lord* (London: Cassel and Co., 1939), pp. 174–5.

81 Symons, *Horatio Bottomley*, p. 75.

82 The chair was known to Bottomley as "the extracting chair".

83 Symons, *Horatio Bottomley*, pp. 111–12; Tenax, *The Rise and Fall*, pp. 37–8.

84 Felstead, *Horatio Bottomley*, pp. 4–5.

85 Hyman, *The Rise and Fall*, p. 93.

86 'Macavity: The Mystery Cat' in T. S. Eliot, *Old Possum's Book of Practical Cats* (London: Penguin, 1939), pp. 37–8.

6

SENSUALIST

To view Horatio Bottomley at the age of 40 is to see a great bear of a man. His mouth was set in a scowl, but he also had a pleasing smile which had extracted him from many scrapes already. He wore the morning jacket of the successful entrepreneur and had the true businessman's talent for extravagant spending. His properties included a large home in rural Sussex ("the Dicker"), a flat at 56a Pall Mall, two or three secret flats inhabited by girlfriends, and Bell'Aria, a six-bedroom villa in the Alpes-Maritime near Monte Carlo, where Eliza and Florence Grace Bottomley were sent each summer.[1]

The Dicker had started life as an ordinary country cottage with two downstairs rooms and two bedrooms. Rebuilt several times by Bottomley, by the turn of the century it had accommodation for 30 guests, as well as gardens, stables for racing horses and an artificial lake. It required six gardeners, half a dozen indoor servants, two chauffeurs – Bottomley was a fan of the motor car[2] – and horse-trainers and other staff.[3] To pre-empt bankruptcy Bottomley made sure that estate and furniture were registered in the names of relatives,[4] and similar provision was made to disguise the ownership of his horses.[5]

Bottomley saw a role for himself as a patron of the theatre. One theatrical investment supported Fred Horner's comedy, *The Bungalow*. It played at Toole's Theatre near Charing Cross and the *Manchester Guardian* said that the cast "did every possible justice to it and gave it as good a chance as it could hope to have. Its plot, like its reception, was rather mixed, and its complications are so elaborate as almost to defy relation in anything short of a volume".[6] The play was not a commercial success.[7]

Horner became more ambitious. He purchased a paper, the *Whitehall Review*. He stood as a Conservative candidate for Parliament in 1900, he was elected. But association with Bottomley, Bottomley's money and Bottomley's methods did him little good in the end. The editor of *Truth*, Henry Labouchere, alleged that

DOI: 10.4324/9781003306085-6

Horner had paid bills with cheques that bounced. Horner sued for libel but lost, and was declared bankrupt.[8]

Successful in the same election was another Bottomley associate, Harry Marks. He (so his critics claimed) had secured election by staging free dinners with entertainments for potential voters in Thanet. He had paid grocers in his constituency to distribute free parcels of food, milk and coal, saying they were gifts from the Conservative candidate.[9] Within the constituency were many insurance clubs for those threatened with unemployment. Marks became a member of every one, contributing to their funds.

Bottomley also stood in 1900, as the Liberal candidate for South Hackney, a marginal constituency which had been held for the Liberals for several years by Sir Charles Russell. The election saw national consolidation for the Conservatives, buoyed by the success of British troops in South Africa, and the capture of Pretoria from their Boer opponents. The Conservatives had gone into the election with a majority in the House of Commons of 319 and left with one of 338 – an advance for them, but a result close enough to allow Bottomley hope for future victories. Three weeks after this election, a conference in Bradford announced the formation of a Labour Representation Committee with 130 delegates, representing 861 members of the Fabian Society, 9,000 members of the Social Democratic Federation, 13,000 members of the Independent Labour Party, and 540,000 members of sponsoring trade unions.[10]

Neither Horner's success nor Bottomley's near miss at the polls diminished the latter's desire to be associated with the theatre. He invested in Arthur Law's play *The Judge*, in which the leading man was the comedian William Penley. A former draper, Penley had enjoyed his first theatrical success, two decades before, playing the foreman of the jury in Gilbert and Sullivan's *Trial by Jury*. At a drunken lunch, Penley complained to Bottomley that the other members of the company were getting too many laughs and his part was suffering. Bottomley passed on the instruction that the others were to tone down their performance in Penley's favour. Perhaps unsurprisingly, the production flopped.[11]

Next Bottomley leased the Lyceum Theatre for a run of *Hamlet* with actor and theatre manager Johnston Forbes-Robertson in the lead. Three years previously, George Bernard Shaw had reviewed him in this role: "Nothing half so charming has been seen by this generation. It will bear seeing again and again".[12] The public agreed, as did a further round of positive reviews, [13] and by end of its run the production had netted Bottomley £5,000. He then leased the same venue for *Macbeth*, again with Forbes-Robertson playing the lead.[14]

Wine

At the Dicker, Bottomley was drinking champagne at breakfast, lunch, and all through the evening.[15] Perhaps surprisingly, given his sensualism, his preferred brand was Pommery Nature, the first mass-marketed Brut champagne, with a dry taste, almost bitter at a time when most champagnes of the period were sweet. If Bottomley or one of his friends was suffering fatigue, toothache or stress, Pommery was the cure.[16]

Good wine had of course to be matched by fine food. The writer Theodore Felstead was in the Piccadilly Hotel, dining with friends when he saw Bottomley in his pomp arriving at a neighbouring table. "I remember when the waiter brought Bottomley his bill, a nice heavy one it must have been, for there had been champagne and caviar, lobsters and salmon *ad lib*, he never even looked at it". Bottomley scrawled his name on the bill's back, gave a £1 tip, and "waddle[d] out as only the redoubtable Mr Bottomley could do. One of my companions remarked, 'By Jove, if only I could do that!'"[17]

Frank Harris recalls the enthusiasm with which Bottomley drank his champagne and enjoyed the company that came with it: "To see him lunching... with two of three of his intimates... with a pretty chorus girl on one side and another siren opposite, while the waiter uncorked the fourth or fifth bottle of champagne, was to see the man as he was".[18]

Sport

Bottomley's next extravagance was sport. He regarded himself as an athlete; he enjoyed playing both billiards and tennis at the Dicker. He had hustled his way around a billiards table since his 20s, when he had often played at a club on Fleet Street, posing as the "green-coated stranger", and betting against the club's newest members.[19]

Bottomley organised annual cricketing competitions at the Dicker between the villagers and a team composed of printers from London. These contests were remarkable for the large quantities of alcohol offered – before the game – to the visiting team's best players.

But the sport in which Bottomley took the most sustained interest was horse-racing, and this is the one with which he is most associated. Early in his business career, and in his various legal adventures, he had had dealings with many barristers and judges who were enthusiastic horse-riders, including Sir Charles Russell. Among the stories told about Russell is the following. Even when serving in the Cabinet as Attorney General, he continued to do private work as a barrister. One morning he was sitting with a friend in chambers, already robed, waiting to be summoned to his next case. The friend pointed out a large pile of outstanding opinions waiting to be written. Russell replied that he did not like to begin work which might have at any moment to be broken off. He then picked up his pen: "I asked him what he was doing, and he told me that he was trying to make a list of the four best horses that had ever existed for a prize offered by the *Sporting Times*".[20] Here was an evident link between social prestige and legal and political power. Bottomley determined to make a quick name for himself through investing in racing.

During his gold-mining adventures, he announced to the press that he had acquired a stable of racehorses, with the intention of winning the Epsom Derby or the Grand National. Not long afterwards, he addressed an audience of company shareholders:

> A friend who called upon me yesterday said, "I hope you are not going gambling on horse-racing". I think my answer was to the point. I said, "Heaven knows I have too much gambling in the City, to want to gamble when I get out of it".[21]

Bottomley's hope for the Derby was a horse called Hawfinch, grandson of the stallion Ormonde, who in 1886 had won his owner the Duke of Westminster the "Triple Crown", the 2000 Guineas, the Derby, and the St Leger, ending his career unbeaten. Despite this success, Ormonde was almost sterile, getting only 11 foals in 16 years at stud.[22] Hawfinch had an ambling, unbalanced canter, and one journalist described him as a "great lengthy, lanky chestnut, with ample bone, a malformed though perfectly sound near hock, and curious knees... no-one ever saw anything less like a winner than he then appeared".[23] But he won the Dewhurst Plate at Newmarket, and Bottomley had invested £5,000 in him. However, rather than leave matters to his trainer Harry Batho,[24] Bottomley insisted on attending training sessions, often with friends, and demanding the horse perform for them. Batho, well aware of the insecurity of his own position, did not stand up to his employer. "I wanted to see a Derby trial every time I went to the stables", Bottomley would later admit, "with the result that on Derby Day itself the poor animal was more fit for the kennels than the race".[25] Hawfinch led the Derby for just 100 yards, before fading badly.

One of Hawfinch's rivals at Newmarket had been a mare called Nun Nicer. Bottomley remembered the name, and one of his favourite horse-racing stories began at Epsom, at The Oaks in 1898, and the favourite for the upcoming race was Nun Nicer. Bottomley was in the presence of an MP and his 19-year-old daughter. "Tell me, sweet maiden", he purred, "why, when this race is over, the name of the winner will remind everybody of you?" The young woman smiled back. Bottomley then watched with horror as the favourite faded and was beaten by its rival, Airs and Graces.[26] Bottomley was of course married and double the age of the woman with whom he was flirting.

Women did not necessarily bring him luck trackside. "One of the biggest bets I had", Bottomley recalled, "was on a horse I ran at Epsom". Bottomley was watching as the horses neared the post, his still in contention – until his hopes seeing the finish were ruined by the lady at his side, who "gave a pull at my arm and in dulcet tones observed, 'Oh Mr Bottomley, do get me some more strawberries'".[27]

Weeks before the 1899 Grand National, Bottomley bought a mare, Gentle Ida, from her celebrated owner, the trainer and solicitor Harry Dyas. With odds of 4/1, Gentle Ida was the pre-race favourite, and leaving nothing to chance, Bottomley kept her in Dyas's stable rather than risk her among his other horses at the Dicker. "On the Turf some men achieve greatness by raising their own

stock", wrote one wag, "while yet others achieve it by purchasing red-hot fa-
vourites on the eve of big races".[28] But Bottomley once more failed to record
a victory. Gentle Ida fell, and to compound the defeat, Manifesto, the eventual
winner, was also from Dyas's stable. Bottomley had picked the right trainer but
bought the wrong horse.

Bottomley often bet as much as £10,000 on a race.[29] Whether he lost or won,
he wanted to be discussed in the papers. Gambling was part of his plan to raise
his profile, "Try to imagine a King of England", Bottomley once wrote, "who
didn't go racing. Why there would be a Republic in a week".[30] This association between betting and the politics of the people was one to which he often
returned:[31] "There is rarely a dispute between the bookmaker and backer, and
if there is they have their tribunals whose word is law. The freemasonry of the
Turf is wonderful. All men are equal on it and under it. It is one of the most absolutely national democratic institutions in the whole country and has done more
to humanize men and to do away with silly social distinctions than anything else
I know".[32]

Another sporting interest was in boxing. On occasion he promoted contests,
including the search for a challenger to the heavyweight world champion Jack
Johnson. Johnson, the first black heavyweight champion, was the son of a freed
slave and one of the sport's greats. He had fought over 70 professional bouts,
winning his title from Tommy Burns before a crowd of 20,000 at the Sydney
Stadium in Australia. Boxers all over the US challenged him, promising by defeating him to save the honour of the white race. When he defeated the former
champion, James Jeffries, the victory saw rioting in 50 cities. When Johnson
refused to fight Bottomley's nominee, Bottomley produced documents claiming
to prove that Johnson's victories depended on his rivals agreeing to throw their
bouts.[33] Johnson ignored him.

In literature – Bottomley and his kind

Edwardian fiction produced at least two further characters showing some resemblance to Bottomley. The first is flower girl Eliza's father Alfred Doolittle, in
George Bernard Shaw's *Pygmalion*. Eliza's ascent from poverty forms the heart of
that play, but if she is one of the deserving poor, the same cannot be said for her
father, as he acknowledges:

> I don't need less than a deserving man: I need more. I don't eat less hearty
> than him; and I drink a lot more. I want a bit of amusement, cause I'm a
> thinking man. I want cheerfulness and a song and a band when I feel low.[34]

The play is remembered for the efforts taken by Henry Higgins, a professor of
phonetics, to improve Eliza's diction, but her father Alfred also secures social
advance. Through the intercession of a society of philanthropists, he is given an
income of £3,000 a year, after which he returns from the wings, his dustman's

clothes swapped for a dazzling silk hat and patent leather shoes. He complains of his treatment. Before, Higgins had been alone and the professionals ignored him. "When I was a poor man and had a solicitor once when they found a pram in the dust cart, he got me off, and got shut of me and got me shut of him as quick as he could". It had been the "same with the doctors: used to shove me out of the hospital before I could hardly stand on my legs, and nothing to pay". Now that he had become rich, he was never alone. "A year ago I hadn't a relative in the world except two or three that wouldn't speak to me. Now I've 50, and not a decent week's wages among the lot of them".[35]

This is not to say Shaw had Bottomley in mind, rather that Bottomley and Doolittle were recurring Edwardian types. If we consider the solicitors eager for Bottomley's business or the 50 friends and relatives wanting to visit with him at the Dicker, these afflictions were the common experience of the newly rich. When Shaw wrote about Alfred's unwanted sponsors in the Moral Reform World League, he drew more on his own time among Fabians[36] than on Bottomley's links, via George Jacob Holyoake, with the Owenites. Bottomley too had grown up poor and had become rich. But where Doolittle seemed somewhat regretful at his ascent, Bottomley was distinguished by the exuberance with which he demanded it.

And then there's Toad in Kenneth Grahame's *The Wind in the Willows*. This anti-hero is the owner of a magnificent country house who squanders money and drinks too much champagne. While Bottomley sang his own praises figuratively, Toad is more literal:

> The world has held great Heroes,
> As history-books have showed
> But never a name to go down to fame
> Compared with that of Toad![37]

Grahame was obsessed by what he considered to be the declining morality of the times. Finance was under attack from an alliance between the new rich and the working classes – neither of whom had any right to rule. In 1903, five years before the book was published, Grahame, then Secretary of the Bank of England, had been shot at by an intruder to the bank, who was found by the court to be a madman of "Socialistic views". He had an almost-equal contempt for Radical Liberalism. To the poet and essayist Arthur Quiller-Couch, a Liberal-voting acquaintance, Grahame wrote, only half in jest, that he would not wish him luck "in your nefarious designs on our savings, our cellars and our garden-plots".[38]

In *The Wind in the Willows*, Grahame warns against ostentatious spending, which might tend to encourage envy among the poor. Toad has come into money without learning how to behave with it. He is conceited and aimless; first he gives up boating for a horse-drawn caravan, then when a motorcar startles his horse, he determines to buy one for himself. In all he crashes seven cars, spending a fortune on fines, before being tried and sentenced to 20 years. At one point, Grahame sets out the justice Toad deserved: "The brutal minions of the law fell upon the hapless Toad; loaded him with chains, and dragged him from the Court House, shrieking, praying, protesting; across the market-place". There, the people mobbed him, "the playful populace, always as severe upon detected crime as they are sympathetic and helpful when one is merely 'wanted', assailed him with jeers, carrots, and popular catch-words".[39] On the same sentence goes, for another 300 words of coughing sentries and time-worn stairs, of mastiffs, rack-chambers and private scaffolds, a pastiche of fake medievalism that expands on (and mocks) the punitive institutional fury waiting for Toad and his kind.

Toad is not a wholly dislikeable character. Like Bottomley, he is loyal to his friends and capable – at least in the passing moment – of admitting his crimes, acknowledging their harm and promising he would never do anything of the kind again.

The book is more than a satire on what Grahame called "gentleman in difficulties", or on the risks posed by the excessive consumption of the leisure class.[40] It was also a message to Grahame's young son Alastair, and a warning as to how an upright person should behave in relation to their contemporaries. In a key passage, Rat explains to Mole: "There are a hundred things one has to know which we understand all about and you don't as yet. I mean pass-words, and signs, and saying which have power and effect and plants you carry in your pocket, and verses you repeat, and dodges and tricks you practise". All of these were "simple enough if you know then, but they've got to be known if you're small, or you'll find yourself in trouble".[41]

"They've got to be known if you're small": one message of *The Wind and the Willows* is that children must learn their responsibilities; another is that the mindless rich who throw away their capital on mere pleasure will be the best propaganda for the socialists.[42]

Bottomley's biographer Peter Green has argued that the man who inspired Toad was none other than Horatio Bottomley, whose "flamboyant, gabby, vulgarian" politics were a source of particular distress to Grahame.[43]

Bottomley might have accepted that one side of his personality embodied the conspicuous consumption of Edwardian capitalism, but he was also (in his own mind) the Radical, advocating the tearing down the homes of the rich. The novel splits these two elements of his personality apart. When a mob comes to plunder Toad Hall, it is led not by Toad but a hostile crowd of weasels and stoats. Whereas Bottomley was insisting that these two groups of people – the rich and the Radicals – could co-exist.

One answer is that the same person cannot be both, in real life or in literature, or at least not in *The Wind and the Willows*, which is more satisfying and truer to life than the stories told by Bottomley. If he was Toad, he could not also be a weasel. He was no advocate of wealth redistribution; he wished to own Toad Hall by right, with the support of the establishment and of the law. No twisting of labels could make him a revolutionary.

Bottomley and his vows

Much of Bottomley's extravagance revolved around women. Tommy Cox, another employee (and Bottomley's friend since his teenage years), was tasked with renting West End flats and inviting Bottomley's mistresses to live in them. Bottomley showered them with gifts, taking more care to keep them ignorant of each other than to hide them from his wife. "For a public man", Houston complained, "he was amazingly reckless in his feminine friendships. Repeatedly I have had to point out to him – not always with any effect – the unwisdom of travelling while on public business with a lady to whom he was not married".[44]

Bottomley's wooing involved the woman's entire family. He would pester his dates to invite him back to their parents' home for supper and then soften his palate with a generous accompaniment of champagne. He was, after all, used to high-class dining.

Houston insists the affairs were unconsummated: "Never once, during my 13 years of closest association with him, night and day, did I see him in a situation that would have compromised his honour as a husband and a father".[45] Yet as so often with Bottomley, it would be wrong to take this declaration on trust. In one pre-war case, Bottomley was named as the co-respondent in Edward Aubrey Courtauld Lowe's divorce petition against his wife. Mr Lowe[46] told the High Court that his wife had committed adultery with Bottomley at the Dicker, in London and at hotels in Edinburgh, the Isle of Man and Ostend.[47]

Mrs Lowe is an important figure in Bottomley's life; though when she appears in the newspapers of the day, she always appears under her stage name of Peggy Primrose. By his own account, he had spotted her at Romano's at the age of 24, as a chorus dancer in a comedy, *The Dollar Princess*. So besotted was he that he hid with her for a week, neglecting all his business activities.[48] According to Houston: "He was lunching at Romano's Restaurant when a radiant girl of rather less than 20 years walked into the restaurant with a gentleman". The woman was "perfectly dressed, with merry laughing eyes [and] delicately modelled features". Bottomley whispered, "What a pretty girl! What a fine figure!"[49]

They met. Afterwards, he and Peggy Primrose continued to dine at Romano's, so often indeed that on a subsequent visit Peggy's husband was able to attack Bottomley as he left. "I gave him one, two, three and knocked him flat on the pavement. After he got up, I hit him again". Despite the presence of a witness who saw everything (a taxi driver invited by the husband to observe), Bottomley declined to press charges.[50]

Mr Lowe issued proceedings against his wife for divorce. Peggy remained with Bottomley throughout the court case. He paid for rooms for her at Bedford Court Mansions, where they entertained actors and directors.[51] Peggy was booked for a three-week run as a mimic and dancer at the Middlesex Music Hall on Drury Lane, followed by a straight role in *A Cardinal's Romance*, which ran for 15 performances at the Savoy.[52] Bottomley invested in a spy melodrama *The Hidden Hand*, in Liverpool, and this brought Primrose more work. "Though seemingly rather overweighted in making her first appearance as a heroine of drama", reported the *Stage*, "Peggy Primrose played with unaffected simplicity of style".[53] Later she would star in a farce *The Dear Little Lady*, at the Palace Pier in Brighton, in which a young girl spends the night innocently with the hero. The censor objected to plans to exhibit intimate feminine garments on the stage. Bottomley spent £10,000 on the play.[54]

In all, Bottomley's career-long spending on horse-racing came to £340,000, on "largesse" (i.e. mistresses) £200,000, and on theatrical enterprises £150,000.[55] These were the estimates of Edward Bell, who acted for several of Bottomley's creditors over many years, and whose descriptions of Bottomley's business and other affairs are unsurpassed in their detail.[56] Bell was counting in absolute figures, without inflation. For the rough equivalent in current purchasing power, multiply the numbers by 50[57] – and then perhaps we start to grasp why he quit company promotion for the simpler task of meeting wealthy individuals and extracting their money. No honest employment existed that could have sustained spending on the scale to which Bottomley was accustomed.

Notes

1 After complaining that she had been happier in the old days when she and Horatio had struggled to afford a simple piano. Hyman, *The Rise and Fall*, pp. 59, 69; Houston, *The Real Horatio Bottomley*, p. 84.
2 The cars were eventually sold in 1922 to fund Bottomley's final criminal defence. Felstead, *Horatio Bottomley*, p. 285.
3 Symons, *Horatio Bottomley*, p. 130.
4 Felstead, *Horatio Bottomley*, p. 171. The Dicker itself was formally the property of Bottomley's son-in-law Jefferson Cohn, a City man and racehorse-owner. Symons, *Horatio Bottomley*, p. 133.
5 National Archives MEPO 3 302, undated witness statement of William Lotinga, c. May 1914.
6 'The Bungalow at Toole's Theatre', *Manchester Guardian*, 8 October 1889.
7 Bottomley, *Bottomley's Book*, p. 148.
8 *Times*, 13 July 1906.
9 C. R. Buxton, *Electioneering Up-to-Date* (London: Francis Griffiths, 1906), pp. 77–81.
10 H. Taylor, *Victor Grayson: In Search of Britain's Lost Revolutionary* (London: Pluto, 2021), p. 50.
11 Hyman, *The Rise and Fall*, p. 62; G. Deghy, *Paradise in the Strand: The Story of Romano's* (London: The Richards Press, 1958), p. 193.
12 *Saturday Review*, 2 October 1897.
13 For example, "Mr Robertson... makes, a poetic Hamlet, a noble Hamlet, a Hamlet as Ophelia dreamed him to be, and such a Hamlet as obeys, often exquisitely, his own advice to the players in the matter of elocution. We see, if not the whole of Hamlet, at least a piece of him, rounded off and presented with skill and sympathy". 'Mr Forbes Robertson in *Hamlet* at the Theatre Royal', *Manchester Guardian*, 2 October 1900.
14 Hyman, *The Rise and Fall*, p. 62; Bottomley, *Bottomley's Book*, pp. 147–8.
15 Symons, *Horatio Bottomley*, p. 40.
16 Houston, *The Real Horatio Bottomley*, pp. 91, 95.
17 Felstead, *Horatio Bottomley*, p. 4.
18 F. Harris and J. F. Gallagher, *My Life and Loves* (London: Avalon Travel Publishing, 2000), p. 424.

19 Tenax, *The Rise and Fall*, p. 14.
20 O'Brien, *The Life of Lord Russell*, p. 354.
21 Tenax, *The Rise and Fall*, p. 42.
22 D. Craig, *Horse-Racing* (London: Pelican, 1949), pp. 44–5.
23 *Lyttleton Times*, 16 December 1897.
24 Bottomley housed Batho at Wingrove House in Alfriston, a Colonial-style building in East Sussex.
25 Bottomley, *Bottomley's Book*, p. 123.
26 Bottomley, *Bottomley's Book*, pp. 125–6.
27 Bottomley, *Bottomley's Book*, p. 128.
28 *Judy*, 22 March 1899.
29 Felstead, *Horatio Bottomley*, p. 68.
30 Bottomley, *Bottomley's Book*, p. 130.
31 He told Blathwayt that the egalitarianism of the paddock had first been pointed out to him "in the days of my green youth, when I was an ardent Republican", Blathwayt, *Horatio Bottomley*, p. 33.
32 Houston, *The Real Horatio Bottomley*, p. 176.
33 *John Bull*, 18 July 1914.
34 G. B. Shaw, *Pygmalion* (London: Penguin, 2003), p. 46.
35 Shaw, *Pygmalion*, p. 89.
36 A. West, *A Good Man Fallen Among Fabians: A Study of George Bernard Shaw* (London: Lawrence and Wishart, 1950).
37 K. Grahame, *The Wind in the Willows: An Annotated Edition* (Cambridge, MA: Harvard University Press, 2009), p. 214.
38 K. Grahame, *My Dearest Mouse: 'The Wind in the Willows' Letters* (London: Pavilion, 1988), p. 154.
39 Grahame, *The Wind in the Willows,* p. 107.
40 T. Veblen, *The Theory of the Leisure Class* (New York: Macmillan, 1899).
41 Grahame, *The Wind in the Willows*, p. 129.
42 P. Green, *Kenneth Grahame 1859–1932* (London: John Murray, 1959), p. 150.
43 Bottomley is identified as a model for Toad in P. Green, *Kenneth Grahame*, pp. 142–3; and in A. Prince, *Kenneth Grahame: An Innocent in the Wild Wood* (London: Allison & Busy, 1994), pp. 229–30.
44 Houston, *The Real Horatio Bottomley*, p. 83.
45 Houston, *The Real Horatio Bottomley*, pp. 84, 91.
46 Lowe lived at Takeley in Essex. Born in 1872, he had divorced his previous wife in 1906. *Burke's Peerage, Baronetage & Knightage*, 107th edn (London: Burke's Peerage, 2003), Vol. 1, p. 1349.
47 The divorce was not completed, and it is most likely that Lowe's action was in due course compromised following some payment by Bottomley. National Archives J 77/1131/4332.
48 Hyman, *The Rise and Fall*, p. 127.
49 Houston, *The Real Horatio Bottomley*, p. 36.
50 Symons, *Horatio Bottomley*, p. 132.
51 Hyman, *The Rise and Fall*, p. 179.
52 Peggy was listed in the programme as Peggy Fitzmaurice. Symons, *Horatio Bottomley*, p. 134; *The Stage Yearbook 1914* (London: The Stage, 1914), p. 89.
53 *The Stage Yearbook 1919* (London: The Stage, 1919), p. 89.
54 Hyman, *The Rise and Fall*, p. 200.
55 Tenax, *The Rise and Fall*, pp. 281–2.
56 Bottomley's memoir says of Bell that his firm Carter and Bell did not stand "absolutely at the head of their profession". Bottomley, *Bottomley's Book*, p. 45; Bottomley attempted all sorts of ruses against Bell's firm, including reporting them to the Law Society.
57 Retail price inflation between 1922 and 2020 was 4934%. See www.thisismoney. co.uk/historic-inflation-calculator. Bell gives no separate estimate of Bottomley's spending on champagne.

7

THE GOSPEL OF HUMANITY

In his youth, Horatio Bottomley had acquired the habit of terming himself a Democrat. At the time, the word had real content; he had lived in London on the edge of the same left-wing social circle as some of the country's most important advocates of social reform, including Holyoake and Bradlaugh. More than a decade after Charles Bradlaugh's death, Bottomley gave a speech at the annual dinner of the Bradlaugh Fellowship, in which he recalled his hero in glowing terms: "Wasn't he a dangerous and vulgar agitator, a man who knew no God, a Republican who had dared to impeach the House of Brunswick? So, he stood, without friends, without means, without influence". Despite the contempt of his peers, Bradlaugh was undaunted. "On and on he went, ever hopeful, ever courageous, preaching what he believed to be the true Gospel, the Gospel of Humanity, with Reason for its creed and Human Emancipation for its faith".[1] It would be impossible to mistake Bottomley's admiration here. But it's less clear from the speech what Bradlaugh – or Bottomley – stood for. Did any specific Radical creed still have purchase in 1905, and if it did, were Bottomley's politics influenced by it?

The questions are best answered if we look at the period when George Jacob Holyoake was first taking an interest in politics, the mid-19th century, when the central demand of the workers movement was the extension of the franchise. If workers had the vote, they would elect politicians chosen from the ranks of the workers and amenable to democratic politics: this was the argument. Universal male suffrage was a means to an end – or to several ends. Radicals also believed in the abolition of the monarchy and opposed the privileges of the aristocracy. They called for the separation of church and state. Most Chartists held that political and social institutions should be developed that corresponded to genuine human need. They believed that the principle of inheritance girding up the

DOI: 10.4324/9781003306085-7

monarchy and the House of Lords was irrational; as Thomas Paine had written for a previous generation, the idea of hereditary legislators made no more sense than the idea of a hereditary poet.[2] They supported the rights of oppressed nations, including Poland, Hungary and Ireland, and they opposed consumption taxes, arguing that state spending should be funded by taxing the rich. They had plans for economic redistribution, with land reform on one hand and unions and co-operatives[3] agitating for higher wages on the other. Working-class mutual help would transform a world of factories and slums.

By the turn of the century, much of this had been achieved. Electoral reform in the 1860s had led to no significant change in the composition of the Commons, and the further reforms proposed in the 1880s were never accompanied by the hatred of the rich so evident in Chartism. The power of the church was less than it had been, less through the election of secularists than a proliferation of dissenting chapels and the gradual secularisation of society. As England became a settled, urban country, land reform seemed an irrelevance. The needs of the workers would not be met by parcelling up the estates of the landowners.

Here and there commentators acknowledged a sense of anachronism. In 1874, for example, the year of Austin Holyoake's death, Charles Bradlaugh had been invited to speak in Philadelphia. In the audience was a young Frank Harris, then a young Irish exile studying law in Kansas and far from the cynical man he would one day become. He had encountered European social theory and was convinced that the whole world was about to turn left.

To this youthful opponent of Christian hypocrisy and sexual prudery, Bradlaugh seemed a heroic figure, and his first impressions were favourable. Here was a "giant of man with a great head", Harris wrote, "irregular features and stentorian voice: no better figure of a rebel could be imagined". Yet the longer he listened, the emptier Bradlaugh seemed. In particular he seemed to lack any sense of the harm done by the rich, let alone any desire to tear down their stately homes: "Bradlaugh's speech taught me that a notorious and popular man, earnest and gifted and intellectually honest, might be 50 years before his time in one respect and 50 years behind the best opinion of his age in another province of thought". Social transformation was coming, and Bradlaugh was silent: "In the great conflict of our own day between the Haves and the Have-nots, Bradlaugh played no part whatsoever".[4] Much the same could have been written by Annie Besant, for example, at any point between her conversion to socialism and her subsequent move into Theosophy.[5]

Yet such was the state of British politics in the long period between the decline of Chartism and the rise of New Unionism four decades later, that Bradlaugh's hostility to socialism did no harm to his reputation as the foremost Radical of his day. From the mid-1880s onwards, Radicalism began to be eclipsed. Radicals tended to go in one of two directions: either they looked beyond their old programmes, or else they sheltered in them. Many of the former become socialists or supported the extension of the suffrage. In 1891, the year that Bradlaugh died, George Jacob Holyoake was agitating on public platforms for women's right to vote.[6] Others became reconciled with Liberalism, including Bradlaugh himself, who in the 1880s would oppose compensation for industrial injuries and the demand for an eight-hour day, complaining that these measures interfered with the freedom of employers and workers to draw up their own contracts. As we have seen, Bradlaugh supported the right of the unemployed to speak. But the content of their programme, public works schemes, was objectionable to him.

The weakness of Bradlaugh's legacy was that it left Horatio Bottomley unable to sustain a Radical politics into the 1880s, let alone beyond. The political conflict between mid-Victorian Liberalism and Conservatism had been fought on the terrain of free trade; with the Liberals advocating low taxes and a limited role for government, and the Conservatives championing the owners of agricultural estates. By the 1880s – that is, in the period when Bottomley had taken his first steps in politics – this duopoly was facing challenge from the left. Bottomley needed free trade to be a popular cause, but a growing proportion of the people were demanding a great deal more. The protest movements of the unemployed and strikes by the dockers and others were one sign of the coming rise of labour while politicians espousing municipal socialism were successful. Here too Bottomley was a mere hostile onlooker.

At the start of the 1890s, the Fabian Sidney Webb stood as one of two Progressive candidates for the London County Council. His opening move was an address in the secularists' citadel of South Place Chapel in Finsbury, on the hypocrisy of Christian talk of "Peace on Earth". The manifesto that Webb published, *The London Programme*, proposed pensions, state education, unemployment benefits, the building of local authority owned housing, and the replacement of the Poor Law system with what would evolve into today's National Health Service. By dint of hard work and the breadth of his vision, Webb would become the dominant figure in the Progressive administration that would dominate the LCC for many years.[7]

There is some overlap between the careers of Webb and Bottomley. Both were signalling their debt to post-Chartist secularism; both could win elections with the support of the Liberal Party; both emphasised their support for Temperance as a way of wooing the dissenting Christian voter: Bottomley, as we have seen, by taking the pledge, and Webb by addressing meetings of the Temperance Party before a map of his own design, with the public houses all marked by red dots. He called this "London's scarlet fever", remarking how unfortunate it was that the city had three times more pubs than bakers' shops.[8]

Yet there were also great differences between them. Webb courted such prominent trade unionists as Tom Mann, the leader of the dock strike, creating a special union committee to advise and support Webb's campaign. By the mid-1900s, Webb was also lobbying for a significant reform: the abolition of all London school boards, and their centralisation into a single committee under the control of the LCC, which would at once level up education standards and increase the power of London's metropolitan government. Webb was using elected office to create the institutions for further social reform. Bottomley, by contrast, had no programme beyond the manifesto of the Liberal Party.

In a society where wages were too low to sustain a system of income tax, and where most people were in addition hostile to consumption taxes, the demands of workers for pensions, education and health care could not be achieved without redistribution from rich to poor. The Conservatives may not have welcomed state welfare but they grasped that there was no other basis on which to win elections, so they tried to reconcile social provision with imperial interests. The Liberals accepted reforms but did all they could to slow their pace. What split the Radicals was the relationship with Liberalism – with some becoming socialists and others letting themselves be absorbed into the Liberal mainstream. As with Kenneth Grahame's weasels and toads, the two souls of left-Liberalism could not be reconciled forever.

In the late 1870s it was still possible for the interests of the urban rich and poor to be promoted together, against the rural rich. But 30 years later, the coalition had lost its coherence. And this is why Bottomley's eulogy for Bradlaugh was so vague. To set out precisely what Bradlaugh had achieved would be to highlight the distance between Bradlaugh's lost grandeur and Bottomley's own, far more limited vision.

For the representation of labour – if done by Bottomley

Following the narrow loss at South Hackney in 1900, and hoping to win next time around, Bottomley was determined to keep a high public profile. He spoke at concerts and church services and kept his name in the local press.

In 1902, he bought an evening newspaper, the *Sun* (no connection to today's paper of the same name). It was on the verge of bankruptcy, [9] and Bottomley hoped to build a new readership by the familiar device of reporting crimes, especially murders. The paper often took the side of the accused, as for example William Gardiner, a Sunday-school superintendent accused of murdering a girl in the Suffolk village of Peasenhall. Twice tried without conviction, after the juries failed both times to reach a verdict, Gardiner remained in jail, and Bottomley arranged for submissions to be made to the Attorney General, after which Gardiner was released. In another case, two brothers were charged and convicted of stealing boxes of tea from a van in the East End. Bottomley recruited journalists to investigate the crime, and published evidence that the two men had strong alibis. The Home Secretary pardoned them.[10]

The paper promoted itself as broadly a Liberal newspaper – although in contrast to the majority of Liberal publications it actively supported the Boer War.[11] Bottomley also tried to boost its circulation by recruiting guest editors, including his uncle George Jacob Holyoake, the Test cricketer Ranjitsinhji, the Nonconformist preacher Joseph Parker, and Ben Tillett, former leader of the dock strike. There was a racing column and a lottery of sorts ("Sunspots"), as well as a new idea – an occasional column of workers' news, mainly warning workers against advancing demands based neither on reason nor justice.

One difficulty in South Hackney was the opposition of trade unionists to his candidacy. Hoping to run its own Labour candidate, with trade union backing, the Hackney Labour Representation Association was hostile to him. Bottomley still considered himself a Radical at the furthest left edge of the Liberal Party. It annoyed him that, despite his fond opinion of himself, the unions were holding out for something better.

Hearing that the local branch of the Independent Labour Party was sounding out potential candidates, Bottomley arranged for his friend Ben Tillett to speak alongside him on a Liberal platform. Labour supporters responded by passing a resolution criticising Tillett.[12] So Bottomley adopted a new tactic: instead of wooing advocates of working-class representation he would threaten them. He wrote to Charles Horne, of the Gas Workers and General Labourers Union, saying he would sue him for libel: "You have for some time past been spreading various libellous and slanderous statements concerning me, describing me, amongst other things as an unscrupulous Company Promoter and a City swindler". Such attacks, Bottomley maintained, were motivated by a hostility to his candidature for South Hackney. Refusing to criticise his politics, Charles Horne had "resorted to the cowardly – but at the same time very dangerous – device of endeavouring to malign my personal character".[13] The warning was, at first, vague and general: "I should have thought that, after the result of my recent libel action against Mr. Henry Hess and the *Critic* newspaper, you would have been more careful in your methods".[14] Bottomley soon, however, came to the specifics: "Your action leaves me no alternative but either to apply for an immediate Order for a criminal prosecution, or to impose a Writ against you for damages". That prosecution could only be averted by a public apology. Bottomley enclosed a letter which Horne could sign apologising and retracting his libel, and gave the address of one of his employees who would witness Horne's signature. Should that not be forthcoming, by the following day, "please distinctly understand that, without any further notice whatever, I shall institute either criminal or civil proceedings against you".[15]

The threat worked; the unions took no active steps to put forward their own Labour candidate in South Hackney. But this would not be Bottomley's last attempt to scare them with libel threats. Over the next six years, the unions had repeatedly to raise funds to stop him from suing them.[16]

Bottomley sold the *Sun* in autumn 1904. Meanwhile, the geography of labour representation was shifting from London to the industrial North. Manningham Mill and the launching of the Independent Labour Party in Bradford would shift the Labour movement's focus. The next round of unemployed protests began in Lancashire and Yorkshire. By July 1904, a Manchester Unemployed Committee was marching daily to demand public works. On 31st July, police officers charged a demonstration, arrests were made and Victor Grayson, a leader of the movement, was struck on the head. The next day, he and other protest leaders led crowds to the Town Hall to negotiate their comrades' release.[17] Under pressure, the Conservative government passed an Unemployed Workmen Act, establishing Distress Committees and paying grants to councils and businesses who recruited the jobless.

Bottomley's moment

In the 1906 general election, Bottomley addressed dozens of meetings in Victoria Park and at Hackney Town Hall: "He attended smoking concerts and opened bazaars, made speeches at dances, religious meetings and trade union rallies".[18] As Henry Houston recalls, the pubs of Hackney were his base: "During every election in South Hackney H. B. made a point of lunching and taking his tea at the various licensed houses in the division. Those landlords who had no facilities for providing a meal were not neglected. H. B. would have his lunch sent in and support the house by ordering a bottle or paying corkage for that which he took with him".[19] Everywhere he went, his supporters cheered him.

Midway through the campaign, George Jacob Holyoake died. He was cremated at Golder's Green, his ashes interred in a grave beside George Eliot's. He and his nephew had to some extent reconciled: by inviting Holyoake to write for the *Sun*, Bottomley was signalling his admiration, though there is little indication the older man's sympathy extended beyond such commissions. One of his last published works, a posthumous history of the Co-operative Movement, contains the following passage, emphasising the importance when building co-operative organisations of choosing those who can be trusted to give more than they take:

> Mere intellectual education is no surety for probity. The artistic accomplishments of Oscar Wilde did not make him a desirable companion. Energy, alertness, and business sagacity are often found in a rascal.[20]

It is no stretch to read that final sentence as a comment on Holyoake's unwanted nephew.

Meanwhile in South Hackney, Bottomley's two rivals were an independent Liberal named Riley and the incumbent Robertson. There would be no Labour candidate.[21] A Conservative poster called on electors to "Vote for Robertson and Reputation". Bottomley's team changed *Reputation* into *Repetition*. Another poster read: "Vote for Robertson, your old and tried Member" – until *tried* became *tired*.

The jargon of racing had long entered his business slang. When creditors pursued him, Bottomley would task staff with finding out their "form". When an opponent in court proposed a settlement, Bottomley described them as "tailing off", and would say after a win that he "got over that fence alright".[22] His leaflets were equally full of such figures of speech, with "Sporting intelligence" reporting on the "South Hackney Stakes", and the riders:

> Mr John Bull's HORATIO (dark horse, by Vox Populi out of Fairplay)
> Ms Robertson's HERBERT (grey horse, by Claptrap out of South Hackney)
> Mrs Grundy's RILEY (by Crank, out of His Mind)

Bottomley, "the favourite", was said to "go strong". "He is daily doing some excellent gallops, and yesterday went the full course of the constituency, pulling up sound and well". Herbert on the other hand was travelling badly. The bookies were said to make Bottomley the favourite:

> 20 to 1 on Horatio
> 20 to 1 against Herbert (offered freely)
> 1,000 to 1 Riley (offered).[23]

Bottomley won, with a majority of 3,479. His final act of the campaign was to sue the *Daily News and Star*, which was critical of his candidacy. But the action was dropped when the paper's solicitor, Liberal colleague and occasional fellow teetotaller[24] David Lloyd George, paid him a visit: "There's very little gained by recriminations", Lloyd George told Bottomley.[25]

As Bottomley waited for the opening of Parliament, he must surely have been paying mind to his fellow MPs. The Liberal Party had increased its representation by an astonishing 214 seats, almost all taken from Conservatives. But of greater significance were the Labour candidates. Previously there had been just two. The numbers had increased to 29, elected as a result of a secret pact between Liberal chief whip Herbert Gladstone and Ramsay MacDonald, secretary of the Labour Representation Committee. Chief among these new arrivals would be MacDonald himself, as the new MP for Leicester.

Arriving at Westminster, Bottomley signed the register of new MPs. Like Charles Bradlaugh before him, he made no oath but instead affirmed his allegiance to the Crown. He was 46 years old, with a head like a lion's and long hair falling over his eyes and ears. He "was recognised instantly by the crowds, wherever he appeared".[26]

In Parliament

In Disraeli's *Sybil*, written 60 years before, Lady St Julians remarks on the ambitions of lesser men who secure their election to Parliament without the support of the ruling class: "If they have indulged in hallucinations about place before they enter the House, they are soon freed from such distempered fancies; they find that they have no more talent than other people". The new arrivals learn that "power, patronage and pay are reserved for us and our friends".[27] Bottomley had always had a keen practical idea of the need to cultivate social elites, but winning the interest of his fellow parliamentarians proved a harder task than he had hoped.

Early on he rose to make his first speech. In his own account, it was a modest success; the apprentice slowly winning over a hostile audience: "First, the Irish members applauded my condemnation of the 'Instalment system' of Home Rule, and my suggestion that the usual default clause be insisted on, providing for payment in full upon failure in any instalment". Then, after that, other factions on the Liberal left began to listen to him. "The Labour men took up some of my proposals for taxation, and, by degrees, other sections of the House came around, with the result that the papers were good enough to say that I had done well".[28]

Another newly elected Liberal MP, C. F. G. Masterman, recalled the scene rather differently. On his account, Bottomley "spoke through icy silence: a silence cold and contemptuous which could be felt. He made his little jokes, and no-one laughed. He made his eloquent periods, and no-one cheered". The explanation of the other MPs' hostility was their belief that Bottomley was a rogue: "as a House of men of property there is one crime which damns a politician for ever there. That is the suspicion of financial dishonesty". Bottomley had been humiliated: "It was perhaps the most unpleasant afternoon I have ever spent [in the House of Commons] – far worse than being shouted down".[29]

In his first two years in Parliament, Bottomley raised various proposals, including suggesting a bill to enable the state registration of betting. Bottomley had no draft legislation for it; it was simply an excuse to make a speech.[30] When he spoke on the theme of old age pensions, he suggested that they could be paid for by the collection of sums left dormant in private bank accounts, [31] or by an employers' tax on wages, or by a stamp duty on share certificates. All these ideas for raising revenue were adopted in subsequent decades, but we can hardly credit Bottomley for their introduction. He made no alliances in Parliament. He supported the government as long as he saw the possibility of quick advancement, but then – when he realised how poor his odds were of quick promotion – drifted towards independence. He made himself visible to the newspapers; he behaved as an organising committee of one.

His independence, Houston suggests, was adopted opportunistically: "H. B. discovered in the House that the party to which he belonged was so strong that the only way to attract any notice at all was to display a certain amount of independence. It was not so much a matter of political conviction but parliamentary tactics". Bottomley "was determined to get into the limelight and from that circumstance sprung the policy of independence which has more or less characterised his political career. Had there been more prospects of success along party lines, there is little doubt that H. B. would have been a party stalwart".[32] The way to judge Bottomley's success, Houston goes on, is to apply the standards of the entertainer: "In that respect he was a supreme artist. On countless occasions I have sat behind him on the public platform, watched him from every gallery of the House of Commons, and... although I knew every one of his tricks of oratory, I never lost admiration of his superb artistry".[33]

A proprietor once more

Bottomley's arrival in the House of Commons resulted in his next decision, to launch a weekly news magazine, *John Bull*. Its first issue alluded to its editor's election: "The question is, 'That this paper be now read a first time'. The Ayes have it".[34] With the exception of the *Financial Times*, which was not in the

Bottomley stable long enough for him to have shaped it in his image, *John Bull* was the most successful of all his efforts as an editor.

Within weeks of his election, Bottomley had produced a 24-page dummy issue. He approached Julius Elias, the young head of Odhams Press and invited him to print it. Elias had been born in Birmingham. His father had manufactured jet buttons and brooches until the business had failed, after which he became a newsagent and confectioner. Elias was an office boy: he had worked hard and had pulled himself up from poverty. He was also Jewish and this may have appealed to Bottomley's image of himself as an outsider.

They were very different temperamentally, however. Elias was five foot four, thin and dapper. He had never stopped working hard. He was law-abiding, near-teetotal and utterly faithful to his wife Alice. He approached Bottomley's commission with caution, and was very ready to refuse. His first concern was Bottomley's grand set of chambers on Pall Mall, where the rent was obviously punishing – and thus to Elias a grotesque extravagance. He was also perturbed by Bottomley's offer of champagne. His head spun at the suggestion that any money he put up would be matched by funds from Ernest Terah Hooley, who was still (as Elias well knew) an undischarged bankrupt. A paper edited by Bottomley would sell in large numbers, but would his bills be paid? When he tentatively asked Bottomley whether the first issue could be paid for in advance. Bottomley replied that he was currently without any money of his own.

After a great deal of deliberation, Elias agreed. To celebrate, Bottomley opened a third bottle of champagne – and in the end, Elias allowed himself a reluctant sip.[35]

At first, *John Bull* was a modest publication, just a few pages long, and trading heavily on Bottomley's personal reputation. A column in the first issue, "About Ourselves", is a good guide to what he thought of his new magazine – and of himself. Bottomley began with a seeming nod to Bradlaugh. "The parson and the politician we look upon as necessary evils – the one a spiritual, and the other a temporal, policeman – and we hope for the day when we will have no need for either". If Bradlaugh's tone had been one of hope, however, Bottomley combined that emotion with cynicism. "The majority of mankind we regard not, with Carlyle, as fools, but as children". Bottomley explained how he chose his magazine's title, "We liked the ring of it; it suggested common sense and warm blood, and no humbug".[36] To give these messages a visual expression, Bottomley placed a cartoon of John Bull on the front cover, dressed in union–jack waistcoat, top hat, riding gear including crop, and with a dog: this John Bull was corpulent and aggrieved, but also set on change.

Bottomley and Labour

One theme of Bottomley's time in Parliament was his failure to make any positive impression on those immediately to his left, the Labour MPs. In broad terms, the tenor of his politics was tending away from Labour and the causes allied to it.

He always had an eye on personal advancement, and from this perspective, there seemed no good reason to seek allies to his left. There is one further reason for the hostility. Already by 1907–08 the Labour Party was tending to split into left and right factions, with the right ascendant in Parliament. Perhaps surprisingly this was also the wing that was most hostile to Bottomley. This was unexpected in the sense that the likes of Ramsay MacDonald were ostensibly closer to him, sharing Bottomley's instinctive patriotism and his deference towards employers and the wealthy.

A way to explore Bottomley's relationship to the different Labour factions is through the career of Victor Grayson, the firebrand elected to the Commons in July 1907 as member for the Colne Valley Labour League. The Labour right distrusted him. He was a socialist and a recent veteran of unemployed protests; he was not a trade unionist nor supported by any significant group of unionised workers. This seat had previously always been held by the Liberals, and his victory seemed to presage a sharp left turn in the popular consciousness. Both the Conservative and the Liberal parties were, after all, devices to ensure that political power was retained by the propertied. Ever since the reforms three quarters of a century before, both parties had feared that the extension of the franchise would end with a Parliament dominated by workers and the poor. Grayson's final election message could not have been clearer in its appeal to these groups: "To the electors of Colne Valley. I am appealing to you as one of your own class... I do not believe that we are divinely destined to be drudges. Through the centuries we have been the serfs of an arrogant aristocracy". With the rise of industry, a new class of exploiters had emerged: "We have toiled in the factories and workshops to grind profits with which to glut the greedy maw of the Capitalist class. Their children have been fed upon the fat of the land... A vote for the Landowner or the Capitalist is treachery to your class".[37]

Bottomley's initial response to Grayson may well have been dislike. Here was a stranger storming into Parliament within 18 months of Bottomley's own arrival. He was two decades younger and a greater novelty. Unlike many other Labour MPs, Grayson was committed to social redistribution, demanding its achievement as a matter of urgency. In his maiden speech, he derided the grant of a £50,000 pension to Lord Cromer, who had served as Consul-General of Egypt. How could Parliament grant this extravagance, he asked, at a time when the "unemployed are walking the streets"?[38] The Clarion, a left-wing paper, dubbed him the "First Socialist MP".[39] The older man had seen the future – and it hurt.

Yet the longer Grayson was in Parliament, the more complex his situation must have seemed. He was not part of the Parliamentary Labour Party, and was therefore just as isolated in the Chamber as Bottomley. In October 1908, intending to force Parliament to discuss assistance for the unemployed, and to move business immediately to a discussion of works of employment,[40] Grayson had attempted to disrupt a debate on pub licensing. He was escorted from Parliament by the Sergeant at Arms. The last MP to have been so treated was Charles Bradlaugh. This connection must have struck Bottomley, because the next day, when Grayson resumed his protests, Bottomley crossed the floor and attempted to speak to him. Grayson refused his assistance or mediation.[41] He continued his protests – and was suspended.

Grayson's protest had been directed both against Parliament as an institution, and also against the leaders of the Parliamentary Labour Party. He criticised the latter for spending their days on schemes to make themselves appear respectable to nonconformist Liberal voters, and to those who shared the Liberal party's sense of the great cultural divide – between Anglicanism and dissident Christianity, between personal extravagance and thrift. To Grayson's mind, this was all inadequate. In the face of the real distress suffered by millions of unemployed workers, action was needed. Outside Parliament, he had the backing of George Bernard Shaw, [42] and of the Independent Labour Party. Press reports predicted he would soon take over that party.[43] But within Parliament he was isolated and ignored.

Ben Tillett, the dockers' leader who had been Bottomley's columnist, renounced the Labour whip, announcing that he was joining H. M. Hyndman's Social Democratic Federation. He published a pamphlet making the opposition between these two styles of left-wing politics explicit. Titled "Is the Parliamentary Labour Party a Failure?" the short book denounced Labour for reverting to an older form of politics little distinguishable from Liberalism. Labour, he complained, was ignoring the "great tragedy of starvation as represented by the millions unable to find work". Instead it made itself subservient to the "Nonconformist-Temperance-Liberal Party". But the Liberals were not interested in the workers, and Labour put no pressure on them: "The lion has no teeth or claws, and is losing his growl, too; the temperance section being softly feline in their purring to Ministers and their patronage".[44]

The pamphlet was poorly edited and jumbled together various incompatible complaints, but certain recurring criticisms emerge. One concerns temperance. Tillett was accusing his leaders of chasing Nonconformist voters by supporting their demands for reduced opening hours and tougher conditions on pub licensing. This instinct of banning a harmless pleasure, he was saying, was a bad one. Yes, it might appeal to Nonconformist religious voters – but it would lose Labour support in the rest of the country. Another was simply a lack of nerve. Labour was there to help workers, to make it easier for unions to organise and to improve conditions for those who could not work. But it was just too timid to help its own people. Finally he accused the leadership of being star-struck by those people with greater social power.

Contrast this with a second short book, Ramsay MacDonald's *The Social Unrest*, published in 1913. MacDonald had been one of Tillett's targets, and he too was concerned with the same question, namely Labour's failure, since entering Parliament, to stamp its values on society. But this, he insisted, was not Labour's fault alone. It was the product of massive social processes which none of the parties had yet grasped. The real evil facing society, he insisted, was not capitalism, nor the trade unions whose members had become more militant, despite the press criticism they were subject to. Rather, MacDonald argued, Britain had until recently been ruled by an aristocracy remarkable for their wisdom, intelligence, manners, and good taste. The tragedy was that men of breeding were being displaced by the new rich: "The decay of good-breeding and clean, serious living was everywhere apparent, from Turkey trots[45] to lounging in gold clubs". Everywhere, the new spirit was apparent. "You went out to dine where of old you spent a quiet evening in pleasant conversation, and behold, you were hurried through the peaceful after-dinner smoke and rushed to a card-table to gamble the rest of the night". As a visitor, "you knew you were but an encumbrance, and you departed as quickly as possible, never to return". Women, in particular, were toys in the hands of the new consumption, they "caught the new pursuit, and during rubber and other gambling booms freely used social influence to add to their ability to spend lavishly".[46]

MacDonald's analysis follows closely to Tillett's analyses – save that the values are reversed. For Tillett, Labour was spending too much time worrying about drinking and gambling. In his eyes, private extravagance could be ignored as long as the bargaining power of labour rose. For MacDonald, gluttony, as the greatest evil, was a far more revealing guide to Britain's failings than the suffrage question or the rights of unions.

One reason why the independent Liberal Horatio Bottomley could reach no working compromise with a Labour Party led by Ramsay MacDonald is that, for the latter, Bottomley incarnated everything wrong with British life. He was the sort of person who, by drinking to excess and joking about horse-racing, was making life unbearable for everyone else.

Class, nation, Bottomley

Why *John Bull*? As coined by the Scottish writer John Arbuthnot in a series of 18th-century pamphlets, later republished as *The History of John Bull*, the original character had been an imagined cloth merchant, bringing lawsuits against the kings of France (Louis Baboon) and Spain (Lord Strutt), and other enemies.[47] Arbuthnot, a satirist associated with Swift and Pope, was a Tory opponent of Whig wars in Europe, who wished Britain to withdraw from these conflicts, leaving businessmen to get on with the task of making money.

Towards the end of the 18th century, an attempt had made to turn the character into a Whig. In the *Gazeteer and London Daily Advertiser*, he became an opponent of the then Tory government, complaining that the Scots paid less tax than the English. John Wilkes, in *North Briton*, charged that Bull had been "choked by inadvertently swallowing a thistle".[48]

From then until the middle years of the 19th century, Bull would become a cross-party signifier of the wisdom of the English. Tories, Whigs and Radicals all appealed to him, on the basis of two assumptions: first that he was a patriotic Englishman who disliked foreigners, and second that what he most disliked about government was taxes.

In the 1850s–60s, John Bull appeared often on the pages of *Punch*. He had become the pure, patriotic Englishman, in one famous 1859 cartoon seen standing in front of a Christmas pudding in military uniform, with a rifle in his hand. A bulldog is at his right side, ready to go into battle with his master. But he was less of an imperialist than an isolationist. He disliked wars because they meant higher taxes on beer, tea, spirits, tobacco and cigars.[49] His fattening, and his growing satisfaction with the world around him, were products of the same historical dynamics which were undermining Radicalism, and converting the defence of the over-taxed middle classes into a partisan Conservative message.

On the cover of Horatio Bottomley's magazine, the character was as corpulent as the *Punch* cartoon of the 1850s, with a turned-up collar, black boots and a bulldog pawing at the ground. In another cartoon from 1906, we see him walking through a canning factory. By then the Liberals had been in power for four months, but the great man was already offended by the stench and the mess his leaders were making: "war scandals, taxation, rates, party politics, monopolies..."[50] Scandal and corruption, Bottomley maintained, were a chronic feature of Edwardian Liberal government. The magazine abhorred the party system, advocating an administration of businessmen to replace the politicians.[51] It also opposed Lloyd George's reforms of taxation, insisting that luxuries such as gambling and horse-racing should be taxed, not personal income. The visual image that was the publication's brand was fused with that of its owner-publisher-editor: "Pudgy, pompous, curly-haired", *Time* magazine claimed: "Horatio Bottomley looked like John Bull. To millions of Britons he *was* John Bull".[52]

Meanwhile the paper set out to incarnate an Englishness that required it to dismiss the virtues of every other nationality. In the third issue, the "Foul French" are described as "corrupt, tyrannical, bloodthirsty, sycophantic, unmannerly, treacherous and lecherous". A companion piece says of the Germans: "All character has long been battered out of them, they are all machine-made, with lives and habits fashioned in the same ugly mould... They are enslaved, body and soul, by hordes of offensive officials who in their turn are the vassals of other bureaucrats... Their language is the harshest and clumsiest in the world".[53]

"At the end of the Victorian age the mob had no paper", the magazine *English Review* wrote in 1922. "In feeling, Bottomley belonged to this class". His writing was sentimental, easy and conversational. In all these ways, it was popular:

> He took the inarticulate thoughts of the mob for his text and wove them into a journalese which seemed to be, or at any rate came to be regarded as, Biblical in its derivation... He megaphoned the passions, prejudices and hates of the mob.[54]

This account assumes, as Bottomley himself did, that when the people formed themselves into a crowd ("a mob") they could not express themselves save in hatred.

In fact there were many sorts of crowds in late Edwardian England, and their politics often pushed back against Bottomley's conception of the people. Between 1910 and 1914 there was a near-continuous series of strikes and lockouts. Between January and April 1910 a third of the miners in Northumberland and Durham were on strike. In October, 102,000 cotton spinners in Lancashire were locked out by their employers. The following month 50,000 boilermakers from all across the country were also locked out, after their employers sought to end unofficial strikes, obtaining agreements for a return to work from the union executive, only for mass meetings at Newcastle and Edinburgh to reject the proposed deal. These gatherings were not at all Bottomley's idea of England: they were demanding increased pay, better conditions and control over the conditions of work. The editor of *John Bull* would concede the rights of labour *in general*, but never *in particular*.

In November of the same year several hundred suffragettes marched from Caxton Hall to Parliament Square, where police officers attacked them. The women fought back; banners were torn from their hands by officers; when Ada Wright was struck to the ground one man stood above her prone body to defend her. This was a rowdy mob, but its values were those of equality: the extension of votes to women on equal terms to men.

The suffragettes had no place on *John Bull*'s island. Nor did trade unionists, nor such advocates of working-class Ireland as James Larkin or James Connolly, nor the thousands in Liverpool, Birmingham and London who followed them. Also excluded were the Jews, and all migrants who came crowding through the ports. Bottomley's conception of a valued crowd had no place for any of these unruly social movements.

We might see this as a failure of imagination on his part, a claim to speak for the whole people, while at the same time ignoring millions of his fellow men and women. That would be correct, but insufficient. The more troubling thought is that Bottomley's myopia and his popular success were bound up together. For the effect of the demand for Irish freedom was not just to mobilise thousands of people in that demand's support, but also crowds opposed to Irish independence – the thousands who listened to Conservative ("Unionist") orators, or who marched against Home Rule in Belfast. As well as the socialists, there were thousands of people (among them some workers) who became hostile to wealth redistribution. Alongside the suffragettes were similar numbers of people motivated by their hostility to the extension of the vote to women. Bottomley built an audience for *John Bull* out of the polarisation between the Edwardian left and right, and because he offered a platform to the latter. Being an opponent of people's rights may not make a politician unpopular. It did Bottomley no harm at all.

Bottomley and his friends

Bottomley could draw on his allies for copy. Frank Harris wrote leader articles for him, as did Theodore Dahle. Bottomley's column "The World, the Flesh and the Devil" allowed him to flatter or to condemn politicians, company directors, judges and magistrates. One Open Letter was addressed to King Edward VII: "With Your Majesty on the throne, Parliament is almost a redundancy. You are more of a democrat than most of its members".[55]

Within weeks of launching *John Bull*, Bottomley faced the old question of how much of his old Radical programme endured. On its launch, the magazine praised Charles Bradlaugh and the free-thinkers[56] – but this annoyed David Powell, a backer who had purchased £10,000 worth of shares in the publication. Powell communicated his displeasure to Bottomley via Hooley. Bottomley replied to Hooley: "D'you really think I care tuppence about Bradlaugh or anyone else? If you want us to preach orthodox religion, then by all means let's have it". The theme of *John Bull*'s next issue was the blood of Christ.[57]

One of the most important contributors was the paper's racing correspondent, William Lotinga, who wrote a page or more of "Racing Notes and Ideas", as well as offering tips – as Larry Lynx – for *John Bull*'s competitor, *The People*. Other regular columnists included the spiritualist A. P. Sinnett and the travel writer Herbert Vivian.[58]

Bottomley dictated an Open Letter to Sir Henry Campbell Bannerman, then the Liberal Prime Minister and his own party leader in Parliament, chiding him for leading this party with lethargy: "In view of the fact that the Liberal Party has been returned by an overwhelming majority, the country expects you to instate new and vigorous policies. Enough of this fooling! As you are strong, be Brave, Wake up!"[59]

At the centre of the magazine were City and sporting pages. The latter complained of rogue bookmakers, the former dealt with smaller companies, and there were also once more Bottomley's familiar replies to correspondence:

> A bank and betting scandal – W. A. (Birkenhead) – We can see no good purpose to be served by giving publicity to the facts to which you refer.
> London and Paris Exchange – R. W. (Keighley) – Have nothing to do with these marginal investments.[60]

The enemy was not so much politicians as a class as those who had snubbed Bottomley that week; not lawyers in general but those who had represented his opponents; not the rich *en masse* but any businessmen who he judged weak and vulnerable to blackmail.

Disgruntled former employees of prominent businesses were encouraged to write in to complain of malpractices, and an initial answer would be provided in the "Letter Bag": "Loco (Gateshead) – You 'understand' that on the Cheshire Lines Railway between Warrington and Manchester they are short of 30 plate-layers. In some gangs there are only two left". *John Bull* noted that such lax practices were dangerous to safety, and concluded by appealing to the public for more information: "Perhaps somebody can tell us whether you understand correctly".[61] Bottomley would approach the relevant firm explaining that it was his duty to investigate, and drop the hint that enquiries would end only if the company agreed to advertise in *John Bull*. When threatened in this way, Harrods and Lyons both agreed to pay him.[62]

Bottomley and Elias fell out for the first time. The latter was accountable to his fellow directors at Odhams. He began every meeting by observing that never in their entire history had any contract been as lucrative to them as their present association with *John Bull*. That may be so, the directors would reply, but this association with Bottomley was bad for them personally. The minutes record the conflict. "The matter was fully discussed", one records. Another noted a resolution: "This board views with great concern the increasing tendency of *John Bull* to attack well-known commercial firms, and desires the Managing Director [Elias] to represent to the management of *John Bull* the danger of this practice".[63]

Bottomley attacked prominent individuals. One was Annie Besant, who he characterised as a "spurious religious teacher, preying upon the intellectual slavery of her hypnotised disciples". Bottomley accused her of having recruited into the Theosophical Society an "army of morbid moral degenerates", by which he meant lesbians, "whose teachings are calculated to undermine the character and sap the manhood of our race".[64]

The magazine *Modern Man* accused *John Bull* of blackmail. Bottomley sued for libel and was represented by F. E. Smith. *Modern Man* successfully pleaded justification, citing the bank Warings, which had been threatened by the magazine, and Bottomley had to pay costs.[65]

Such setbacks did nothing to dampen his enthusiasm for fraud. When the Charing Cross Bank collapsed in 1910, it was revealed among its (considerable) debts that its managing director, Alfred Carpenter, had loaned Bottomley £12,000. When other newspapers were printing stories that Carpenter's bank was in trouble, Bottomley had appeared on his premises, £52 in cash and various share certificates in hand. All he wanted, Bottomley explained, was a small loan on these securities. Carpenter well knew the value of Bottomley stocks – as well as the risk to his business that Bottomley represented. "My dear Bottomley, they're worthless", said Carpenter. "So is your bank", Bottomley replied. Carpenter granted the loan.[66]

Bottomley also agreed to fund the defence of Charles Crippen when he was charged with murdering his wife, in return for the murderer's account of his trial. After his conviction, Bottomley demanded that Crippen's solicitor Arthur Newton secure the confession. This project was scotched by the prison governor, but Bottomley wanted a scoop, and dictated the confession that Crippen should have made. Brought before the High Court, Newton was struck off the solicitors' roll,[67] and two years later, caught in another fraud, he was sentenced to three years in jail.[68] Bottomley, who had instigated the forgery, escaped without censure.

The People's Budget

The House of Commons was as divided in this Parliament as that institution has ever been. Britain was no longer the world's leading industrial power but one power among equals, with the United States and Germany catching up with her. The two main parties were facing this very differently. To the Liberals, the answer was just as it had been in Gladstone's day: to be a mercantile and a trading power. Exports should be dear, imports (above all corn) should remain cheap. An absence of tariffs on imports and exports would protect both employers and workers. Free trade would be accompanied by those measures of social reform that were necessary in principle (to help the majority who were poor) or desirable on grounds of expediency (the promise of social reform would firm up voters' support for Liberal candidates).

The politics of free trade had dominated in Parliament for six decades, but on the Conservative side new alliances were emerging. Joseph Chamberlain had been President of the Board of Trade in Gladstone's government, but as an opponent of self-government for Ireland and a newly recruited Conservative, he had launched a campaign for Imperial tariffs. His suggestion was that Britain could preserve economic ascendancy by forming a closer economic union with Canada, Australia and India, charging taxes on imports from beyond the Empire. This would restore the economy and would also fund more dramatic reforms, such as pensions (already adopted by Bismarck's Germany), providing a solid and patriotic basis to welfare. Without such a policy, Chamberlain warned, the great employing industries of Britain (cotton, the mines) would fail, with millions forced into poverty.[69] Many Conservatives endorsed this line, though not yet the national party, which remained committed to free trade.

As Chancellor of the Exchequer, Lloyd George introduced a "People's Budget" to pay for both old age pensions and new Dreadnoughts for the navy. The funds were raised by taxation on alcoholic spirits, a higher income tax for those earning in excess of £5,000 a year, and further taxes on land. The Conservatives had a majority in the Lords: they declared the budget unconstitutional. Lloyd George responded with fire of his own, describing the Lords as "five hundred ordinary men chosen at random from amongst the unemployed".[70]

This budget encouraged rebellion across a fault line extending from labour reform, via pensions, as far as Irish politics – where the Liberal government was moving towards devolution.[71] Conservatives encouraged the Army officers to rise up against Home Rule.[72]

Set against the deepening hostility between the two main parties, there is something of the dilettante to Bottomley's record as an MP. He adopted a number of public causes, for example he complained about the Post Office's policy of franking letters publicising unlawful lotteries.[73] He proposed a tax on titles. He complained about the lengthy periods served by prisoners on remand. He spoke on free speech, kleptomania and pub licensing.[74] In fact he was willing, or so it seemed, to speak on every topic except for the great issues of the day.

He began a new organisation, the John Bull League, to reform a system tainted by party, replacing it with one embracing "common sense business methods". It was in the course of this campaign that Bottomley would spot and recruit Henry Houston, the autodidact son of a railway worker who would become one of his key fixers. The League's first meeting was held at the Albert Hall, with 20,000 people present, including the following MPs: the lawyer F. E. Smith (Conservative), Richard Bell (Lib-Lab), Colonel Hall Walker (Conservative), Mr Condon (Irish Nationalist) and Edward Hemmerde (Liberal).

Of these various allies, Smith in particular requires explanation. Dark-haired, in his late 30s, a brute of a man famed among his contemporaries for his love of horses, [75] his very long cigars, [76] and his arrogant courtroom manner, [77] Smith was one of the most militant of Conservatives, arguing that Lloyd George's budget, and the Liberal government, lacked legitimacy. Bottomley, it should be recalled, was still a Liberal Member of Parliament. And here he was allying with this most strident of Conservatives.

Bottomley – for hire

There was another general election in January 1910 and the contest in South Hackney is narrated by Houston, a recent recruit to Bottomley's payroll. The government had been in power for four years, and was losing popularity. The MP recruited a group of supporters, not just the old hands from previous campaigns, but also the journalist William Lotinga and William Ramsey, a one-time lecturer for the National Secular Society, and co-defendant, almost 30 years before, alongside Bradlaugh in one of his many blasphemy trials.[78]

Bottomley's Conservative opponent was a barrister named Conway Wertheimer, and Bottomley made frequent reference to his foreign origins. When the Conservatives booked Joe Chamberlain's son Austen, Bottomley responded by hiring a squad of 50 men paid three shillings each, with boots heavily soled and heeled and weighted with iron nails. On the day of the meeting, they rose one after another, and clattered by the longest route possible to the meeting doors. As the chair shouted "Silence", the first man returned, declaring that he was going as quietly as he could. Then he left, as loud as before, whereupon a second man rose. The speaker lost heart and the meeting was brought to a premature end.[79]

As the election approached, Bottomley issued proceedings against Mr W. Parker, secretary of the Hackney Trades Council, for libel. The claim would be dropped a month later, after Bottomley secured re-election.[80] The contest was inconclusive: despite a swing of more than 100 seats from the Liberals to the Conservatives, the former retained a majority – provided the 71 Irish and 40 Labour MPs continued to vote with them.

In March, the House of Commons debated whether a second elected chamber should be established in place of the House of Lords. Bottomley said that the problem was not how the chamber was elected, but the dominance of the two main parties and their use of patronage: "The Member who barks… gets a knighthood, and, having got into the titled class, he considers it no longer genteel to make himself conspicuous in the public eye. The Member who bites but does not bark is forced out of public life".[81]

If this speech was intended to antagonise the managers of his own party, in other ways Bottomley went further. On 13 June he wrote to the Conservative social imperialist Edward Goulding, an admirer of Chamberlain's campaign for tariff reform, [82] exploring the possibility that both he and *John Bull* could be persuaded to defect. As he was short of cash at this time, the offer was made in blunt commercial terms. He insisted that a comparable offer already existed for him to deepen his relationship with the Liberal Party: "an influential section of 'our side' of the House is desirous of securing a substantial interest in *John Bull*, the only stipulation being that I remain 'sound' on the Land and Constitutional Questions". Bottomley insisted that remaining a Liberal did not suit him. "I do not like the atmosphere of the proposed alliance, and I would infinitely rather enter into relations with some of *your* friends".

The whole point of this scheme, Bottomley acknowledged, was that it was intended to pay off his debts. After a long struggle, he explained, "I have now finally shaken off the aftermath of my old City business". Accordingly, "I *am* both willing and desirous to place an interest of from £10,000 to £20,000 in my journal, in which I have at present the whole of my capital. Will you follow the matter up?" As this would in effect be a commercial contract (his defection to the Conservatives in return for a five-figure payment), Bottomley emphasised the profitability of his magazine. Even a loan, he suggested, could be sufficient. "The paper is the greatest success of modern journalism, the circulation approximating half a million and the advertising income approximating a thousand a week, and the profits being sufficient to easily pay 20 percent dividend upon the shares and to leave ample Reserves in hand".[83]

In the end nothing came of this and its author remained a loudly declared partisan of the Liberal party. Moreover, his entourage continued to feature such characters as the free-thinker Ramsey, recruited to his cause on the basis of Bottomley's connections to Bradlaugh.

It had been a proposal with no meaningful chance of success. In Bottomley's day, just as our own time, it was not unknown for politicians to offer their services for sale. But those who could be bought, then and now, were MPs capable of masking their defection under the pretence of some great issue of principle. Bottomley's terms were just too blatant.

If negotiations had broken down, the Conservatives could have leaked the correspondence and stood against him. In an atmosphere of intense partisan voting, and polarisation along party lines, with no one trusting Bottomley, Liberals or Conservatives, it is hard to see how he could have defended his seat.

The reason Bottomley considered this ruse was that his creditors were in the ascendant. The most threatening was Robert Master, a former Indian Civil Servant who had backed several of his schemes. After several years of silence, Bottomley had written to him: "I have been going over the names of my old supporters and it struck me that I might now be able to do something for those people who have lost money in my companies. Would you mind letting me know approximately the amount you consider you are out of pocket and I will see what I can do towards recouping your loss".[84] Master met Bottomley, as he recorded in his diary: "Walked to Mr Bottomley's chambers in Pall Mall. Took me to a small hotel in Coventry Street where we had much champagne and unnecessarily gorgeous lunch".[85]

At this meeting Master purchased £90,000 of shares from Bottomley, investing in Carter's Deep Leads, Southern Counties Stores Hedon Park Estates and Bottomley's Investment Trust & Agency, a range of company names suggesting that Bottomley had a wide portfolio of capital investments spread across different sectors. Yet when the matter came before the Courts, it was accepted that all were worthless. Master said nothing of any of this to his daughter Eleanor Curtis, but on his death, she learned that her inheritance had been dissipated. She then instituted her own proceedings against Bottomley.[86]

Bottomley promised to honour the debt in full; but then paid nothing. He promised shares in exchange for the debt, and Mrs Curtis declined the offer. He attempted to bribe her solicitors. Once it became clear that Bottomley was to be subject to a criminal prosecution, his tactics changed. A burglar stole into the offices of Mrs Curtis' solicitors, Dade & Co. in Queen Victoria Street. They took nothing of value – except Mr Master's diaries. Six months later, there was a second burglary. Once again, the thieves proved strangely discerning; all that was stolen was the personal correspondence sent by Bottomley to Master.[87] Despite such tricks, Mrs Curtis won, the jury awarding her £50,000 plus costs in 1911.

Bottomley's distancing from his party was not however just a matter of frustrated ambition, or a need to raise funds quickly. Also at play was his hostility to the direction of travel in which his party was heading. Liberal policy was tending towards social reform, the fights over the budgets and the convergence with Labour over issues of social policy must have brought echoes of the old debates between Hyndman and Bradlaugh. In that controversy, Bottomley had been no socialist. Bradlaugh had supported Irish Home Rule, so too had Bottomley in the 1880s, but the image he wanted to create of himself was as a patriot. That implied putting the rights of the English above those of Ireland, and maintaining the Empire. The great issues of the time were pushing Bottomley towards the Conservatives.

For the moment, Bottomley continued to play for time. Over the course of 1910 the Liberal party in Hackney had split into pro- and anti-Bottomley factions. During a further general election in December 1910, the party ran against Bottomley a Liberal schoolteacher, one Mr Roberts. One Liberal paper, the *Daily News*, called on its readers to back Roberts.[88] The Conservatives, meanwhile, delayed in nominating a candidate – perhaps waiting to see whether Bottomley was running, as he had proposed, as a pro-Conservative independent. Cox, Ramsey, and other members of Bottomley's claque were sent into battle, with orders to force Roberts' supporters off the streets. But Roberts' supporters came off rather better, to his alarm, than his own men.[89] In the last days of the election campaign, the Conservatives at last picked a candidate of their own. Though

Bottomley might well have lost in a straight political contest with Roberts, he emerged as the winner in a three-sided fight.[90]

Bottomley's chafing against the party system, in the form of the John Bull League, was not original to him. Instead he was articulating views that were becoming common. Elected alongside him was the poet Hilaire Belloc, another Liberal MP frustrated by his inability to impose himself on his fellow MPs. In February 1911 Belloc published *The Party System* as a critique of the established setup, complaining that parties were dominated by their front benches and that differences between them were minimal, as the Liberal and the Conservative leaders were joined by ties of class, education and even marriage. Both parties were controlled by a small group of the super-rich, into whose hands all power had passed. Parliament was in an advanced state of decay, wrote Belloc, calling it "no more than an opportunity for highly lucrative careers". The traditional programme of the Chartists and the Radicals had been the enfranchisement of the remaining adult population, payment of MPs and the limitation of parliamentary sessions – but these measures could not have saved it: "The degraded Parliament may ultimately be replaced by some other organ", Belloc wrote. But he concluded that no more legitimate body "appears to be forming". Until it did, Britain should be counted as one of the fallen nations that had lost control of their destiny.[91]

The Party System is little known today, but it was widely read in Edwardian England and it influenced the interwar right. In 1957, Belloc's own biographer Robert Speaight would characterise it as a book of superficial appeal based on a glib misunderstanding. As an MP for just four years, Belloc felt equipped to write as if he understood Parliament and the English ruling class, in history, in the present, and for all time. It is true, Speaight argues, that the parties in the Edwardian House of Commons demanded much greater discipline from their MPs compared to 50 years before, but this was for a specific reason, the existence in the Commons (since 1874 and prior to 1914) of the Irish Home Rule party, whose seats ensured that almost any Conservative or Liberal government would also be a minority government. In those circumstances, the desire to sustain governments compelled greater unanimity. As for Belloc's notion that little by way of political differences continued to separate the parties, that may have been true in 1906–10. But it was untrue after 1918, when Labour would supplant the Liberals as the main opposition party, bring closer the possibility of nationalisation and greater social spending. In both these regards, Speaight argues, Belloc's was a shallow critique, the views of an egotistical privileged elite beginning to grasp that a democracy would, over time, reduce their social and class privilege. Speaight accuses Belloc of paving the way for fascism.[92]

Bottomley's diagnosis was every bit as pessimistic as Belloc's. He told constituents in the Hackney Empire that his "idea of the function of a Member of Parliament is that of a parliamentary counsel; his duty is to criticise the Government of the day and get the best he can out of it for not only his constituents but for the whole nation. That is practically impossible under the present party system".[93]

At another public meeting, he described the Commons as "played out… quite possibly an illegal assembly" and claimed that the "musty, rusty, corrupt system" needed replacement by "business government".[94]

This latter phrase would be picked up again in the 1930s and by the same politicians that Speaight was warning against. The idea was that some nominated individual, whether the King, the Prime Minister or a military dictator, be given supreme power to nominate ministers to a government of capitalists. The idea assumes that those who did not desire to live under this new corporate oligarchy could have their votes taken away without difficulty. And that the social violence needed to break democracy was a price worth paying to achieve dictatorship. However, Bottomley's authoritarian instincts were to some extent blocked by his difficulties as a politician: his lack of money or dependable allies. Unlike Belloc, he did not have the literary talent to make dystopia seem desirable. A crisis on an unimagined scale would have to break out before Bottomley's plans had any prospect of fruition.

Notes

1 Bottomley, *Bottomley's Book*, p. 166.
2 T. Paine, *Rights of Man* (Whitefish, MT: Kessinger, 1998 edn), p. 37.
3 This helps to explain why, for example, the Chartist Fergus O'Connor was a consistent advocate of land schemes. He wanted to show that workers could run large agricultural estates along co-operative lines.
4 F. Harris, *My Life* (New York: Frank Harris, 1925), Vol. 1, pp. 221–2.
5 Taylor, *Annie Besant*, p. 247.
6 Holyoake/2/40, Bishopsgate's Institute.
7 R. J. Harrison, *The Life and Times of Sidney and Beatrice Webb 1858–1905: The Formative Years* (Houndmills: Palgrave, 2000), pp. 210–12.
8 Harrison, *The Life and Times*, p. 212.
9 A typical headline was, 'Murdered Family, Babe and Mother Rest Together. Buried Quietly at Bow. Scene at the Cemetery this Morning', *The Sun*, 4 January 1903.
10 Hyman, *The Rise and Fall*, p. 81; Felstead, *Horatio Bottomley*, p. 63.
11 Causing one Radical publication, *Reynolds's Newspaper*, to oppose Bottomley's candidature in South Hackney. 'Cockneyisms', *Reynolds's Newspaper*, 24 June 1900.
12 Labour History Archive and Study Centre, LP/LRC/6/209-211/1-4.
13 Letter from Horatio Bottomley to Charles Horne: enclosed Form of Apology and Retraction in respect of Horne's alleged libel and slander, 24 February 1903, Hackney archives, D/S 52/8/1/1.
14 Bottomley to Horne, 24 February 1903.
15 Bottomley to Horne, 24 February 1903.
16 Charles Horne & W. Parker v Horatio Bottomley (1903–09), and W. Parker Defence Fund Committee (1908), Hackney Archives, D/S/52/8/1 and D/S/52/8/1/5.
17 Taylor, *Victor Grayson*, pp. 36–40.
18 Symons, *Horatio Bottomley*, p. 68.
19 Houston, *The Real Horatio Bottomley*, p. 105.
20 G. J. Holyoake, *The History of Co-Operation* (London: Fisher Unwin, 1906), Chapter XLV.
21 The party's ostensible absence did not prevent Bottomley from threatening to sue Hackney Labour activists, see Labour Party archives. Hackney LRA (W. Parker): LP/GC/1/159-160, 1906 Mar 1–2.

22 Hyman, *The Rise and Fall*, p. 50.

23 Hyman, *The Rise and Fall*, pp. 74–5; Symons, *Horatio Bottomley*, p. 69.

24 As discussed in Chapter 4.

25 Felstead, *Horatio Bottomley*, pp. 77–8; Bottomley, *Bottomley's Book*, p. 63. Bottomley later remembered this incident in correspondence with his former opponent, Bottomley to Lloyd George, undated but 1923 or 1924, Parliamentary archives, LG/G30/2/62.

26 R. J. Minney, *Viscount Southwood* (London: Odhams Press, 1954), p. 75.

27 B. Disraeli, *Sybil* (London: Penguin Classics, 1985), p. 261.

28 Bottomley, *Bottomley's Book*, p. 70.

29 Symons, *Horatio Bottomley*, p. 70.

30 Bottomley, *Bottomley's Book*, p. 71.

31 This proposal was revived by the incoming Conservative-Liberal coalition in 2010.

32 Houston, *The Real Horatio Bottomley*, p. 106.

33 Houston, *The Real Horatio Bottomley*, p. 101. Compare the verdict of the *New York Times*, "He might perhaps have been a political boss, had a machine been available. But in politics he was ever on the doorstep, and Bottomley's party never exceeded himself". *New York Times*, 4 June 1922.

34 *John Bull*, 12 May 1906.

35 Minney, *Viscount Southwood*, p. 80; Houston, *The Real Horatio Bottomley*, p. 153.

36 *John Bull*, 12 May 1906.

37 Taylor, *Victor Grayson*, p. 78.

38 Taylor, *Victor Grayson*, p. 94.

39 Taylor, *Victor Grayson*, p. 84.

40 Works of employment were public works to keep the unemployed paid and active, thus providing an actual job, unlike modern benefits.

41 Taylor, *Victor Grayson*, p. 119.

42 Taylor, *Victor Grayson*, p. 121.

43 Taylor, *Victor Grayson*, p. 141. Grayson lost his seat in 1910, and failed in later attempts to return to politics. He would end up as a minor writer for Bottomley's publications, prior to his mysterious and still unexplained disappearance in 1920.

44 B. Tillett, *Is the Parliamentary Labour Party A Failure?* (London: Twentieth Century Press, 1908), pp. 1, 13.

45 This was a dance craze.

46 R. MacDonald, *The Social Unrest: Its Cause and Solution* (London: T. N. Foulis, 1913), pp. 36–7.

47 J. Arbuthnot, *Law Is a Bottomless Pit* (London: John Arbuthnot, 1712).

48 M. Taylor, 'John Bull and the Iconography of Public Opinion in England c. 1712–1929', *Past and Present* 134 (1992), pp. 93–128, 103.

49 Taylor, 'John Bull', pp. 118–19.

50 Taylor, 'John Bull', p. 121.

51 Given Bottomley's own record as a businessman, it is not unkind to speculate that such a system would have placed Bottomley in power and forced millions into poverty. Business government was however explained, rather differently, by Bottomley's biographer Blathwayt: "A Business Government simply means a Government that would conduct the affairs of the government on a strictly business basis. A soldier at the War Office, a sailor at the Admiralty, a banker as Chancellor of the Exchequer..." Blathwayt, *Horatio Bottomley*, p. 36.

52 'Death of John Bull', *Time*, 5 June 1933.

53 Hyman, *The Rise and Fall*, p. 85.

54 'The Moral of Horatio Bottomley', *The English Review*, July 1922.

55 *John Bull*, 12 May 1906.

56 It also satirised the believers. For example, "Charitable Christian Protestants are going about saying that the Anarchist outrage was a judgment upon Queen Ena for

changing her religion. But as the outrage failed, Catholics are justified in retorting that she was preserved as a reward for embracing the true faith". *John Bull*, 16 June 1906.

57 Hyman, *The Rise and Fall*, p. 88.
58 All published in *John Bull*, 16 June 1906. Despite his brave past, Tillett was a notoriously bad judge of character; in the 1930s, he was an admirer of Oswald Mosley, the leader of the British Union of Fascists.
59 *John Bull*, 16 June 1906.
60 *John Bull*, 21 July 1906.
61 *John Bull*, 31 January 1914.
62 Symons, *Horatio Bottomley*, p. 85.
63 Minney, *Viscount Southwood*, p. 94.
64 J. Dixon, *Divine Feminine: Theosophy and Feminism in England* (Baltimore, MD: Johns Hopkins University Press, 2021), p. 55.
65 Tenax, *The Rise and Fall*, p. 97; Symons, *Horatio Bottomley*, p. 118.
66 Felstead, *Horatio Bottomley*, p. 138; Tenax, *The Rise and Fall*, p. 96.
67 Darling was amongst other things a former Conservative candidate (in 1885) for Bottomley's seat of South Hackney.
68 Felstead, *Horatio Bottomley*, p. 187.
69 Chamberlain's predictions were of course to be vindicated, but only from the 1920s onwards. The 1931 National Government replaced free trade with protection. The country returned to free trade only after 1979, and in the dramatically different conditions of the Thatcher premiership.
70 *The Times*, 10 October 1909.
71 The government was dependent after 1910 on Irish Nationalist support for its Commons' majority.
72 The classic account is G. Dangerfield, *The Strange Death of Liberal England* (London: Serif, 1997 edn), pp. 269–80.
73 Lotteries would play a large part in Bottomley's business life after 1914.
74 Bottomley, *Bottomley's Book*, p. 78.
75 For Smith's participation as rider in the Pegasus Club, Hawkes, *Bench and Bar*, pp. 79–80.
76 A cartoon of him drawn in 1901 shows Smith in a tweed jacket, matching plus fours and a cigar almost as long as his riding boots. Hawkes, *Bench and Bar*, p. 63.
77 Just two of Smith's exchanges with judges convey a sense of his personality: "Mr Smith, having listened to your case, I am no wiser". "Possibly m'lud, but much better informed". And, "What do you suppose I am on the Bench for, Mr Smith?" "It is not for me to attempt to fathom the inscrutable workings of Providence". J. Campbell, "Smith. Frederick Edwin", *Dictionary of National Biography* (Oxford: Oxford University Press, 2004), Vol. 51, p. 113.
78 J. M. Robertson, *Charles Bradlaugh* (London: Watts & Co., 1920), p. 87.
79 Hyman, *The Rise and Fall*, p. 126; Houston, *The Real Horatio Bottomley*, p. 109.
80 Tenax, *The Rise and Fall*, p. 93.
81 HC Deb 31 March 1910 Vol. 15 cc1544–1545.
82 Goulding was known in Parliament as "Joe's Man Friday". A. Sykes, 'Goulding, Edward Alfred', *Dictionary of National Biography* (Oxford: Oxford University Press, 2004), Vol. 23, p. 81.
83 Bottomley to Goulding, 13 June 1910, Parliamentary archives, War 2/16.
84 Felstead, *Horatio Bottomley*, p. 80; Symons, *Horatio Bottomley*, p. 128.
85 Felstead, *Horatio Bottomley*, p. 81.
86 Symons, *Horatio Bottomley*, p. 129.
87 Felstead, *Horatio Bottomley*, pp. 83–4.
88 S. Koss, *The Rise and Fall of the Political Press in Britain* (London: Fontana, 1990), p. 586.

89 Houston, *The Real Horatio Bottomley*, p. 111.
90 Koss, *The Rise and Fall of the Political Press*, p. 586.
91 H. Belloc and C. Chesterton, *The Party System* (London: Latimer, 1911), pp. 150–8, 185, 201; R. Speaight, *The Life of Hilaire Belloc* (London: Hollis & Carter, 1957), pp. 302–6.
92 Speaight, *The Life*, p. 306.
93 Tenax, *The Rise and Fall*, p. 107.
94 *John Bull*, 3 August 1912.

8

THE SPELL OF WORDS

From 1910–14, Bottomley instructed many lawyers and encountered many more. Among them was the best-known barrister of his day,[1] Sir Edward Marshall Hall, whose celebrity stemmed from his defence in 1894 of the Austrian prostitute Marie Hermann. Hermann was accused of murdering a client, and in his closing speech, Marshall Hall turned to the prisoner: "Even this woman", he declared, "was at one time a beautiful and innocent child. Gentlemen, I almost dare you to find a verdict of murder. Look at her, gentlemen of the jury, look at her! God never gave her a chance... won't you?" The press had been convinced this was murder and that Hermann would be hanged – but she was instead convicted of manslaughter.[2]

In the second 1910 election in South Hackney, Marshall Hall was speaking on behalf of the Conservative candidate[3] when a heckler asked if he was not also a friend of Bottomley, at that moment being investigated for fraud. "I meant to say no word of him", Marshall Hall began, "but now his name has been thrown at me I will. I hope from my heart that he will be able to disprove the allegations made against him".[4] One reason Bottomley was able to sustain such a friendship, despite Marshall Hall's greater status, was that Bottomley excelled at skills that barristers considered their own. He was very often the instigator of a court case, seeking compensation for libel or unpaid debt. Whether plaintiff or defendant, he most often won.

There are many tales about his success in court. It seemed nobody could lay a finger on him. In 1911 he was sued by T. W. H. Crosland, author of such books as *The Unspeakable Scot*. Crosland declined to appear in court or give evidence. Bottomley was represented by Mr F. E. Smith, and played up the plaintiff's cowardice, taunting him and threatening to call him as a witness for the defence. He attacked Crosland from the witness box as an "undischarged bankrupt under circumstances of a peculiarly disgraceful character". Crosland's counsel asked

DOI: 10.4324/9781003306085-8

Bottomley to say how many times he himself had been served with applications for bankruptcy: "With the utmost pleasure", was the instant reply, and Bottomley said that he had fought over 200 claims in the shape of bankruptcy petitions. At the conclusion of the case, the jury found Crosland but awarded him only one farthing in damages. He was refused costs, and the judge remarked that the case should never have been brought.[5]

In another case Bottomley was examined by the Official Receiver, Mr Harold De Vaux Brougham, on the winding up of his Joint Stock Trust. He was asked 3,000 questions.[6] Had he, for example, ever inspected the reports provided by his accountant Dalston Easum?

> Bottomley: No, not a single figure. Never seen them in my life.
> Brougham: Did you not take an interest in them?
> Bottomley: No, I had sufficient confidence in Mr Easum as an accountant.[7]

Brougham made the mistake of pressing on with the same question. Bottomley claimed that even his own chequebook had not been his own. Rather it was at his employees' disposal.

> Brougham: Everybody helped themselves to your money as they pleased?
> Bottomley: Yes, in connection with this Company, as they are doing now in connection with the liquidation...[8]

Any potential investor (the likes of Henry O'Hagan) would have been horrified by Bottomley's account of such a lax and haphazard way of doing business. But Bottomley was uninterested in the view of his business contemporaries. What he grasped was the importance of a legal win; that was all anyone would remember. And the wider the blame went for the collapse of his business, the less the chance of any negativity attaching to him personally.

Following this cross-examination, Bottomley was summonsed to appear before the Justices at the Guildhall on a charge of conspiracy. The barristers prosecuting him were Horace Avory[9] and Richard Muir, with Bottomley once again represented by F. E. Smith. Avory read out a passage in which Bottomley told his shareholders that it was desirable to have one dominant personality on the board. Bottomley's response: "Quite a little classic. I rather like it. It reads splendidly. I did not know I could speak so well".[10]

One particular difficulty faced by this prosecution was that Bottomley had so jumbled up his files. It was impossible to reconstruct how the shares of the Joint Struck Trust had been allocated to their purchasers. A dismissed clerk named Levie was called to give evidence against his former employer. Bottomley asked him was his purpose in making such claims blackmail. Levie denied it. Bottomley asked why he had been dismissed. Because he was too honest to do the dirty work asked of him, replied Levie. However further questioning produced an admission: he had in fact been dismissed for drunkenness.[11] Bottomley then produced letters, written after dismissal from Levie to Bottomley, in which the clerk had expressed first deep gratitude to his former employer, then begun asking for money. When his pleas were ignored, he had become more menacing. When they were rejected, he approached the Official Receiver. As Levie's credibility was dissipated, Bottomley's stable cheered their champion.[12]

The prosecution called more than 100 witnesses, though some testifying as victims of Bottomley's frauds claimed still to believe in his good intentions. As one said: "I have always thought a great deal of you, Mr Bottomley". Another had purchased 27,000 worthless shares, yet he believed the charges were "absolutely unfounded". A third told the court that he would take up more of Bottomley's shares if given the chance.[13]

Bottomley remained good-humoured, and his closing speech stressed his left-wing pedigree: "Radical and Democrat as I call myself; I am one of those who honestly has always revered the traditions, the prestige, and the power of this corporation".[14] Sir James Ritchie dismissed the case, and Bottomley left the court in triumph. "It will be a long time before anybody dares to prosecute Bottomley again", the prosecutors were heard to say.[15]

Bottomley and the joy of litigation

Few besides lawyers enjoy a day in court, yet Bottomley spent an extraordinary portion of his life being cross-examined on his business dealings, years in all. He was not always the defendant; he was often the plaintiff. What sort of person consents to such torture?

Bottomley had certain advantages open to few other non-lawyers. First, he had spent three years as a young man taking down court cases in shorthand, an unofficial training every bit as thorough as most barristers had undergone. Second, he had acquired a large retinue of paid supporters to cheer his every word from the public gallery. Authority rests less in anything intrinsic to a person than in their relationship with others. Just as the naked Emperor with his uncritical courtiers, so it was with Bottomley. None would point out the invisible cloth. Members of the public deferred to him, barristers followed, and so did judges.

Bottomley was also a master of the dark art of stopping a case before it came to court at all. Sometimes he offered shares by way of settlement; sometimes he agreed to settle for the sum owed, on condition that all allegations were publicly withdrawn. When more drastic measures were needed, an opponent's barristers or solicitors might be offered bribes not to appear against him – and not all of them declined.

In one prosecution an accountant had been hired to investigate his papers, as a potential expert witness against him. Bottomley discovered that this man was so financially strapped that he had had to sell his own furniture. He appeared at his home and blackmailed him with the threat of exposure as a debtor.[16] Five ledgers of documents essential to the prosecution vanished, burned by Bottomley at the Dicker.[17]

When *John Bull* was sued for libel, F. E. Smith was counsel for the paper, and Bottomley represented himself "in person". In general, barristers are taught to be "nice" to social superiors and inferiors alike, since when you are polite to someone, they are more likely to agree to whatever you ask. This respectful culture is magnified a hundred-fold before a judge. Barristers never interrupt judges, and almost never make jokes at a judge's expense or speak out of turn in court. But a party unrepresented by a lawyer is often allowed to disregard such conventions. If they make a joke, the judge may not hurry to silence them. If they interrupt another witness, the judge will leave the interruption unchallenged. Not unless the misbehaviour is obvious and repeated will a judge intervene. Bottomley enjoyed behaving as little like a barrister as he could, so as to present himself as the court's rule-breaker.

Opponents feared that if *John Bull* lost a case, Bottomley would close the paper. This is why they kept suing him alongside his paper. If damages were also ordered against the man, he could not dodge them by declaring bankruptcy – a bankrupt may not remain an MP, and if there was one thing Bottomley treasured it was his seat in the Commons.

A. E. Bowker was a barrister's clerk and watched Bottomley and F. E. Smith: "To listen to their closing addresses to a jury was a study in itself. 'F. E.', with that whiplike tongue, sarcastic and searing. Then the bold Horatio, nimble witted, humorous with a most powerful turn of rhetoric, convulsing the Court with his witticism".[18] Most accounts end here, in admiration. Bowker observes the flaw: "It was young Douglas Hogg[19] who spotted the weakness of issuing writs against both Bottomley and the publishers, and plaintiffs started to issue them against the publishers only… and his 'in person' advantages were reduced to nil".[20]

Platt v Rowe – and its aftermath

Three years after Bottomley had entered Parliament, an 80-year-old investor named James Platt brought a claim against a stockbroker, Mr Rowe, from whom he had bought a number of Bottomley's Joint Stock Shares, at a total price of £20,000. Bottomley was a witness for Platt and was cross-examined by Frank Russell. Bottomley accepted that Platt had in his possession duplicate (i.e. void) share certificates, but argued that they were issued in error, and innocently.[21] The court ordered Bottomley to repay Platt all sums owed to him. Bottomley's conduct, according to Mr Justice Swinfen-Eady, had been "wholly irregular and illegal".[22]

In June 1911, Eleanor Curtis's case against Bottomley concerning the estate of her father Robert Master reached the High Court, and Mrs Curtis was awarded £50,000 in damages. Blaming the jury foreman, describing him as an alien who spoke no English,[23] Bottomley petitioned the Court of Appeal, but without success.

On 28 November 1911, the Official Receiver brought an action for damages arising out of Bottomley's transactions as chairman of the Joint Stock Trust and

Financial Corporation Limited. The case was heard between 11 January and 1 February 1912, heard once again by Mr Justice Swinfen-Eady. As usual Bottomley appeared in person. Frank Russell represented the creditors of the Selected Gold Miners of Australia Ltd. Bottomley's evidence repeated his argument in *Platt v Rowe* – that he had lost control of the share certificate numbering system, and that this was an innocent mistake, caused by the poor administration of subordinates.[24]

Russell in his concluding remarks argued that Bottomley had invented a new form of property, a "springing and shifting share, a share which shall at the will of Mr Bottomley or his clerks shift and turn from Mr Bottomley's into my share, will turn from a fully paid share into an unpaid share or partly unpaid share, or more marvellously still will turn from an issued share into an unissued share".[25] Bottomley was found liable for fraudulent breach of trust.

This same year Bottomley sued the Prudential Assurance Company for libel. *John Bull* had published a dozen articles attacking the Prudential, claiming that members of the public had been tricked by its agents, and that it had also cheated its own employees. Over 100 agents were said to have killed themselves or attempted suicide.[26] Bottomley's motives in waging this campaign are obscure: it may be that some genuine scandal had been reported to him and he was in campaigning mode. Or it may be that the man who had bullied money out of Harrods and Lyons considered the Prudential a pushover.

Bottomley complained that the Prudential had described him as a fraudster and a blackmailer. But he then became more cautious, taking no steps to bring the claim to a hearing. He did send an emissary with the message that if the case did not settle, further attacks would be on their way. This was a misstep, allowing the Prudential to counterclaim. When Bottomley failed to defend his own case, they sued and obtained judgment and £1,500 costs.

J. M. Astbury, who had also represented Mrs Curtis, was the Prudential's barrister. In preparation for this hearing, Astbury had approached Bottomley's former financier Osborne O'Hagan: "He has a way of dealing with you gentlemen of the Bar which not only floors you, but also wins the sympathy of the judge and jury", O'Hagan told him. "The only way to beat him is to control yourself: smile when he scores of you or insults you, but keep pegging away... You must keep your temper with him".[27]

This advice Astbury followed. His cross-examination lasted four days, exploring much that Bottomley preferred still be hidden, including the extravagance of his household at the Dicker and the large sums leaving his company accounts to pay his friends. The trial also saw an exchange between Bottomley and one of the Prudential's witnesses, that formidable solicitor Edward Bell. "You look at me in such a tragic way", Bottomley complained. "You always take my memory away. You scowl and frown at me and bite your lips". As Hooley was serving a month in prison for contempt of court, Bell asked Bottomley if he had visited him. "I will come and see you one day", Bottomley responded.[28] At the end of the case Bottomley was found in contempt of court and fined £100.[29]

In 1912, Bottomley applied to the High Court for a declaration of bankruptcy. He also applied, on 16 May 1912, for Stewardship of the Chiltern Hundreds, the traditional method of resigning a seat in the House of Commons. A by-election took place eight days later.

Over the coming weeks, F. E. Smith would regret his friend's removal from Parliament: "His House of Commons style was almost ideal, self-possessed, incredibly witty, and distinguished equally by common sense and tolerance. His absence has impoverished the public fund of gaiety, of cleverness, of common sense".[30] Labour leader Ramsay Macdonald is rumoured to have commented that this downfall had long been coming to the magnate.

Bottomley was bankrupt. He had lost the one thing he prized most: his seat in Parliament. His friends wondered how and whether he would recover.

Notes

1 Unusually among his contemporaries, Marshall Hall preferred golf and pheasant shooting to horse-riding; Hawkes, *Bench and Bar*, p. 56.
2 M. Lewis, 'The great defender, Sir Edward Marshall Hall', *Law Society Gazette*, 13 July 1988.
3 Hall was the Conservative candidate in the same election for East Toxteth in Liverpool.
4 Tenax, *The Rise and Fall*, p. 93.
5 A. F. Bowker, *Behind the Bar* (London: Staples Press, 1951), p. 57. Counsel for Mr Crosland suggested that the true figure was 211 bankruptcy petitions. Felstead, *Horatio Bottomley*, p. 175.
6 Tenax, *The Rise and Fall*, p. 72; Hyman, *The Rise and Fall*, p. 99.
7 Easum, it will be recalled, had been Bottomley's accountant at least since the Hansard Union.
8 Tenax, *The Rise and Fall*, pp. 75–6.
9 Avory was the senior prosecuting counsel at the central criminal court; his previous prosecutions had included Oscar Wilde (1895), the Jameson raid plotters (1896), and Adolph Beck (also 1896), wrongly convicted of fraud based on dubious identification evidence. He was another horseman, and former President of the Pegasus Club. Hawkes, *Bench and Bar*, p. 33.
10 Symons, *Horatio Bottomley*, p. 90.
11 Hyman suggests that Bottomley had arranged to get Levie drunk in order to justify dismissing him. Hyman, *The Rise and Fall*, p. 102.
12 'The Bottomley Case: A Confidential Clerk's Evidence', *Manchester Guardian*, 8 January 1909.
13 Symons, *Horatio Bottomley*, p. 94.
14 Felstead, *Horatio Bottomley*, p. 158.
15 Symons, *Horatio Bottomley*, p. 96.
16 Symons, *Horatio Bottomley*, p. 88; Felstead, *Horatio Bottomley*, p. 114.
17 In court, Bottomley would later blame their disappearance on Edward Bell.
18 Bowker, *Behind the Bar*, p. 56.
19 Later Lord Hailsham.
20 Bowker, *Behind the Bar*, p. 107.
21 Tenax, *The Rise and Fall*, pp. 88–9.
22 Symons, *Horatio Bottomley*, p. 97; Tenax, *The Rise and Fall*, p. 90.
23 Symons, *Horatio Bottomley*, p. 119; Tenax, *The Rise and Fall*, p. 100.
24 Tenax, *The Rise and Fall*, p. 103.

25 Symons, *Horatio Bottomley*, pp. 118–19; Tenax, *The Rise and Fall*, p. 105.
26 *John Bull*, 29 April 1911.
27 Symons, *Horatio Bottomley*, p. 128.
28 Symons, *Horatio Bottomley*, pp. 129–31.
29 The contempt is the threat of litigation Bottomley knew had no prospects: the further (bogus) claims he would launch unless they settled.
30 W. Camp, *The Glittering Prizes: A Biographical Study of F. E. Smith, First Earl of Birkenhead* (London: MacGibbon & Kee, 1960), p. 140.

9

PATRIOT

Bottomley would remain a bankrupt for the next six years – yet his prospects were not as bleak as they seemed. *John Bull* was still in print, and its proprietor's disgrace had little effect on its sales. Indeed by autumn 1912 it was claiming that it now had 1.5 million subscribers.[1] Bottomley was prone to exaggeration; his strategy was to make himself seem bigger than he was, and the Advertisers' Protection Society records just 400,000 registered sales per week at this point.[2] But the magazine was more successful than any of its rivals: *Pearson's Weekly*, *Titbits*, *Answers to Correspondents*. It was also paying Bottomley generously.

As after the Hansard trial, Bottomley had the choice of pausing to reflect and acknowledge fault, or of pressing on regardless. Once more he saw no need for contrition, and focused on increasing the income his magazine brought him. *John Bull* introduced a feature called "Bullets": readers were given a phrase to which they were asked to reply; the first and last words of the reply had to include two letters from the original phrase, the replies judged the best winning awards. The best answer for "In the Swim" was "Miles Without Smiles". With each answer a reader had to send in a six-penny postal order, for a prize of £500. To cover its stated costs, the scheme therefore needed several thousand people to contribute.[3] We should not assume that the prize was paid out on every occasion, as announced. However the readers were sending in their sixpences every week.

John Bull also continued its campaign for "business government", including proposals after the 1912 national coal strike to ensure no repetition of such action. The Board of Trade would mediate and make proposals to Parliament. Were the workers to refuse the government's suggestions, soldiers would be sent in, with powers to jail any striking workers.[4]

Around this time, Bottomley was on holiday at Carlsbad in Switzerland, when an admirer came to see him. A Birmingham-based printer, Reuben Bigland had worked himself up with difficulty, his father having died when he was young.[5]

DOI: 10.4324/9781003306085-9

He had been a boot-black, a match-seller, a pantry boy and a house decorator.[6] The owner of the Homer Press, Bigland wanted *John Bull* to run a sweepstake on the Derby. This was riskier than it might sound, as lotteries were then illegal in England. Indeed, section 41 of the Lotteries Act made it an offence even to publish a proposal for the sale of any chance in a lottery. But such a difficulty could be avoided, said Bigland, if the tickets were sent to Switzerland for printing – and if the paper advertising the sweepstake limited itself to remarking in general terms that such a sweepstake existed, including information on how tickets could be bought.

Bottomley met Bigland and quizzed him on his plan. Far more experienced than his new acquaintance in evading the law, Bottomley asked just enough of Bigland to give his co-conspirator the impression he was to be involved. But the magnate was not given to sharing, [7] and Bigland was soon recording his disenchantment. Henry Houston sees the breakdown of the relationship as characteristic of Bottomley's contempt for subordinates: "The man whom he regarded as safe he treated lightly; the doubtful man he showered attention upon".[8]

John Bull ran a sweep on the 1913 Derby, organised from Switzerland by Harry Bennett, one of Bottomley's stable. Bottomley made £150,000; Bennett received £5,000; Bigland nothing. Bennett was informed that his services were no longer needed for any future sweepstakes. Bottomley was doing everything himself. Bennett and Bigland met to commiserate: "Horatio wants the middle and both ends".[9]

In summer 1913, open conflict would break out between Bottomley and Elias. Bottomley's printer was so exhausted by his partner's lax ways with money that Odhams was applying to court for the magazine to be placed in receivership. Elias complained that *John Bull* was being run improperly, and shares had been issued on Bottomley's say-so, diminishing the company's value without any other director having approved them. On 30 July the application was withdrawn. Bottomley apologised. He had underestimated Elias, a mistake he would not make again for many years. Of all his close allies, the printer was the one who was best placed to thrive without Bottomley's assistance.

Further sweepstakes would follow, on the Grand National and the FA Cup, all to the same pattern. *John Bull* would announce the existence of a foreign lottery, publicising its terms to its readers and promising huge prizes. Bottomley's associates arrived in Switzerland or France to handle the correspondence. One or two *bona fide* winners would be publicised. A lucky retainer perhaps received their cut. Various smaller prizes[10] went to members of Bottomley's stable: to Houston, to Cox, even to Bottomley's valet George Wade. All other moneys found their way into Bottomley's own pocket.

For all their suspicions concerning these overseas operations and agents, the law enforcement agencies lacked a source in his camp. Any prosecution would have to be directed against Bottomley himself. But following Bigland's original plan, *John Bull* never announced the lotteries. The magazine limited itself to reporting that someone was organising them.

In March 1914, the Metropolitan Police sought a legal opinion from Wontner and Sons (the forerunners of today's Crown Prosecution Service) as to the merits of a prosecution. The solicitors replied: "We cannot recommend having a fall with Mr Bottomley upon such vague and flimsy material".[11]

John Bull ran a sweepstake on the 1914 Derby, which would be won by Durbar II. It was reported that the first prize, of £25,000, had gone to a Madame Gluckman, a blind lady living in Toulouse. The sum was drawn on an account with the London Joint City and Midland Bank, and a copy of the cheque was reproduced in *John Bull*. As it happened, Mme Gluckman was the sister of Saul Cooper, and Cooper was a member of Bottomley's entourage. She was indeed blind – which may explain why she ended up receiving just £280 in cash rather than the full sum owed. To hide her from press enquiries, Bottomley took her to Paris.[12]

Bottomley deposited £25,000 in the account of his Northern Territories Syndicate Limited.[13] "A few more sweeps like the Derby one and I'll be able to pay off all my debts and get back to the House of Commons", Bottomley told Houston.[14]

The National Anti-Gambling League proposed that he should be prosecuted for fraud. The Metropolitan Police were interested, but as one officer confided to his seniors: "There is no proof in the possession of the police that the John Bull Derby sweepstake is fraudulent or that it is controlled by Bottomley".[15] Nevertheless an investigation was launched, and in May 1914, Bottomley was prosecuted and fined £25 for publicising the Derby sweepstake. The prosecutor was Travers Humphreys, who had once acted for Oscar Wilde. Bottomley appealed the conviction to the High Court. Six months later, the judge at the appeal – Mr Justice Darling, [16] a regular participant in the Bar's annual horse-riding competitions – quashed the conviction. Within the meaning of the Lotteries Act, an article in a newspaper that favourably mentioned and gave information about a sweepstake upon a horse race was not the "'publication of a proposal or scheme for the sale of tickets in an unauthorised lottery". Hence neither editor nor newspaper were guilty of an offence. "Bottomley argued the case extremely well", Humphreys wrote: "As well indeed as any member of the Bar could have done".[17]

Yet the overall picture was one of stagnation. Bottomley's tastes were too extravagant. He could not satisfy them except by setting out further schemes, each threatening to end in loss or imprisonment. He needed a victory on a new scale if he was to rescue his finances.

Redemption

In summer 1914, Bottomley was planning *John Bull*'s response to the assassination of Archduke Franz Ferdinand and the Austrian ultimatum to Serbia. He had travelled to Austria before, and favoured that country over the quarrelsome peoples of the Balkans demanding independence. Indeed, he had campaigned for several years against Slav nationalism: "To Hell with Serbia!" his magazine declared: "Why should Britain shed her blood to save a nation of assassins? Let Serbia be removed from the map of Europe".[18] But by 4 August 1914, Britain was at war with both Germany and Austria, and the whole weight of the Empire was being employed to protect the rights of small and gallant nations.

In August 1914, Bottomley was on holiday in Belgium with 20 racehorses.[19] When war was declared, Bottomley made a show of offering the horses to the Belgian government for its cavalry; cheaper for him than paying for their passage home.

Back in England, Bottomley went into the *John Bull* offices. His magazine continued to denounce Serbia, claiming to have in its possession a document from the Serbian Secret Service planning the Archduke's murder. As late as 8 August, four days after Britain declared war, *John Bull* was still supporting Austria and Germany against their enemies. As patriotic crowds formed[20] and as the women of the National Service League began handing out white feathers to those who had not yet volunteered, [21] *John Bull* was on the wrong side.

Then on 15 August Bottomley's magazine joined the patriotic war effort. In place of the usual cartoon on its masthead – John Bull as a farmer – it featured a sailor with the words *HMS Victory* on his cap. "Do you recognise him now?" the magazine asked.[22] The next issue led with an article: "The Dawn of England's Glory. The Day Has Come". "It is not necessary to be a soldier", the paper continued, "but it *is* necessary to be a MAN".[23]

As Bottomley told Houston, "Whatever I have been in the past, and whatever my faults, I am going to draw a line at 4 August 1914, and start afresh. I shall play the game, cut all my old associates, and wipe out everything pre-1914". "Including the women?" asked Houston. "Including the women", Bottomley insisted.[24]

The first recruiting meeting for the war effort was held with Lord Birkenhead speaking alongside various MPs. Bottomley was not invited. "We must have a big meeting", he told Houston.[25] He approached the London Opera House (today the Royal Opera House) to book a meeting for 14 September: "*John Bull's* Great Patriotic Rally for recruiting".

Bottomley began his speech with the dangers facing Britain, the most serious being the emergence of the German navy. This and all other dangers facing the country he blamed on the "party system of government". He called for a different system of politics, with all power placed in the hands of a leader, a "man conversant with the details of his work" and with the ear of the people.[26] Bottomley told his listeners that the war was not of Britain's making – but that if they were determined it could be brought to a speedy end: "Its duration depends upon you. It depends upon those who are wanted to go to the front, the more there are, the sooner will the enemy see the folly upon which he has embarked and sue for terms of peace". It would end with German warships in British hands, its Empire partitioned and its Kaiser dethroned. He called on every man present to sign up for the army and to thereby hasten the coming peace.[27]

Bottomley claimed that 5,000 had attended his rally, with a further 20,000 turned away.[28] We should allow for his habitual exaggeration: the venue's capacity was just 2,500. In any event, larger venues offered themselves to him, including the Albert Hall (capacity 5,300). Houston claims that the latter was so tightly packed that it took Bottomley two hours to make a way into his own meeting.[29] George Bernard Shaw watched one of his performances: "It's exactly what I expected; the man got his popularity by telling people with sufficient bombast just what they think themselves and therefore want to hear".[30]

One of Bottomley's war poems gives a flavour of his wartime patriotism, its sentimentality and its insistence on the unambiguous wonders of war:

> Why is the red blood flowing – why do the women weep?
> Why have our dear, long-lost brothers gone to their long last sleep?
> Come, comrade, come – consider: let's look things in the face,
> For this is more than a war, mate – it's a call to the human race.[31]

In January 1915, Bottomley wrote to Prime Minister Asquith to offer his services as Chief Recruiting Officer. Asquith replied, "Thank you for your kind offer, but I shall not avail myself of it at the moment. You are doing better work where you are".[32] Bottomley decided to consider this a promise of official employment in due course.

Others were experimenting with similar oratory, though with less success. F. E. Smith was considered the "democratic orator-in-chief of the Tory party", and had collaborated with the novelist Arthur Conan Doyle on a recruiting pamphlet, *To Arms!* In this, Smith rebuked the industrial cities of the North, who "send tens of thousands to cheer their representatives on a football field, but are unmoved by the terrible experiences of our men on the field of battle". But as he confided to friends, such rhetoric left its intended audience unmoved. The more he attacked the Liberal government, the more the country clung to its leaders. Bottomley, Smith had to acknowledge, was doing a far better job than he was.[33]

Between 1915 and 1918, Bottomley would deliver 340 public lectures. At the urging of various patriotic associations, Bottomley also spoke at 20 formal recruiting meetings. In his mind, the lectures were distinguished from the re- cruiting meetings. The latter he spoke at for free; the lectures, by contrast, were money-raising ventures, and advertised as such. A venue had to be booked and travel paid for – but all further takings Bottomley pocketed himself.

He delivered his patriotism in a rough formula according to the generosity of the audience. When takings were less than £75, Bottomley would end with a subdued call on the name of the King. The band would then strike up the National Anthem, and Bottomley would bow and leave. But when he was up by more than £75, his audience were rewarded with a more stirring finale. At its crescendo, he would shout, "When this great nation emerges from its period of trial – as please God it will – we shall stand erect shoulder to shoulder before the world, and declare with one voice that Britain is the 'Land of Hope and Glory'".[34] The band played Elgar's music, with Bottomley's voice rising until overwhelmed by the audience singing with him the litany of imperial expansion: "*Wider still and wider...*"

On the best nights – where the profits were in excess of £100, meaning an audience of 1,000 people – Bottomley would end his oration, his voice thundering, with the speech he had first made at the London Opera House. The war, he would declare, was the destiny of the Anglo-Saxon Race, promising death to traitors, to aliens, to every enemy of the King.

These great patriotic assemblies were the glory of Bottomley's life, and a historian can only note their two chief consequences. First, their star made money in abundance. Second, where he did persuade men to volunteer, he contributed to a war in which more than 16 million people were killed. Thousands of those deaths would not have happened without him. In every city, those signing up at his urging would return as invalids, if they returned at all.

Bottomley and the left

Britain needed to change, Bottomley argued, so as to enable the total war that victory required. A different sort of society was needed – one that showed no compassion to its left-wing and pacifist enemies within. Under a business government, Parliament (that "played-out institution") would be abolished in favour of military rule.[35] Bottomley's old opponents (trade unionists, socialists, the Irish...) were candidates for imprisonment or worse. So when miners struck in 1915, Bottomley and *John Bull* insisted that any worker following suit must be "arrested, treated as deserters and punished according to martial law".[36]

The magazine had long traded on insinuations that this or that business was being improperly run. In the conditions of war, such accusations carried far higher stakes. Several large companies were so scared of Bottomley that they felt it needful to advertise their patriotic credentials in *John Bull*. Lyons and Bovril bought space to insist their directors were British rather than German. De La Rue (which made pens) used *John Bull* to attack their rivals Waterman's, suggesting that Waterman's wares were sold through an Austrian firm, L & C Hardmuth. Waterman's took out a full-page ad to deny the allegation.[37] It would be a safe bet to assume that such advertising was pricier than it had been prior to the war.

Bottomley's newfound patriotism was wiping from public memory all taint of the outstanding allegations against him: his bankruptcy, his business affairs in Austria, even his support for Austria over England in the first week of the war.

When a minority of politicians spoke out against the slaughter, he raged against them. His chief target was Labour politicians. He had never understood socialism and never forgave the Labour Party for breaking with the Radical Liberalism of his youth, which is to say with the most left-wing belief then to hand. Even as he announced his continued loyalty to the left, he could not accept that the political tradition that first shaped him had been outflanked. Had he not, since his youth, been labour's staunchest friend?

In February 1915, *John Bull* named Labour leader Ramsay MacDonald (along with Keir Hardie) as one of two leaders of a "pro-German Campaign" in Britain.[38] In the following issue, Bottomley published an article by A. G. Hales. One incident in particular during the German invasion of Belgium had become a key justification for the war. The nuns of Brabant had been ordered to strip, it seems, to prevent men from hiding among them – and this had been transformed in the telling into the rape of thousands. Privately, MacDonald had cast doubt on such stories. Such doubt, Hales argued, was itself a crime. Girls of tender age had been ravished. In that context: "It is hard to believe that a British member of Parliament would lower himself to whitewash criminals in uniform, and I hope that Ramsay MacDonald can step forward and vindicate himself against the charge to which I have referred".[39]

In summer 1915, *John Bull* demanded that MacDonald be tried for treason, "and that he be taken to the Tower and shot at dawn".[40] Macdonald described Bottomley in the Commons as a "man of doubtful parentage, who lived all his life on the threshold of jail".[41]

The attacks became more personal still. Aware of how hurtful his own parents' death and his youthful poverty had been to him, Bottomley chose to declare that MacDonald, as well as being a liar, had been born a pauper and a bastard:

> "James Ramsay Macdonald", MP for Leicester, late "leader" of the Labour Party, late member of a Royal Commission, under the seal of His Majesty… libeller and slanderer of his country [is] *the illegitimate son of a Scotch servant girl.*[42]

As MacDonald wrote in his diary: "The first time I had ever seen my registration certificate was when I opened the paper… Never before did I know that I had been registered under the name of Ramsay and cannot understand it now".[43] MacDonald's closest ally at this time was Keir Hardie. *John Bull* renamed him "Kur" – with Bottomley proposing he be locked in a psychiatric hospital.[44] At this bitter attack on his friend, Hardie suffered a stroke.[45]

Meanwhile, *John Bull*'s registered sales carried on climbing. In July 1915 they reached a consistent million for the first time, and continued to grow strongly.[46]

Bottomley and the Germans

Bottomley allowed no distinction between Germany the state and her people, even as increasing numbers of the latter were demonstrating their opposition to war. He considered all Germans evil: "If by chance you should discover one day in a restaurant that you are being served by a German waiter, you will throw the soup in his foul face, if you find yourself sitting at the side of a German clerk, you will split the inkpot over his vile head".[47] There could be no restraint against such an enemy: "War is the eagle's business, with neck outstretched and beak stern for combat, with talons outspread ready to fasten in the back of the foe and never lose hold until every drop of blood has dripped from the quarry".[48]

In Bottomley's view of the world, this was not a matter of nationality alone, but one of race. A person born in England to a German father and an English mother was outside the British race. They too had no right to remain in Britain – and no right to live at all.

Bottomley's campaign would reach its pitch in mid-1915, following the sinking on 7 May of the passenger ship HMS Lusitania, in which 1,198 people died: 785 passengers and 413 crew. Many of the crew were from Liverpool, and the Irish districts in the northern parts of the city. The first attacks occurred there on the evening of the sinking, on businesses with German-sounding names: Fischer's, Dimler's, and Deeg's.[49]

Bottomley's response appeared in *John Bull* on 15 May. He proposed that German people in Britain should be made to wear badges when they left their homes. And this display of their inferiority was just the first step in his plans. As soon as it could be done, they should be deported. If that was impossible, he urged his readers to wage a "blood feud": "You cannot naturalise an unnatural beast – a human abortion – a hellish freak. But you can exterminate it".[50] Nor was extermination a mere linguistic flourish. He had put careful thought, not just into the point of principle (that all Germans in Britain be killed), but into how to kill them – without wasting the precious resources needed for the war. "I should welcome the formation of a National Council of Righteous Retribution – a National Vendetta, pledged to exterminate every German-born man (God forgive the term!) in Britain – and to deport every German-born woman and child". Bottomley proposed to go beyond deportations: "I would put in the field an army of Zulus and Basutos and other native and half-civilised tribes – and let them run amok in the enemy's ranks. I would give them all the asphyxiating gas they wanted".[51]

As we re-read this passage today – with its joy in the gassing and extermination of civilians – we must remember that *John Bull* was at this time the best-selling weekly news magazine in Britain. At least some of its two million readers could be expected to act on such calls. "On the same day that Bottomley's article appeared", writes Panikos Panayi, the historian of the Anglo-German community, "riots broke out through the country".[52] No doubt Bottomley was tailing public opinion as much as he was leading it. Nevertheless here was a senior British journalist-politician demanding that thousands be murdered.

Germans were attacked in Poplar, in Deptford, in Keighley and in Crewe. British nationals with German-sounding surnames found themselves having to advertise their Englishness in the press. "I, William Andrew Utz", one such announcement read, "am a British-born subject. I was born at 42 High Street Poplar... I have been in the business of a butcher for many years, following my father in his long-established shop at the said 42 High Street Poplar".[53] Bankers gathered in their top hats on the steps of the Stock Exchange to pass a motion: "No Germans must be left in the City of London". Smithfield porters hung signs from their necks: "No business transacted with Germans". In Poplar crowds swarmed into the houses of those suspected of harbouring Germans.[54]

The novelist D. H. Lawrence was horrified. His wife Frieda had been born in Metz in Alsace-Lorraine, and three months after the sinking of the Lusitania, he would write to his friend Cynthia Asquith, warning that the whole ruling class of England was mired in selfishness and deceit. It needed to be swept aside. Or, "if we continued in our bad spirit, we shall have Horatio Bottomley for our Prime Minister before a year is out".[55]

Bottomley and the people

Bottomley's message was that Britain had been brought low by internal enemies, both political (trade unionists, Labour supporters, pacifists) and racial (Germans or "Germhuns" and Austrians or "Austrihuns").[56] The war was a glorious opportunity for national rebirth: "Those who are the real victors have the greatest right of all to a say in the peace which is to follow war – in the great awakening and reorganisation that will come from the soil of rebirth".[57]

To counteract a threatened strike by shipwrights, Bottomley was invited to stage a great meeting on the Clyde, where 5,000 workers listened as he pledged that the relationship between employers and workers would have to change: "Half the work of bringing about a better understanding between masters and men – between Capital and Labour – has been done by the war itself". In future, "You will find new Rules of Trade Unions and Employers' Federations on a more humane basis; you will find brotherhood and humanity covering the whole relations in the financial, commercial, and industrial field".[58] When the speech was over, Bottomley contacted the employers offering to send his words to their shipwrights. Names were supplied. Instead of his speech, Bottomley sent a form for the 1915 *John Bull* Derby sweepstake.[59]

In the 30 years since he had been Bottomley's co-worker at *Youth*, Alfred Harmsworth had become the greatest newspaper proprietor of the age. He had been ennobled with the title Lord Northcliffe, and ran the *Daily Mail*, *The Times*, the *Observer* and other papers. He approached Bottomley with the offer of a series of articles in a new publication, the *Sunday Pictorial* (which was conceived as a Sunday counterpart to the existing *Daily Mirror*). Bottomley obliged, producing piece after piece modelled on his speeches. He demanded £150 per article, an extraordinary fee when most workers earned £3 or £4 per week. Nor was this just an extra platform for him. The *Pictorial* was advertising the services of its new celebrity correspondent and calling for his immediate promotion to a government post: "Is there a strike to settle? He can pour oil on troubled waters... Yet his great talents are mostly used 'unofficially'. There is much work that Mr Bottomley could do. He is a force in the State... His services should be utilised more and more by the Government".[60]

By December 1915, Northcliffe's *Evening News* had taken up the call, covering London with placards reading "Bottomley wanted". Houston, ever in attendance, records: "It was the moment for which H. B. had waited and longed. I believe he would have bartered his soul and ten years of his life for the honour of leading the country to victory in the war".[61] Yet even as the possibility of this call to greatness welled up within Bottomley's mind, it never quite happened. Days were spent at King Street, with Houston, and friends bearing flowers. But while Asquith was indeed considering new appointments, no offer came Bottomley's way.

This same month he also began campaigning against a proposed Central Control Board of Liquor Traffic, intended to introduce stricter licensing laws. The John Bull League being dormant, Bottomley set up a new organisation, the League of the Man in the Street.[62]

He was also attempting to call a new independent party of the right into being, pledging his support for Noel Pemberton Billing's candidacy at the by-election in January 1916 in Mile End, just three miles from South Hackney. Pemberton Billing had resigned from the Royal Naval Air Service and was demanding air raids against Germany. Another supporter was Ben Tillett, now an eager supporter of the war.[63] Coming within 380 votes of defeating the Conservative candidate, Pemberton-Billing afterwards stood in a by-election in Hertford, where he was elected. He also founded a weekly journal, the *Imperialist*, which combined attacks on the party system with claims that secret German conspiracies had already overrun the country. Bottomley then repeated and inflated Pemberton Billing's claims, complaining of the "Unseen Hand" that controlled the unions and the Labour Party.[64]

Bottomley was an outrider in the war effort, his lectures mainly raising funds for him personally. His methods were clumsy and obvious, and no doubt senior politicians were criticising him behind closed doors for the excessive nature of his attacks on ordinary Germans and pacifists. Yet he was starting to be recognised in establishment circles. By bullying their enemies at no risk to the government, he was serving the interests of Britain's rulers. Even as they benefitted, they could disassociate themselves from him.

In 1916, the journalist and actor Raymond Blathwayt published a biography. It opens with a talk Blathwayt had been giving to an audience on the virtues of the Bible and John Bunyan. A soldier asks him which magazine men should read. Blathwayt had stalled, but the soldier continued: "What about *John Bull*? We think a lot of Bottomley in the Army". Blathwayt went on to dub Bottomley the "uncrowned King of England", gushing that he knew of "no man who could so well fulfil the popular ideal of a Leader... as he would do".[65] This was high praise, though not from an independent voice (his publisher was Odhams, who still printed *John Bull* every week, their most lucrative contract).

Bottomley used this book to distance himself further yet from Holyoake and Bradlaugh. Just seven years earlier he had called Bradlaugh his "ideal public man".[66] Since then, the tone in dealing with his parents' generation had changed: "They never seemed to get any further", he told Blathwayt, "they didn't seem to accomplish anything". He said, "There were moments when I felt, as many others must have felt, that I'd rather be a pagan suckled in a creed outworn, so might I have glimpses that would make me less forlorn. There was nothing half so lonely and hopeless as [their] creedless atheism".[67] In this small act of violence against his family, we can see Bottomley taking the final steps towards (what he was convinced would be) his victory. Once offered a position in the cabinet, he would in that moment be released from his past, his shame. He would cease to be what he had always hated: a former orphan.

Victory and downfall, both in reach

Yet Bottomley continued to accumulate enemies. Following the disclosure of MacDonald's parentage, the Labour MP received dozens of letters of support, including one from Bottomley's former ally Reuben Bigland.[68] Earlier in the same year, Bigland had written to remind Bottomley of an old debt of £50. The reminder went unanswered. Resentment would perhaps have dwindled had he not then by chance met with another journalist with his own reasons to have harsh thoughts towards Bottomley: William Lotinga.

In return for 2800 shares in *John Bull*, Lotinga had sold *Lotinga's Weekly*, his sports newspaper, to Bottomley. The shares (said Bottomley) were worth £2 each, and there was also promise of an annual salary of £1,000. But the two had fallen out, and Bottomley had revealed that the shares were worth just 10 shillings. Lotinga was down £4,200, plus several months' salary. Having sued unsuccessfully,[69] he was dismissed from the *People*.[70]

Over tea at a café near Holborn's Red Lion Street, he and Bigland shared stories of their humiliation. Bigland agreed to print a pamphlet Lotinga had written exposing Bottomley. Soon the few sceptics in Bottomley's audiences had access to the following account: "I need now only mention a *few* of his victims – usually very old or very young men – with "round" figures as the amounts of which he robbed them. Thomas Hill (£80,000), James Platt (£50,000), R. S. Master (£83,000), Joseph G. Smith (£70,000)..."[71] A second pamphlet followed: *What Horatio Bottomley Has Done for His Country and the Wounded Soldiers*. Its 24 pages were blank.[72]

Bottomley offered a reward of £50 to discover the printer's name. Lotinga named himself and demanded the £50. He was not paid, so he sued. The case was listed for a hearing on 23 February 1916, but it never took place. The day before trial Bottomley paid up. Lotinga gave the money to the Red Cross.[73]

Bottomley offered to tour the country with cabinet ministers, making speeches to keep up the public's flagging morale.[74] On 18 December 1916, Lloyd George became Prime Minister, with three press lords in his government, including Lord Northcliffe and his brother Lord Rothermere. But Bottomley was still not one of them. As he spent his war plotting his own advancement, others – with equal determination and ingenuity – were starting to plot his downfall. The more his name was discussed, the greater the target became for his critics.

Bottomley published a prospectus of his own: *Who Is Mr Bottomley?* After 12 hours of negotiation at a solicitor's office in Great Marlborough Street,[75] he reached an agreement with Lotinga for his silence, in return for full payment of the old debt of £4,200. As Houston records, the journalist was thus neutralised – but not appeased. Lotinga "carried his animosity to the grave, and when his will was read, it was found to contain certain clauses warning his son never to have anything to do with 'that scoundrel Bottomley'".[76]

In February 1917, Bottomley organised a presentation to Julius Elias of a portrait of the Odhams owner.[77] He was shoring up the support of a key ally. In May 1917, he even met Bigland, paying him £50,[78] after which the two once more resumed their unlikely alliance. At times, Bottomley would tap Bigland for cash. Over the next two years, so Bigland later claimed, he had loaned Bottomley more than £10,000, without interest.[79]

A tin of bully

When Bottomley visited the front to boost morale in September 1917, and even though he was on official business, looked after by the Army throughout this tour of duty, the *Sunday Pictorial* paid £1,000 towards his expenses. His articles home struck an unfamiliar, cautious tone: "I could not but marvel at the satire upon civilization which directed all this energy and enterprise and capital to the destruction of life and property instead of into channels for the happiness and welfare of mankind".[80] Was it dawning on him that those he had called to serve were suffering in the wet, the cold and the hunger of the trenches?

Or was he just missing his champagne? Houston describes his patron as listless in the four days he spent without Pommery, and local villages were scoured for anything suitable. He travelled to Amiens, where his party finished off six bottles. Bottomley declined to return to HQ, sending a telegram: "Sorry I cannot get back, am in the bosom of my family".[81]

In the trench newspaper *BEF Times* Bottomley was known as "Cockles Tumley", his patriotic reporting satirised as the outpourings of a ravenous blowhard: "I've been in the support line which is much more dangerous than the first. I've been in Div. HQ which is more dangerous still... I have learnt that there's a lot of meat in a tin of bully. I have learnt that an army biscuit is tough to crack". From such ignorance followed a shallow optimism: "Every German prisoner I spoke to said the same thing. I can't tell what it was, but THE WAR IS WON... I will write more when my head is clearer. I must go now and have my photo taken in a gasbag and tin hat".[82] Bottomley was little more than a brief amusement to the soldiers. They had other and worse enemies, but they nevertheless grasped one thing far better than any of Bottomley's civilian sycophants: the dishonesty of his public persona. Bottomley knew nothing of the war and cared little for it. He saw it as a means of settling scores and getting rich.

Meanwhile he spoke out against doddering generals, the scandal of Dutch neutrality, the toleration of conscientious objectors, and the workers "slacking" when they should have been making arms. His favourite target was war-profiteers: "What is to be said of the man who is making money out of the war by fashioning military equipment and yet [does not fight]... A man who cannot take the risk of dying for his country is not fit to live in it".[83]

In November 1917, the Assistant Secretary to the Cabinet Thomas Jones was dining with various well-connected figures; editor of the *Times* Geoffrey Dawson, MP for Plymouth Waldorf Astor and his wife Nancy, Secretary of State for Foreign Affairs Arthur Balfour. Several "irresponsible controllers of the Press" were said to have been "doctoring the news", Jones recorded in his diary – and Bottomley's was one of the names that came up.[84]

The War Cabinet would soon have a genuine reason to fear Bottomley. In early 1918, Horatio learned that Prime Minister Lloyd George's son Richard was engaged to Roberta McAlpine, daughter of Conservative donor Sir Robert McAlpine. *John Bull* asked whether "McAlpine (the Army Contractor) be a relative of a famous politician?"[85]

The reports were of particular concern to the Prime Minister. Lloyd George had long had to face down accusations of corruption. Before the war, he, Attorney General Sir Rufus Isaacs and Postmaster General Herbert Samuel had all purchased shares in American Marconi, before it was to profit from a government contract.[86] After the war ended, Lloyd George would be accused of raising money for himself and for his party by the reckless selling of peerages to war profiteers.[87] Any exploration either of the McAlpine's relationship to him or McAlpine's success in obtaining government contracts could have caused real trouble for him.

Over the next few weeks *John Bull* was full of praise of the Prime Minister, with no further mention made of the embarrassing gossip.[88] In place of barbed hints of scandal, the paper became constructive, proposing for example a series of changes to the rationing system. Bottomley had made lurches of this kind before, first questioning the patriotic standing of this business or that, then applauding them. Always previously, the reasons for the change of heart had involved gifts of money. But this time Bottomley was once again angling for a public position to crown his wartime activity.

Early in 1918, he was invited to Downing Street, where they discussed food distribution.[89] Bottomley suggested that a Director of War Propaganda was needed, making his ambitions as overt as he dared, and Lloyd George flattered him, insisting that he already played that part. In the company of admirers afterwards, Bottomley boasted that he had been offered a post in the War Cabinet – and had graciously refused.[90]

Meanwhile the patriotic speeches continued – though with a discontented edge. On 28 April 1918, Bottomley spoke at the Albert Hall to a vast audience, with Edward Marshall Hall in the chair. By this stage of the war, Russia was no longer a protagonist: the Bolsheviks had signed the peace treaty of Brest-Litovsk with the Germans. This withdrawal allowed Germany to release many hundreds of thousands of men to fight against Britain and France in the West, and the conflict remained in balance.[91] All this Bottomley blamed on the politicians. Britain should never have allowed Russia to leave the war. Bottomley went on to suggest that Britain could have achieved a knock-out victory as long ago as the previous summer, but had been held back by the cowardice of her leaders. "We waited, dissipated, and frittered our resources all over the world". If the politicians had listened to him: "We should have concentrated all our attention on the Western theatre of war, and we would have crushed the enemy into dust, and [the German soldier] would have had no time to trouble about Eastern ambitions". Bottomley claimed to have told Sir Douglas Haig the same. Lloyd George's friend William Sutherland wrote to the Prime Minister, warning him to keep a careful eye on such rumours.[92]

Bottomley was not the only figure on the British right insisting that Britain's seeming failure to secure her war aims might be explained by secret knowledge. Noel Pemberton Billing warned of a conspiracy of German agents spreading an anti-war message. In May and June 1918, Pemberton Billing was on trial, accused of criminal libel against the actress Maud Allan. She had performed in Oscar Wilde's play *Salome*. Pemberton Billing alleged that she was a central figure within what he called a "cult of the clitoris", a group of 47,000 people propagating "evils which all decent men thought had perished in Sodom and Lesbia". A mysterious Black Book contained the names of these homosexuals and Jews – two categories Pemberton Billing believed could not be separated.[93] The German authorities were supposedly threatening to expose them, unless they opposed the war. The main prosecution witness was Lord Alfred Douglas, once Oscar Wilde's lover, now determined to prove himself an unflinching enemy of anything connected to the playwright, "the greatest force for evil that has appeared in Europe in the past 350 years".[94] Pemberton Billing was acquitted.[95] The judge was Mr Justice Darling, later to preside over two of Bottomley's trials.[96]

This victory encouraged Pemberton Billing's allies. One of them, the antisemite Henry Hamilton Beamish, was a contributor to Pemberton Billing's *Imperialist*, warning in its pages that a revolution in Germany would be the work of a secret Jewish conspiracy: "The real writing on the wall is in German but the characters are Hebrew and the descriptive whole is known to the world as Yiddish, the camouflaged tongue of the Bolsheviks".[97]

Bottomley tried to outbid his allies by demanding that Germany pay every penny of Britain's war debts – a sum Bottomley guessed at ten billion pounds. "We'll have an indemnity", *John Bull* wrote, "if it takes a thousand years to pay it".[98] The demand was picked up by others: first at the *Times*, then the *Express* and the *Evening Standard*, then by a group of Conservative MPs styling themselves the "National Party". In Dundee, Winston Churchill told voters that "practically the whole German nation was guilty of the crime of aggressive war".[99]

As the right grew, so did the left. Members of the Independent Labour Party and the British Socialist Party (successor to Henry Hyndman's SDF) discussed unifying into a single party.[100] Pre-war forms of organising were also returning. In 1918, six million days of work were lost to strikes, and the weapon was adopted by some who had never shown any sympathy for the labour movement. In August 12,000 police officers struck, to win within three days a pay rise of 13 shillings per week and a pension for police widows.[101]

Outside Bottomley's meetings a new pamphlet was being sold, written by the shorthand copyist Clarence Henry Norman, a member of the Independent Labour Party, the Society for Abolition of Capital Punishment and the Penal Reform League. Norman was a conscientious objector, one of 16,000 in Britain to refuse conscription.[102] Imprisoned, he had fought with his jailors. Confined to a straitjacket, he was force-fed through a nasal tube. From his cell, he smuggled out his words: "Mr Horatio Bottomley has never ceased to claim that he is the best interpreter of the mind and morals of the ordinary hard-working decent British citizen". He listed all the times Bottomley had been exposed as a swindler, and concluded: "With that we leave Mr. Horatio Bottomley, only reminding our readers that nothing could be more conclusive proof of the rottenness of British democratic and political life than the fact that such a man is consulted by the rulers of this country".[103]

Bottomley's scheme to stop publication of this document was typically two-faced. First, he had Reuben Bigland find a Midlands printer, John Greaney, who for £50 printed ten copies of it.[104] Then Bottomley sued Greaney for libel, with the case heard by Mr Justice Darling on 20 July 1918. Greaney declined to attend. His barrister argued that the damages should be low: "Whatever may be the result of the case, Mr Bottomley may leave the court at all event with the certainty that in one respect he has performed a public service, and that is by the skilful and temperate manner in which he has conducted his case".[105]

Bottomley's closing speech acknowledged Greaney's poverty, but continued to insist that he had been wronged. He reminded the jury of his own distinguished record of war service, and complained that the leaflet made "such public work as I am doing less effective than one would wish it to be".[106] He was awarded damages of £500.[107] Behind the scenes, his chequebook helped Greaney pay this, throwing in a further £200 for services rendered.

The victory was widely reported, and seemed yet another triumph. But the very fact that he had been forced to litigate – especially when targeting someone of a limited public name, safely locked up in prison – was a sign that all was not well. War had made Bottomley rich and had cleansed his public reputation. But was there no clear route to maintain this? What future beckoned, for a man approaching his 60th birthday? As it was, even after the Armistice in November, Bottomley opposed peace in Europe: "There can be no peace until every slaughtered babe and every outraged woman is avenged in German blood".[108]

Notes

1   Hyman, *The Rise and Fall*, p. 135. As late as summer 1910, Bottomley had used the smaller figure of half a million subscribers when proposing to sell a share of the magazine to the Conservative Party, Bottomley to Goulding, 13 June 1910, Parliamentary archives, War 2/16. There are good reasons to think that the sale of *John Bull* must have increased during the war; there are no good reasons to assume that it trebled from 1910 to 1912.
2   H. Cox, and S. Mowatt, 'Horatio Bottomley and the Rise of John Bull Magazine: Mobilizing a Mass Audience in Late Edwardian Britain', *Media History* 25/1 (2019), pp. 100–25.

3   Symons, *Horatio Bottomley*, p. 137.
4   Cox, and Mowatt, 'Horatio Bottomley'.
5   "From my childhood days", Bigland wrote, "I have been a fighter". Bigland, *Bottomley!!!*, p. 3. One common story is that Bigland had been at Mason's Orphanage at the same time as Bottomley. Felstead, *Horatio Bottomley*, p. 10. But neither Bigland nor Bottomley ever mentioned this connection themselves and given what friends they were to become – and what enemies – this is surely something that one of them would have recorded directly.
6   Houston, *The Real Horatio Bottomley*, p. 248.
7   Symons suggests that Bottomley was already considering a sweepstake when Bigland put the idea to him, another reason perhaps why Bottomley was disinclined to pay for the idea. Symons, *Horatio Bottomley*, p. 142.
8   Houston, *The Real Horatio Bottomley*, p. 124.
9   Houston, *The Real Horatio Bottomley*, p. 195. The phrase has its echo in literature. In H. G. Wells' novel, *Tono-Bungay* (London: Macmillan, 1909), the narrator's fraudster uncle complains of the newspaper man Boom, "He wants everything, damn him! He's got no sense of dealing" (p. 298).
10 National Archives MEPO 3 302, undated witness statement of William Lotinga, c. May 1914.
11 National Archives MEPO 3 302, letter from Wontner and Sons to Commissioner, 14 March 1914.
12 Kilday and Nash, *Shame and Modernity*, p. 69. When the police interviewed Cooper about this, six years later, he said, "My memory is not good... I don't remember if I saw the cheque for the prize money or not. I can't remember whether she gave me any of the money. I can't remember if I took her to Mr Bottomley or not". National Archives MEPO 3 302, witness statement of Saul Cooper, 30 June 1920.
13 Tenax, *The Rise and Fall*, p. 124.
14 Hyman, *The Rise and Fall*, p. 143; Symons, *Horatio Bottomley*, pp. 148–9.
15 National Archives MEPO 3 302, file note, 11 May 1914.
16 Darling had indeed proposed the formation of a club, which became the Pegasus Club, to organise the regular hosting of these races. Hawkes, *Bench and Bar*, pp. 18–19.
17 *Bottomley v DPP* (1914) 79 JP 153; T. Humphreys, *A Book of Trials* (London: Heinemann, 1953), p. 83.
18 *John Bull*, 8 August 1914.
19 Houston, *The Real Horatio Bottomley*, pp. 60–2.
20 Albeit not quite in the number that is often suggested, I. Birchall, 'The Vice-Like Hold of Nationalism?', *International Socialism* 78 (1998), pp. 138–42.
21 Kilday and Nash, *Shame and Modernity*, p. 23.
22 *John Bull*, 15 August 1914.
23 *John Bull*, 15 August 1914.
24 Hyman, *The Rise and Fall*, p. 150; Symons, *Horatio Bottomley*, p. 160.
25 Houston, *The Real Horatio Bottomley*, p. 62.
26 *Bottomley's Battle Cry! A Speech on the War Crisis Delivered at the London Opera House on 14 September 1914* (London: Odhams, 1914), pp. 6–7. In another context, Bottomley termed this figure a "Cromwell", "We want another Cromwell in Parliament – a man of iron, a man of dauntless courage... A Cromwell who would close every inlet to Germany that is reached from the sea and starve the Germans as the Germans starved the French..." H. Bottomley, *Great Thoughts of Horatio Bottomley* (London: Holden & Hardingham, 1917), p. 38.
27 *Bottomley's Battle Cry*, pp. 1, 15–16.
28 Hyman, *The Rise and Fall*, pp. 151–4.
29 Houston, *The Real Horatio Bottomley*, p. 64.
30 Holroyd, *Bernard Shaw*, p. 464.
31 Symons, *Horatio Bottomley*, p. 175.

32 Hyman, *The Rise and Fall*, pp. 155; Symons, *Horatio Bottomley*, p. 176.
33 Camp, *Glittering Prizes*, p. 90.
34 Hyman, *The Rise and Fall*, pp. 158.
35 Bottomley, *Great Thoughts*, p. 55.
36 T. L. Thomas, *A Letter to Horatio Bottomley* (Manchester: Blackfriars Press, 1916), p. 5.
37 Symons, *Horatio Bottomley*, pp. 165–6.
38 *John Bull*, 13 February 1915.
39 *John Bull*, 20 February 1915.
40 *John Bull*, 19 June 1915.
41 Hyman, *The Rise and Fall*, p. 132.
42 *John Bull*, 4 September 1915.
43 D. Marquand, *Ramsay MacDonald* (London: Richard Cohen, 1997), p. 191.
44 C. Benn, *Keir Hardie* (London: Hutchinson, 1992), pp. 348–9.
45 "As regards the elder criminal, we are not sure that a madhouse is not his proper place, for there have been evidence for years past of incipient insanity, fostered and encouraged by that overweening conceit which is one of its recognised symptoms". Symons, *Horatio Bottomley*, p. 168.
46 Cox and Mowatt, 'Horatio Bottomley'.
47 Hyman, *The Rise and Fall*, p. 160.
48 Bottomley, *Great Thoughts*, pp. 51–2.
49 'Anti-German Riots', *Liverpool and Merseyside Remembered*, undated.
50 *John Bull*, 15 May 1915.
51 P. Panayi, *The Enemy in Our Midst: Germans in Britain during the First World War* (London: Berg, 1991), pp. 233–4.
52 Panayi, *The Enemy*, pp. 234.
53 C. Holmes, *John Bull's Island: Immigration & British Society 1871–1971* (Houndmills: Macmillan, 1988), pp. 97–8.
54 'Clear out the Germans, Say the People', *Daily Sketch*, 13 May 1915.
55 J. T. Boulton (ed.), *The Selected Letters of D. H. Lawrence* (Cambridge: Cambridge University Press, 1997), p. 103.
56 *John Bull*, 18 November 1916.
57 Kilday and Nash, *Shame and Modernity*, p. 72.
58 Symons, *Horatio Bottomley*, p. 178.
59 Symons, *Horatio Bottomley*, pp. 188–9.
60 Hyman, *The Rise and Fall*, pp. 168–9.
61 Houston, *The Real Horatio Bottomley*, p. 89.
62 Taylor, 'John Bull', p. 124.
63 Searle, *Corruption*, p. 256.
64 Symons, *Horatio Bottomley*, p. 187.
65 Blathwayt, *Horatio Bottomley*, pp. 3, 35.
66 Bottomley, *Bottomley's Book*, p. 165.
67 Blathwayt, *Horatio Bottomley*, p. 12.
68 Lotinga to MacDonald, 29 September 1915, and Bigland to MacDonald, 24 October 1915, both in National Archives, PRO 30/69/1241.
69 National Archives MEPO 3 302, undated witness statement of William Lotinga, c. May 1914.
70 Symons, *Horatio Bottomley*, p. 189; Bigland, *Bottomley!!!*, p. 42.
71 *Answers to John Bull*, 30 October 1915.
72 Bigland, *Bottomley!!!*, p. 44.
73 Tenax, *The Rise and Fall*, pp. 140–1.
74 Hyman, *The Rise and Fall*, pp. 176–7.
75 Felstead claims that the negotiation was arranged by an interested third party, a bookmarker named Thomas Henry Day. So determined was Day that the two sides should settle that he locked them in his solicitor's office insisting that they would not be allowed out until they had agreed terms. Felstead, *Horatio Bottomley*, p. 183.

76 Houston, *The Real Horatio Bottomley*, p. 190.

77 Dalziel owned *Reynolds's News* and the *Pall Mall Gazette*.

78 Symons, *Horatio Bottomley*, p. 192.

79 Hyman, *The Rise and Fall*, p. 182; Symons, *Horatio Bottomley*, p. 193.

80 Hyman, *The Rise and Fall*, p. 184.

81 Houston, *The Real Horatio Bottomley*, p. 97.

82 *The BEF Times*, 8 September 1917.

83 Bottomley, *Great Thoughts*, p. 13.

84 T. Jones, *Whitehall Diary: Volume 1: 1916–1925* (Oxford: Oxford University Press, 1969), p. 39.

85 *John Bull*, 5 January 1918.

86 Marconi's British subsidiary was building a wireless station for the navy. J. Campbell, *Pistols at Dawn: Two Hundred Years of Political Rivalry from Pitt & Fox to Blair & Brown* (London: Jonathan Cape, 2009), pp. 151–2; Robb, *White-Collar*, p. 171.

87 One estimate is that the postwar sale of peerages netted a cool £3 million for Lloyd George's political fund, a fund matched by an equal cut for Lloyd George's then ally, the Conservative Party. A. J. P. Taylor, *English History 1914–1945* (Oxford: Clarendon Press, 1965), p. 188.

88 Tenax, *The Rise and Fall*, p. 147.

89 Henry Houston had been working for Lord Rhondda for several months at the Ministry of Food, and had sent Bottomley several proposals for reform.

90 Symons, *Horatio Bottomley*, p. 200; Houston, *The Real Horatio Bottomley*, p. 69.

91 R. Prior and T. Wilson, 'Haig, Douglas', *Dictionary of National Biography* (Oxford: Oxford University Press, 2004), Vol. 24, p. 463.

92 W. Sutherland to Lloyd George, 28 April 1918, Parliamentary Archive, LG/F/93/2/7.

93 Searle, *Corruption*, p. 264.

94 For Douglas's role in promoting antisemitic conspiracy theories after 1918, C. Holmes, *Antisemitism in British Society 1876–1939* (Abingdon: Routledge, 2016), p. 144.

95 N. Halifax, 'Homophobia in the First World War', *Socialist Review*, February 2015.

96 Darling would also play a significant part in the history of the far right, by in 1919 awarding damages of £5,000 for libel in favour of Sir Alfred Mond and against Henry Hamilton Beamish, then the most prolific publisher of antisemitic literature in Britain, and the founder earlier that year of a party, the Britons, whose members included the novelist Nesta Webster and the future founder of the Imperial Fascist League, Arnold Leese. Beamish responded to the decision by fleeing to South Africa, doing considerable damage to his nascent movement of organised antisemites. Holmes, *Antisemitism*, p. 144; N. Toczek, *Haters, Baiters and Would-Be Dictators: Anti-Semitism and the UK Far Right* (Abingdon: Routledge, 2016), p. 47.

97 'The Black Book', *Jewish Socialist*, spring 1989.

98 R. E. Bunselmeyer, *The Cost of the War 1914–1919: British Economic War Aims and the Objects of Reparation* (Hamden, CT: Archon Books, 1975), p. 115.

99 Bunselmeyer, *The Cost of the War*, p. 117.

100 D. Renton and J. Eaden, *The Communist Party of Great Britain since 1920* (Houndmills: Palgrave Macmillan, 2002), p. 7.

101 C. Rosenberg, *1919: Britain on the Brink of Revolution* (London: Bookmarks, 1987), pp. 24–5.

102 Kilday and Nash, *Shame and Modernity*, p. 32.

103 Hyman, *The Rise and Fall*, p. 188. The article was originally published in *Forward*, the paper of the Independent Labour Party, Felstead, *Horatio Bottomley*, p. 215.

104 Bigland, *Bottomley!!!*, p. 53; Tenax, *The Rise and Fall*, pp. 147–8.

105 Tenax, *The Rise and Fall*, p. 322.

106 Houston, *The Real Horatio Bottomley*, p. 189.

107 Symons, *Horatio Bottomley*, p. 201.

108 B.-S. Rodman, 'Britain Debates Justice: An Analysis of the Reparations Issue of 1918', *The Journal of British Studies* 8/1 (1968), pp. 140–154, 142.

10
THIEF

"When the end of the war came", Houston recalls, "H. B. was eager to exploit his wartime popularity". Bottomley yearned to be back in Parliament: "He sent for me on Armistice Day and his first words were, 'Houston, there will be a general election in a few weeks, and I shall not be ready. There are many thousands of pounds to be found before I can obtain my bankruptcy discharge'".[1] Houston was told to contact Bottomley's creditors.

Bottomley had not saved the proceeds of his lectures. He possessed the charm of his voice, plus new share certificates that he proposed to exchange for his old debts. Incredibly, some of his fatigued creditors were willing to accept them, jam in the future over stale bread now. The day before nominations closed for the December 1918 general election, Bottomley was in court, with £25,000 in cash and £9,000 of war stocks.[2] He remained £50,000 in debt[3] but his bankruptcy was discharged, freeing him to stand once again in South Hackney.

John Bull published a "Black List" of 70 of his most notorious enemies. None of them, he insisted, must be elected: not Sir John Simon, not Charles Masterman, not Herbert Samuel. Simon had once prosecuted him; Masterman and Samuel were prominent Liberal politicians. In addition Samuel was Jewish – he had used his membership of the War Cabinet to lobby for the creation of a Jewish state in Palestine, and was a particular and a frequent target on the far right. But as always pride of place among the anathemas went to Labour candidates, including George Lansbury, Philip Snowden and Ramsay MacDonald.[4]

Hector Morison, the incumbent Liberal MP, was not contesting the seat. Though an Independent, Bottomley was expected to vote with the Conservatives – or even to their right. While no actual pact had been concluded, no voter could have identified any policy on which his views were distinguishable from the Conservatives, and they ran no candidate against him. However the Liberal

DOI: 10.4324/9781003306085-10

Party did: one Arthur Henri. Through the combination of his renewed personal reputation, his magazine and the tacit endorsement of the Conservatives, Bottomley secured a massive majority: three quarters of the 14,000 who voted.

His allies urged him to dominate the Commons, by raising targeted questions and proposing legislation. For a while, Bottomley played along with them, but the strategy left him and them both dissatisfied. As Houston recalls, "The old dynamic energy [had] petered out, and only on rare occasions could he be spurred into a big effort. Even then he was a mere shadow of his former self. Frequently I drafted questions that would have brought him into prominence, but he was generally too lazy to be in the Chamber to ask them".[5]

His authority was declining, as can be detected in a comment made by *Punch* on a poster that advertised *John Bull* on the basis of a Bottomley article: "Why I didn't go to the Bar". "Perhaps", *Punch* unkindly suggested, "it was after hours".[6]

In truth, Bottomley grasped better than Houston where his skills lay: he was a propagandist and an organiser. Houston also missed the urgency at issue: for Bottomley, time was essential. He was still trying to trade the wartime profile of *John Bull* into personal advancement. As a patriotic newspaper owner at a time when the entire nation was required to be mobilised in support of the war, the war had made his opinions uniquely important. The risk was that as civilian life reasserted itself, he would be less relevant.

Postwar Britain was changing in other ways too. This had been the first election in which women could vote, albeit only those over 30. Among the young, there were many more women alive than men. Values were altering. If sexual discussions were not exactly frank yet, they were more open. In her 1925 novel *Mrs Dalloway*, Virginia Woolf's character Septimus was tired, disillusioned and old (though still younger than Bottomley): "People looked different. Newspapers seemed quite different. Now, for instance, there was a man writing quite openly in one of the respectable weeklies about water-closets... And then this taking out a stick of rouge, or a powder-puff, and making up in public".[7] The overwhelming sense was less a pride in what Britain had achieved than horror that so much had been sacrificed for so little. "Everyone has friends who were killed in the war", she wrote.[8]

British troops were still active in Europe. Britain, it said, was on the brink of starting a new war. A National Committee for the Hands-Off Russia Movement was created in London in January 1919.[9] Mutinies among British troops were reported. In Derby, the Labour leader W. R. Raynes announced at the May Day rally in 1919 that he supported demands for a withdrawal of the soldiers. Russia, he said, "had to fight to work out its own emancipation without Czars and capitalism". Elsewhere Raynes gave his support to the Soviet educational policy: "If that is Bolshevism then I am a Bolshevik". *John Bull* called him a "dangerous fool and an unholy liar", regretting that he was not in the range of a gun. "Derby should spew such a man... out from its midst".[10] Lead had become Bottomley's favourite remedy.

This same month, Bottomley announced the launch of a new political party, The People's League, to represent the "People" against organised Labour and organised Capital. Without committing to his campaign, several MPs took an interest, one of these being Oswald Mosley, himself the secretary of the 40-strong "New Members' group" of MPs.[11]

The vice-chairman of Bottomley's League was Sir George Makgill, an emigrant to New Zealand who had returned to Britain on his father's death. Makgill was the founder of the British Empire Union, [12] and the best short guide to his politics is his novel *The Red Tomorrow* (1919), in which a further world war gives rise to a communist revolution led by social outcasts blaming capitalism for their personal failure, urged on by German agents preaching Bolshevik doctrine, who are identifiable by their thick accents and "strongly-marked Semitic features".[13] The origins of this uprising lie in London's underworld, with its "congenital criminals" distinguishable by their foreign racial origins: "Above all, and permeating all the various sinister movements, were everywhere Jews, German and Austrian, Polish and Russian, Spanish and Levantine – Jews in every secret society, Jewish Anarchists and Communists especially". Britain was awash with professional spies, and all of them were racial outsiders: "Jewish foreign police agents [were] spying on the spies – subtle, treacherous, immoral and cruel as Orientals, but always capable. A race of parasites, infesting every class and country and yet, by sheer ability, making themselves indispensable at all".[14]

A later chapter describes the insurrection that Makgill so feared: as "vast crowds" flow towards Whitehall, with the police all "played out", across London "bands of armed men with red flags seemed to spring up, wearing red rosettes and guarding all the railways stations, central telegraph and telephone offices and power stations". This terrifying vision could have been averted, wrote Makgill, if there had been "one man – a real man... A man who'd have taken hold of the situation and shown a strong hand".[15]

At the war's end Makgill had established the Industrial Intelligence Board, a private security apparatus built up to spy on the British left. Several of its operatives combined work for him with membership of the various British fascist parties – or else with spying for MI5. His activities were funded by the Federation of British Industries, the Coal Owners Association and the Shipowners Association.[16] To Bottomley's party he brought his own antisemitic paranoia, plus a talent for organising greater even than Houston's, and thanks to him, the People's League won the support of a number of middle-class campaigning groups, including the British Constitution Association, the National Security Union and the National Unity Movement. The League's policy statement declared that "Socialism and Syndicalism, Communism and schemes of Nationalisation are to be uncompromisingly opposed". It stood for the "encouragement of good relations between employers and workmen, and the discouragement and prevention of lightning strikes and direct action".[17]

Bottomley's favoured approach was to attack the honesty of others: Labour activists for their belief that workers' wages could keep on rising and Liberals for their naïve enthusiasm in the newly formed League of Nations. Bottomley claimed that the best antidote to Bolshevik revolutionism was that patriotism which enabled the domination of broad swathes of the middle-classes while permitting a few selected workers to flourish, so long as the latter's demands remained modest. Strikes were legitimate when curtailed by law, he insisted: subject to a regime of secret ballots, for limited purposes only, and ending with no significant increase in wages. In other words Labour must be restricted and Capital set free.

He attacked waste and bureaucracy. He insisted that the British presence in Ireland was a civilising mission. He wanted Britain to be an Empire. He wanted transport links to be opened and obsolete railways closed down. He was in favour of the cinema, of Premium Bonds, and of the proposed monument to the Unknown Soldier. He believed in lower inflation and reduced welfare spending. All Bolsheviks in Britain were to be jailed. A new party was needed to rule Britain with the patriotism the crisis required. The problem would be establishing such a force, for, without it, Bottomley was nothing. To create the political conditions for a new organisation of the right, Bottomley needed money, and more than ever before.

Harvesting the millions

Edward Bell estimates that Bottomley's lifelong earnings from his journalism were £227,500, most of this made during the war. The patriotic lectures and other government subsidies he estimates as worth a further £37,000.[18] Yet Bottomley was still short of funds. In the months after the armistice he launched his most ambitious money-making scheme, which worked by confusing government schemes to reflate the economy with his own interests.

The government had issued a Victory Loan. As an example of its popularity, in the villages of Great and Little Leigh in Essex, a War Savings Association was set up with the support of the local clergyman Canon Tancock. Within weeks, almost the entire population of the town had subscribed, including many agricultural workers and domestic servants with only modest savings.[19] This pattern was repeated across rural England.

Bottomley was not involved in this scheme. But a notion had occurred to him, perhaps as a result of a question he had put to Chancellor Austen Chamberlain in the Commons. He had asked whether the government would remove the wartime restrictions on beer if he, Bottomley, guaranteed a subscription of £100 million in Victory Bonds. Chamberlain had responded, "I expect my honourable friend to get me that amount in any case".[20] The answer was vague enough to allow Bottomley the pretence that he had official backing.

In June 1919 he founded his Victory Bond Club ("the Club") from his Westminster flat at 26 King Street. The government's Victory Bonds ("Bonds") cost £5 each. Subscribers to the Club could purchase shares for £1 each, when Bonds cost £5. The Club would then purchase the same value of government bonds, so that ownership of a Club Bond would be akin to ownership of one fifth of a Victory Bond. Because the Club was so much cheaper, it was accessible to those without savings, and Bottomley pledged to return all shares for their full value on request. He said he would charge nothing for administration. Subscribers would get, they were promised, all the benefits of the government bonds but for a fraction of the price.

On the date the Club opened, Bottomley's main personal bank account contained just £7.[21] As the Club money came in, he took the largest sums for himself, pocketing the cash and keeping no record, or else spending it as it came in.

By September 1919, the Club was making regular payments to Bottomley. Eight cheques of £1,000 or more would be paid to him in the next eight months, with a further seven, of between £1,000 and £25,000, paid to members of his entourage: Houston received £1,000, Bottomley's horse trainer £1,000, and sums amounting to around £10,000 went to a man called James Kerr, who was doing business for him in Ostend. Another £30,000 was sent to Paris for the benefit of Laura Rogers, who had been living at Sackville Street near Piccadilly; the Metropolitan Police believed her to be Bottomley's mistress. A further £4,800 in cash went to Peggy Primrose, yet another £1,100 to Laura Rogers, the same to Bottomley's pet MP Charles Palmer, plus £100 to a bookie and £20 to Romano's restaurant.[22]

These funds allowed Bottomley to launch a John Bull Bank, offering interest rates of 6 to 8 percent. As proprietor and governor, Bottomley promised to use this new institution to promote the interests of discharged servicemen and impoverished small owners: "The modern tendency towards amalgamation on the part of the leading banks had the effect of cutting out the small capitalists from the banking facilities. The old private banker who was in close personal touch with his customers, has almost entirely disappeared".[23]

Other securities purchased with the Club's money and held in Bottomley's name included shares in *John Bull*, shares in the race courses at Plumpton and Brussels, the lease of an antiques shop at Victoria Street, a factory intended to manufacture John Bull fountain pens, and a German submarine, the Deutschland, which he bought from Noel Pemberton Billing.[24] In a fit of conscience, £25,000 was sent to the Official Receiver, to be distributed to the remaining creditors of his recent bankruptcy.[25] At last Bottomley had funds necessary for him to operate on a scale commensurate with his ambitions.

Old friends; determined enemies

In autumn 1919, Reuben Bigland and Bottomley once more fell out, this time over a scheme of Bigland's to convert water into petrol. He had heard of an invention said to produce petrol in infinite quantities, and had paid £4,000 for a stake.[26] At a demonstration in Newmarket, the inventor had seemed to turn a clear liquid into a fuel. Bigland drove a full half-mile to prove the compound's effectiveness – but this was a mistake. By the time he returned, his audience of potential investors had all left.[27]

Bigland was expecting Bottomley to put £60,000 into the company, his hopes raised by the improvement in the latter's finances. When Bottomley declined,

Bigland was angry. Both men were drunk. "Reuben", said Bottomley, "This is a swindle!" Bigland pleaded with him: "The man is not born of woman who could swindle both you and myself, jointly and severally". Bottomley was amused by this claim, but still refused to offer funds of his own. In a fit of fury, Bigland told him, "From this moment, I shall be your enemy".[28]

Regretting his words, he was again at King Street at 7am the next morning. Bottomley encouraged him to speak to Colonel Grant Morden MP and also to Julius Elias, ringing both men to say that he was sending Bigland over. "No sooner had Bigland left the flat", Houston records, "than H. B. disappeared to the races, and remained out of the way for the rest of the day. That treatment thoroughly nettled Bigland, and he realised that he had little hope of inducing H. B. to come into the scheme".[29]

At this point, it is worth trying to see the two adversaries through each other's eyes. For Bottomley, Bigland was an irritant. Bottomley too had begun as a printer, as a hack journalist and an editor, but since then he had transformed himself. Bigland had proved incapable of escaping his background. Bottomley was aware of the printer's fascination with him, and of his determination to join Bottomley's entourage. He also grasped the harm it would do Bigland to go into open warfare with him, how fearful Bigland was, and how unlikely it was that he would follow through with any plan to topple him.

What Bottomley could not see was the impact his own behaviour was having as an example. For while Bottomley was measuring himself against Bigland, and finding the Birmingham man a mean and inadequate creature, Bigland could do the same thing. The more he saw of Bottomley, the less he feared him: "I don't know whether you have ever met a man who was socially head and shoulders above you, who was a big gun in his own circle… and when you have met such a man have said to yourself, 'Well, where is his cleverness? I could beat him myself!'" Bottomley was a liar, while Bigland told the truth and this, he predicted, would bring him victory. "There is a feeling that you are antagonists, and yet you do not know the cause. Always one feels the man is an impostor, he is not genuine".[30]

Bottomley gossiped with Houston about an evening he and Bigland had spent together before their final break. "My dear Horatio", Bigland had said, "do something so that when you go out you will leave a mark on the history of your country. Help the armless and legless ex-soldiers and thereby build for yourself a monument". As Bottomley told this story, he had shaken his head and smiled at the naivete: "Houston, that man is mad but dangerous!"[31]

Electoral success, but what to do with it?

In October 1919 Bottomley spoke against a government bill to liberalise rules preventing the employment of aliens, proposed in order to recognise French pilots who fought in the war but had not returned home afterwards. Various Conservative "ultras" joined him, including Sir Edward Carson and Sir William

Joynson-Hicks. A meeting was called, and Bonar Law, then the coalition's Lord Privy Seal, reminded the rebels that if they continued with their opposition, the probable consequence would be the resignation of the government, a coalition with Lloyd George's Liberals, dominated by the Conservatives. The rebels were rubbing against the limits of this arrangement. Was the matter of such importance as to bring it to an end?[32] Thus blackmailed, the malcontents withdrew their opposition.

In December 1919, Labour won a by-election in Spen Valley in Yorkshire. The seat had voted Liberal ever since its creation 30 years before, but the party was split, between those who favoured remaining in coalition and those hostile to a government dominated by the Conservatives. The split was such that rival Liberal candidates stood against each other. With a huge turnout, 75 percent, Labour's Tom Myers won a majority of less than 2,000.

Just seven weeks later a second by-election was to take place, at the Wrekin in the West Midlands. Bottomley saw this as a chance to test support for his own brand of populist anti-socialism. He announced that the assistant editor of *John Bull*, Charles Palmer, would stand as an independent. Under the rules of the coalition, Liberals and Conservatives were not standing against one another. The government candidate was a Liberal, John Bayley, the Labour candidate was Charles Duncan, while Palmer was in all but name an anti-coalition Conservative. Palmer beat Duncan by just 500 votes.

In peacetime, *John Bull* had sought to continue as before the armistice, calling for example for a march on Berlin, to prove to the Germans that they had been beaten. But deprived of a defining story, the magazine was forced to find new targets, such as D. H. Lawrence, whose novel *Women in Love* was reviewed beneath the headline, "A Book the Police Should Ban; Loathsome Study of Sex Depravity – Misleading Youth to Unspeakable Disaster". The magazine argued that the novel was an "abomination", which should be suppressed for depicting two men Halliday and Maxim naked and implying that they had slept together. "In the hands of a boy in his teens", this "might pave the way to unspeakable moral disaster".[33]

March 1920 saw Bottomley's 60th birthday. For 15 years, he had hymned the essential goodness of the British middle-classes, lamented the perfidy of foreigners, denounced as humbug all moral vision that claimed to believe in human virtue and prophesied their tumble into degradation. He had built himself an audience. Where once he had raged against the rich and the well-connected, he had become one of them.

The Club: crisis in plenty

The total revenue received by the Victory Bond Club was £1.1 million.[34] The largest part of this, £648,841, was paid to an account with the London Joint City and Midland Bank, with Bottomley and Tommy Cox as signatories.[35] Almost all of this latter sum was taken by Bottomley, but it is not the totality of his personal profit, which also included further sums spent by him in cash, or which disappeared into the accounts of friends and family.

Several flaws with the scheme should have been clear from the outset. The Club had no actual relationship to the Victory Bonds. The government never gave Bottomley permission to purchase fifth-shares in the Bonds. Bottomley might have intended that Club shares would track the performance and dividends of the Bonds, but there was never a mechanism to ensure such a link was being kept. A better-organised investor might have had a blackboard displayed at the Dicker, on which the daily changing prices of the Bonds were chalked. But even this minimum was beyond Bottomley. Moreover, as the Bonds were available on the stock market to be traded, their value might fall. If they did – and assuming Bottomley honoured his promise to buy back unwanted shares at their original price – he would make a substantial loss.

Further, had Bottomley been an honest administrator, he would have charged for running costs. Over a million shares had been purchased in his Club; when a purchase was made, the name of purchasers should have been recorded, with buyers receiving a certificate confirming their purchase. All this – running an accurate list of subscribers, printing bona fide certificates and sending letters to each of a million Club members – would generate expense. If honestly run, the Victory Bond Club would have cost Bottomley a fortune.

Further problems became apparent over time. In return for all the money sent in by subscribers, Bottomley had had to purchase *some* government bonds, which he had, to the tune of £420,000. But their value on the open market had since fallen by a fifth; when Bottomley later had to sell some of them, this was a further loss.

Against this "pot" of £420,000, Bottomley wrote off two losses in the Victory Bonds Club accounts, together totalling £100,000. These signalled acquisition of two further newspapers, the *National News* and the *Sunday Evening Telegraph*, bought with the intention of becoming an even greater press magnate than he already was. But this was yet more foolishness. The second was in direct competition with the *Sunday Pictorial*, which he therefore had to quit, severing a valuable connection. In fact he never put sufficient time into either paper, and both soon folded, costing him considerable time as well as capital.

Time was the commodity that really mattered. To administer the vast sums coming into the Victory Bond Club, Bottomley needed to commit effort and attention – and this he refused to do. Rather than issuing numbered certificates of shares and recording the details of bona fide purchases, Bottomley fell back into his old practice of issuing vast numbers of certificates with scattergun numbering. This left him vulnerable to prosecution for fraud.

Purchasers began complaining, and word began to spread, including to people whose attitudes towards rules were as lax as Bottomley's. Soon he was overwhelmed with false requests, from correspondents who had never contributed to the Club. He paid every such request, it seeming better to pay off a few thousand minor fraudsters than to risk proceedings.

Within weeks of founding the Club, Bottomley grasped the scale of his diffi-culties, calling in his most capable organiser Houston – who described the chaos as the magnate and 12 assistants were overwhelmed by applications for shares. In his King Street headquarters, Bottomley would retire to the waste-paper room and drink: "He endeavoured to cope with an enormous post, and a very consid-erable demand for certificates, without any substantial additions to his staff".[36] In terms of the income raised, this had been one of the most successful share issues in the history of British finance – which should have been cause for delight. But all Houston could see was confusion, piles marked "People who sent in cheques, no tickets received", "Tickets sent and cheques not met", "People who sent postal orders, no tickets received", or "People who stopped their cheques, query tickets sent". There were sacks and sacked of unanswered letters. "There were dozens of them all round the walls of the room, with heaps of correspondence, four or five high, beneath".[37]

Politics, rivalry

As Houston was fixing this mess, he couldn't also be the sergeant of Bottomley's political army. Victory in the Wrekin by-election had been the first test of Bot-tomley's new party. But the pneumonia that Charles Palmer had caught visiting his seat was fatal, and a second by-election was called in November 1920. This time, Bottomley nominated Major-General Sir Charles Townshend, a war hero, while Labour nominated Charles Duncan, a trade unionist who had spent the first two years of the war touring the UK calling on workers to volunteer. Liberals and the Conservatives left the field to Townshend, who won with a majority of 4,000.

The victory was tarnished by the presence at the Wrekin of Bigland, who had published his own pamphlet denouncing Bottomley. In its centre pages was an "Open letter": "I, a poor uneducated species of humanity, in turn a crossing-sweeper, bootblack and match-seller, am urged by some mystic power to cross swords with the great and only Horatio Bottomley". Bigland portrayed his task as the salvation of Bottomley himself: "I just want to unmask you be-fore the world, to cure you of your dangerous vanity, and for your own good, I want your congregation to know the difference between your words and your actions". If Bottomley was a sincere patriot, then this was the time for him to recognise the error of his ways: "The time may come when you would give all you think you have for the chance that is slipping from you for ever – *the chance of doing some good for your country*, if it is only by letting the huge profits of your lectures go to help our wounded soldiers instead of into your pocket".[38]

The pamphlet's title conveys its contents: *The Downfall of Horatio Bottomley MP. His Latest and Greatest Swindle. How He Gulled POOR Subscribers to invest One-Pound Notes in his "Great Victory War Bond Club"*. If its most offensive ele-ment – at least to Bottomley – was its treatment of the feud as a battle of equals, Bigland was also maintaining that the magnate had stolen a million pounds of the public's money.[39]

Bottomley had recently celebrated Armistice Day with a piece in the *Daily Mirror*, which began: "And I heard a Voice from Heaven saying unto me, Write!" Unimpressed by such sanctimony, Bigland sent him a telegram: "And I heard a Voice from Heaven saying unto me, Confess!" Bigland would find Bottomley, hand back a War Bond the financier had given him, "and give myself up to justice". Bottomley had no choice but to meet him. This he did, with Houston and two "six-feet men". Bottomley had reminded Bigland of the £1,000 he had given him before their quarrel: "Pay me!"[40] Bottomley ordered. But Bigland refused: "What about giving yourself up to justice!" Bottomley raged: "Look here Reuben, if I have any more of these wires from you, I shall see that justice overtakes you. You understand that!" His anger frightened the printer and he sent a note to Bottomley. It concluded, "You have won".[41]

Anti-Waste

In the Woolwich by-election in March, Bottomley backed Robert Gee against Labour's Ramsey MacDonald (who had lost his Leicester seat in 1918). A former miner long given to patriotic splits with the socialist left, Gee had served in the war, winning the Victoria Cross. In 1918 he had stood for the short-lived National Democratic and Labour Party, but he was willing to follow the Conservative whip – which left him a little too pro-coalition to be Bottomley's ideal candidate. But he was in every way preferable to the alternative. Bottomley sent in his team to help Gee, who came home first, though his majority was less than 700.

Bottomley's plans were growing more ambitious all the time; but with them grew the list of antagonists, with a rival Harmsworth, Lord Northcliffe's brother Lord Rothermere, arriving as one of them in January 1921. Rothermere put forward Colonel Sir Thomas Polson as a candidate for the Dover by-election, on a manifesto of "Ruthless Economy", and set up the Anti-Waste League after his victory, to run a further 20 candidates in a score of by-elections,[42] among them none other than George Makgill, who would contest East Leyton against the Communist MP Cecil Malone. The League fought to dissolve the wartime coalition government, to shrink the ballooning wartime state, to defeat Liberal projects for better social housing and state education, and ultimately – although this would prove a harder battle – to undo the various social reforms granted by the pre-war Liberal government.

The final Anti-Waste candidate to stand and win was Brigadier-General John Nicholson, in the Westminster Abbey by-election in June 1921.[43] Five right-wing Independents had won parliamentary seats, a palpable caucus including Polson, Nicholson, Major Christopher Lowther,[44] Admiral Murray Sueter and Sir Cecil Beck. Rothermere had been a driving force, but Bottomley, helped by his own election victories and those at the Wrekin, was another, and he still enjoyed certain advantages in this burgeoning rivalry.[45] He could for example intrigue with his fellow right-wing MPs right there in the Commons. On the other hand, Rothermere was wealthier and better-connected, and the *Daily Mail* and the *Daily Mirror*, the jewels in his and his brother's press empires, were read by millions.

Bottomley's allies were an odd mix of generals and company directors, and he wooed them via the services of his hirelings, who were very experienced in fighting elections. Sueter's description treats the relationship as contractual. He was buying Bottomley's time and experience, but what this meant in practice was Henry Houston's electoral acumen: "Knowing little about politics I accepted [this] offer at once. Bottomley came down and made several speeches for me and had great audiences. His organisation was headed by an expert in these matters named Houston". Sueter regarded it all as a fair transaction. "Old Bottomley was perfectly straight with me over money matters, when I had to remunerate his workers. Not a hitch anywhere when I had to settle up their expenses with him".[46]

Growing numbers of Conservative associations supported the broad thrust of the Anti-Waste campaign, while others – among them Oswald Mosley – joined campaigns established in emulation, including a People's League for Economy.[47] "Waste" like "economy" included anything which increased inflation and therefore tended to reduce the differential between the lifestyles of workers and the middle classes. One of the keenest observers of the broader mood in which Anti-Waste flourished was the former Liberal MP C. F. G. Masterman. There were two Englands, he explained. The first, "Richford[48] hates and despises the working classes... Labour only enters its kingdom as a coal supply rendered ever more limited and expensive by the insatiable demands of the coal-miners to work short hours for immense wages". Such suburban, middle-class opinion, "can walk but a few yards and it is in, say, Hoxditch[49] where all the inhabitants are dingy... and the public houses flare at every corner; and it realises that this is the "Labour" against which it is warned by all the supporters of things as they are".[50] This passage shines a harsh light on Bottomley: he was after all still the MP for Hackney South, which included both Hoxton and Shoreditch. And yet in his political scheming he was making himself the partisan of the suburbs in their struggle against their proletarian neighbours.

Anti-Waste was a form of militant Conservatism, and as it chafed at that tradition's limits, it sought to move in from the margins to capture the party. The more successful it was as a slogan, the harder it proved to keep control over its specific partisan content. By the second half of 1921, Conservatives faced with Anti-Waste opponents were producing campaign materials stressing their fidelity to the same goals.

There was also a distinct racial element to the campaign, although the principal target was not so much the poor Jews of the East End than the handful of wealthy West End Jews tolerated by the leaders of the Liberal and Conservative Parties. So when Sir Hebert Jessel, the Conservative candidate for Westminster St George's in June 1921, was defeated by the Anti-Waste candidate James Erskine, the chairman of Jessel's own party, Sir George Younger, was delighted by

Jessel's humiliation, writing that, "Far too many Jews had been placed in prominent places by the present government".[51]

The official Anti-Waste candidate, Erskine, was Rothermere's candidate, while the defeated Jessel, the official Conservative, was with Bottomley. These pioneers of this new strand of militant Conservatism were at odds. What was at stake was not just who controlled the new movement (although this was important) but what counted as "waste", and how to campaign against it. Rothermere's was the longer-term strategy, in which the attack on social reforms would help crystallise middle-class politics around a shared distrust of the poor.[52] He could imagine a political system where the remaining Liberal electorate split between Labour and Conservative, with the latter winning every time, and he Labour's conqueror.

Bottomley's aim was less a reinvigorated Conservatism than the formation of what he called "business government", under which "every editor who either knowingly or recklessly publishes false news will be shot".[53] Ministers should be strengthened and Parliament weakened. He did not want a Britain where Conservatives and Labour alternated in government; he wanted to see Socialist politics banned and advocates of redistribution jailed.

Anti-Waste was a movement to shrink the state, and it was this which Bottomley found hardest. He wanted to see the state spend more money. He wanted the army expanded, he liked to imagine British power extending across the globe and the profits of imperial power making their way into the pockets of certain deserving people, even some who had been poor. Bottomley tended to downplay "the cutting down of pensions and allowances", [54] which he reasoned would alienate as many as it attracted. Even as the leader of a party of Richfords, he did not dare wage war against Hoxditch. His vision was bolder than Rothermere's, and closer to the experiments in right-wing politics emerging in Germany, Italy and Spain.

The eager adversary

Rueben Bigland had no great public reputation and he was far from rich. But despite his recent humiliation, he found the energy to resume his campaign against Bottomley. Where Bottomley could afford dozens of employees, only scattered individuals helped Bigland. But unlike Bottomley he faced just a single enemy, and he was willing to wager everything on this battle. He reprinted 250,000 copies of his anti-Bottomley pamphlet, selling them in Lancashire, Yorkshire, Leicestershire and Nottinghamshire and outside the Trades Union Congress in Cardiff.[55] Sales were encouraging, and he employed three friends to help him.

Bigland attempted to have himself arrested in possession of a War Bond with a value of £500. On 21 June 1921, he appeared before Mr Graham Campbell at Bow Street on the charge of having stolen it. The matter was adjourned twice before a final hearing.

The War Bond had been issued to Northern Territory Syndicates Ltd, and came into Bigland's hands from the possession of his niece. As he told it, he had received it as the designated winner of a sweepstake fraudulently engineered by Bottomley. Campbell accepted that Bigland had not stolen the share from his niece, but was uninterested as to how she had acquired it, [56] and determined that Bigland should be acquitted. Bigland cried out, "I want Mr Bottomley to come into the witness box before I am discharged". But the magistrates refused to hear his complaint. Bigland tried again: "I am representing 250,000 people" – but Campbell discharged the case.[57] Bigland's list of defeats was long and growing.

Houston, Cox and Elias advised Bottomley to ignore Bigland, and seemed at first to have persuaded him. Elias was content as long as *John Bull* continued unhindered. Houston wished not to draw attention to the parlous state of the Victory Bond Club. But Bottomley always had wider concerns, grasping better than any of them that his political career required that he maintain a good reputation. And this in turn demanded that he confront Bigland.

On 29 September 1921, he commenced proceedings for criminal libel. This was a legal doctrine of some antiquity, a crime which had been introduced in the middle ages to prevent public disorder by protecting the great of the realm from slander. It carried a maximum two-year jail term. Bow Street Police Court issued a warrant for Bigland's arrest. On 3 October, Bigland gave himself up to the police and was taken to London for his trial.

The reluctant ally

A hearing before the Police Court determined whether Bigland should stand trial at the Crown Court, which required the prosecution to show that he had a case to answer. The case would be heard before Sir Henry Chartres Biron.[58] Bigland's solicitor was Edward Bell, his tenacious junior counsel being Arthur Comyns Carr. Bottomley was represented by Sir Ernest Wild. As Bottomley knew, so wide a range of attacks on his character was made in the pamphlet that Bigland could not plausibly deny that he intended to damage Bottomley's reputation. So the issue in the case would be whether the allegations were true.

Bottomley grasped the risks. The trial would test whether Bigland could prove his allegations. Bottomley had won many times in court and Bigland had so far always lost. But there was always a chance, however tenuous, that a jury might find the claims justified.

To guard against this, Bottomley had a subtle plan. He accused Bigland of blackmailing him on two other occasions. He claimed that the water-to-petrol scheme had been a sham to cover an extortion, and that during the second Wrekin by-election Bigland had invited others to join with him in blackmailing Bottomley. The MP hoped to have the charges of blackmail heard first. If he won on these, Bigland would go into the libel proceedings as a proven liar and a convict, making it almost impossible for anyone to believe him.

For the moment, the court had to consider both sets of charges together. Did either set of allegations have any prospect of success at trial? In the criminal procedure of the day, this was established by hearing a shorter version of what would be the evidence at the main trial (a "voir dire"). The witnesses were questioned as they would be at the final hearing.

One difficulty for Bottomley was that the judge, in contrast to most he had faced before, had no great admiration for him. Biron was not swayed by Bottomley's jokes and did not smile when his entourage cheered his arrival in court. How many people, Biron asked, had subscribed to the Victory Bond Club? Bottomley could not give an exact figure. Biron persisted. Surely Bottomley must have a record of the number of subscribers?

> Bottomley: We have a record in the books of the bank of every penny received. This is rather like cross-examination from the bench.
> Biron: It is not cross-examination. It is my duty to put questions to get an understanding of what the facts are.[59]

The hearing of the blackmail charge then took a direction that Bottomley had not anticipated. Bigland said that Houston and Hooley had offered him £10,000 and £20,000 respectively to induce him to exit the case on terms favourable to Bottomley. He also stated that Elias, authorised by Bottomley, had approached him with the terms of a settlement under which he would make certain statements and the case would be withdrawn. Bottomley denied all this angrily. Bigland's barrister Comyns Carr was content to allow Bottomley to deny it for now, and to hold back the details for later. But Bottomley had also provided corroborative witnesses: his manservant, his cook and Julius Elias. Each was cross-examined.

The most important of the three was Elias. As owner of Odhams Press and the printer of *John Bull*, he was pedantic, industrious, risk-adverse – and very unlike Bottomley. He also had little experience of court proceedings, so we can imagine the emotions running through his head: anxiety about being in court, guilt, and no shortage of resentment.

Elias began a version of events as scripted; that it was Bigland who had approached him, offering to drop the case if the MP would back him: "Mr Bottomley has refused to let me have £60,000 for my invention and I am determined to bring him to the ground and have told him so". Elias had refused to pay along, he said.

Comyns Carr teased out of him the admission that the idea for the meeting had in fact come from Bottomley, not from Bigland. The next task was to get Elias to admit that the proposal of settling the case had come from Bottomley; that it was in other words a bribe by Bottomley, rather than blackmail by Bigland:

> Comyns Carr: Did you ask him to withdraw the charges he had made against Bottomley and apologise?
> Elias: I did not ask him to.

Under further questioning, Elias admitted that he had told Bigland that if he would offer Bottomley an apology and undertake to issue no more pamphlets, Elias would do his best to get Bottomley to accept those terms. He had given Bigland a sheet of paper and said there were a "few points I have noted which should be cleared up". Bigland had taken the paper to consider, before deciding that he would not to accept Elias's terms. Comyns wrested from Elias that the questions on the sheet of paper had been discussed with Bottomley:

Comyns Carr: Had you discussed them with Mr Bottomley?
Elias: No. I just ought to explain.
Comyns Carr: Just answer the question first. You can explain afterwards.

Elias admitted he had seen Bottomley before his appointment with Bigland and had discussed calling off the case if Bigland was willing to settle. Bottomley said, "If it is to be done, certain points have to be cleared up", and had given him the paper. Elias denied offering money to Bigland if Bigland accepted the proposals. He denied offering the money through Hooley. He denied increasing the offer from £10,000 to £20,000. But these denials carried little weight, since Elias had already changed his story in its key particulars. From what he told the court, the negotiations had been led by Bottomley, who had drafted the key documents. Elias had said enough to expose Bottomley as a perjurer.[60]

Why was Elias such a compliant witness? Bottomley's previous biographers have suggested that he was fed up with Bottomley and in fact wanted him to lose. It is true that he distanced himself from Bottomley after the trial, and went on to have a successful career without him. History treats him as one of the great men of his time, and Bottomley a rogue. Yet the idea that Elias decided in advance to cause Bottomley's fall is unconvincing. The two men had worked together for 16 years; their one public conflict had taken place nine years before and was resolved in weeks. In the witness box, any such plan to bring down Bottomley would have seemed impossibly risky to Elias. He would have to have been certain that the collapse of the Victory Bond Club would affect only Bottomley – who was the most effective of *John Bull*'s journalists as well as its proprietor. There was no good reason to imagine that Elias believed he could distance Bottomley from the magazine without destroying both.

A more plausible way to look at Elias's evidence is that Bottomley had tasked him with something very easy for Bottomley, but very hard for Elias. He was expected to lie, to bluster, to conceal truth with such a shield of manufactured outrage that the judge had no choice but to believe him. Bottomley had played such a game often enough before, and had the personality for it. But Elias had a greater sense of shame. He was the sort of person who would blush in telling a straight lie. He was trying his best to rescue what he could of Bottomley's story. But the performance of the role required by Bottomley proved beyond Elias.

In his closing speech, Comyns Carr accused Bottomley of intimidation, of inciting Bigland to withdraw his attacks, as to let the general public know that he (Bigland) was satisfied there was no foundation to the charges. In fact, said Comyns Carr, "The charge of blackmail has really been brought into this case for the purpose of trying to draw a red herring across the real issues which Bigland desires to have tried".[61]

On 9 November Biron gave his decision. What struck him most, he said, was the gap between autumn 1919 – when Bigland had supposedly attempted to blackmail Bottomley – and autumn 1921, when Bottomley had issued proceedings. If this had been blackmail, Biron determined, Bottomley would not have waited for two years. Biron also criticised Elias, Houston and Bottomley for attempting to negotiate a settlement of criminal proceedings. It was one thing for parties in disagreement agreeing to settle a civil controversy. It was quite another to make allegations of serious and criminal proceedings as a ruse: "Those responsible for the conduct of those negotiations are worthy of, and deserve, the greatest possible blame. It is something like a conspiracy to defeat the very ends of justice". Biron accepted Elias' evidence that Bottomley had written out questions for Bigland. It therefore followed that Bottomley lied. "After carefully considering this case", Biron stated, "and with a due sense of the seriousness of what I am saying, I am unable to believe Mr Bottomley on oath".[62]

The charge of blackmail concerning the petrol scheme was dismissed. But Biron accepted that there was evidence to support the other charges, so Bigland was committed for trial on the libel charge at the Old Bailey and also to the Shropshire Assizes, on the Wrekin charge, of inciting others to extort money from Bottomley. Bottomley had achieved the exact opposite of what he had planned. Rather than tarnishing Bigland, he was the one disgraced. To his misery, he would still have to fight the libel charge, the one with the greatest risk to him.

A play without its protagonist

Bottomley took Peggy Primrose to Romano's for dinner and ordered up the Pommery. Inside, he was suffering. In Comyns Carr he had a determined enemy in court; and it was a shock at last to experience a rigorous cross-examination backed up by a hostile judge. His successes in court had made him seem invincible; that armour was now gone.

"Perish my enemies", crowed D. H. Lawrence in Sicily. Exposed as a swindler, Bottomley could no longer call for the suppression of *Women in Love*.[63] As a further step of revenge, to demonstrate the degradation of the aristocrat Chatterley in *Lady Chatterley's Lover*, Lawrence added the insult: "So cut off he was, so divorced from the England that was really England, so utterly incapable, that he even thought well of Horatio Bottomley".[64]

Bottomley still sought to ensure that the Shropshire case be heard first. What he most feared was Bigland in the Old Bailey pleading justification to the charge of criminal libel. The Victory Bond Club could not be kept out of that hearing. Even with one charge of blackmail dismissed, Bottomley still believed the effect of Bigland's evidence could be diminished – he still expected to win the Shropshire case. If Bigland were convicted there of inciting others to black-mail Bottomley, an Old Bailey jury would be less likely to believe him. But the Shropshire hearing was set for 18 February, and the Old Bailey case was to begin three weeks earlier.

There was also another prosecution to face: Bottomley was before Mr Justice Bailhache for breaches of the Lotteries Act. In fact he triumphed in this skirmish, persuading the court that he had never given orders for the printing of lottery tickets, while Bigland failed to interest the police in a charge of perjury, despite gathering several witness statements to the effect that Bottomley had commissioned Bigland's own Birmingham business to print the tickets.[65]

The battle was being fought beyond the limits of Bottomley's influence. Edward Bell met Chief Inspector Mercer and Inspector Lothero of the Metropolitan Police to establish whether the police had any information of use to his client, Rueben Bigland. Bell took little from this meeting, but it was becoming clear that the police were starting to grasp the need for Bottomley to be prosecuted. As Mercer wrote in his notes: "Bigland gave the Police the names and addresses of persons who are said by him to have been indicated by numbers as prize-winners, including his own niece in Birmingham". Statements were obtained that corroborated this claim. Nevertheless, though not hostile to Bell, Mercer would only allow his officers to be witnesses if they were commanded to do so by court order.[66]

Behind the scenes, the Attorney General held a conference of legal officers. At the conclusion of Bigland's trial, it was decided that the printer be approached for the help he might give in a criminal action against Bottomley.[67]

Bottomley was still fighting. On 10 November 1921 Bell arrived at Bottomley's offices at 26 King Street to inspect the Victory Bond Club's books. Here he was met by Bottomley's solicitor and the Club Receiver, [68] surrounded by a group marshalled by Tommy Cox. Despite the Receiver being a publicly appointed official supposed to protect the interests of Bottomley's creditors, he refused to hand over the accounts to Bell:

> Bell: Do you refuse to produce the books?
> Receiver's solicitor: I do not propose to be cross-examined by you.
> Bell: The Receiver is here, and I ask him where are the books?

The Receiver turned to his solicitor, who attempted to silence Bell. "Do not interrupt", Bell answered. But the solicitor stood his ground.

> Receiver's solicitor: By what authority do you ask the Receiver to produce these books?
> Bell: Under the authority of the subpoena served upon him, and his undertaking, and your letter (making this appointment) which I now produce.
> Receiver's solicitor: The subpoena is dead.[69]

The banks that Bottomley had used to process the Club's takings were the City and Midland and Crédit Lyonnais. They did accept the court orders, and on 4 January 1922 Bell was allowed to see the accounts. He and Bigland at last had enough information to be confident of showing that the Victory Bond Club had been a fraudulent enterprise.

Although he continued to write for *John Bull*, at the start of the year Bottomley passed the bulk of the editing duties at the magazine to Charles Pilley.[70] Despite his woes, the magazine remained full of bluster. His old ally F. E. Smith had become Lord Chancellor: "Dear Lord Birkenhead [Smith's title in the Lords]", one "Candid Communication" began: "I know that you hope to signalise your tenure of the Woolsack by certain sweeping reforms of the legislature, and I am wondering whether the criminal law is within your scope?"[71] Another article complained of the trend for "coloured doctors" – "Chinese, Japanese, Hindoo" or "Negro" – to practice medicine in Britain. "The British Medical Association is powerless to refuse registration to any person of whatever colour, race or religion who qualifies, and therefore it is the plain duty of Parliament to prevent the practice of coloured men".[72]

Days before the Old Bailey hearing opened, lawyers for the two sides met. Bottomley was represented by Marshall Hall. Comyns Carr had with him the papers Bell had collected from the City and Midland bank. On the morning of the trial Mr Comyns Carr who was defending Bigland, came to Marshall Hall's chambers. He had with him a bundle of documents. Comyns showed the papers to Marshall Hall, who demanded to see Bottomley. "We are offering no evidence", he said, "It's the only course to take. And there's nothing you can do about it". Bottomley blustered, but Marshall Hall told him bluntly, "Either you take my advice and offer no evidence, or I withdraw from the case. If you do what I tell you, I'll do whatever I can to help you, but you dare not go into the witness box".[73]

The public – knowing nothing of these behind-the-scenes moves – queued for seats to the trial. Proceedings began with a request from Marshall Hall for more time to study the books of the Victory Bond Club. This request was refused; Bottomley had had months to prepare, said Coleridge. Marshall Hall then announced that the prosecution was offering no evidence.[74] Remarking that the case had come to a "somewhat abrupt conclusion", Coleridge directed the jury to find a verdict of not guilty.[75] A crowd gathered on the steps of the Bailey, where a grim-faced Bottomley addressed them briefly – and left.

The betrayed dead

The refusal to give evidence to support Bigland's criminal prosecution made it look to the world as if Bottomley had something to hide, and that the Victory Bond Club was as bad a business as Bigland had claimed. Bottomley blustered: Bigland, he predicted, would suffer a fall in Shropshire and his own reputation would be restored.

On 24 January 1922, the Director of Public Prosecutions wrote to police officers stationed at all UK ports, warning them to watch in case Bottomley attempted to flee the country.[76] The police also took possession of the notes prepared by Bell and Comyns Carr, preparing to use them as the basis for Bottomley's prosecution.[77]

The Shropshire case started on 18 February, before Mr Justice Darling. During the war Bottomley had been asked by an admiring writer who was his favourite judge. His response: "They are all so nice to me that it is difficult to say, but I am very fond of Darling. Do you know that I have never lost a case against Darling which I personally conducted?"[78]

The charge against Bigland was that he had approached three men a few days before the Wrekin by-election 15 months before, with the aim of extorting money from Bottomley. These three gave evidence. Bottomley did not testify, despite demands by Comyns Carr that he appear. The case came alive on the second day when Bigland was called to the stand and described their relationship, including an incident when Bottomley had fixed a War Stock Combination draw so that Bigland would win a £1,000 prize. "I agreed", Bigland told the court, "to my shame". Such embarrassment was to be a recurring theme. As he told it, Bigland was ashamed to have assisted Bottomley; a repentant sinner.[79]

Bigland admitted fixing the Greaney trial, which had been heard by Darling. As can be imagined, the judge was not happy to have been made so public a fool:

> Darling: You mean Greaney agreed to lose the action?
> Bigland: Yes, he agreed to put up a nominal defence so that really Bottomley would only have to address the jury as to damages. Bottomley got a verdict of £500 and costs, but really, he paid £100 and costs to Mr Greaney.

Grasping that others had made a fool of him and of court proceedings, Darling said only, "I suppose I summed up in his favour, didn't I?"[80]

In his closing remarks, Darling described the Greaney case as a "gross and wicked miscarriage of justice" and discussed Horatio Bottomley's payments to Bigland and their corroboration in the written evidence. But what he suggested the jury focus on was Bottomley's refusal to come forward as a witness: "It is a wonderful, almost incredible story as told by Bigland and it might have been contradicted in one word by the man who is present and must know whether it is true or not". That "one man", was of course Bottomley.[81]

After just three minutes of deliberation, the jury found Bigland not guilty. Before returning to London, Bottomley travelled by train to Birmingham, to find the strength to keep fighting with a visit to Sir Josiah Mason's Orphanage.[82]

In Bigland's first trial, he had accused Bottomley of massive, criminal fraud. Bottomley had offered no evidence in response. In his second trial, Bigland had put on the record detailed allegations of perjury and fraud, and his account had been accepted. The authorities had no option but to prosecute Bottomley.

Attempting to wrest the initiative for himself, on 20 February 1922 he wrote to the Director of Public Prosecutions offering to provide a private explanation.[83] The letter was ignored; he received a summons two days later.

Bottomley attended committal hearings on 22 February. He was charged with fraudulently converting Club funds to his own use.[84] The matter was adjourned to 8 March. This was a true battle at last, and it afforded Bottomley the occasion for some of the most vivid prose of his long career in court. On trial 10 or 15 years before he would shift the subject from his fraudulent business activities to his Radical beliefs, a far safer topic. His politics had moved to the right since then; nevertheless he attempted to repeat this technique; to make the trial a test of his opinions rather than his conduct. "Sir", he told the court, "you must forgive me if I strike a note somewhat unusual in these courts. I have endeavoured to bear up under the charges with a fortitude born of the knowledge that I have done no wrong". He reminded the court of his wartime role: "During the tragedy of Armageddon… [I] became conscious of a new awakening and, putting all the sordid things of the past aside, consecrated [my] whole being to the service of [my] country and of the men who fought and fell in the cause". It was an outrage, he continued, to find himself now on trial. "Week in and week out, by tongue and pen I did my best to inspire our fighting heroes, and to inspirit their dependents. And you are asked to believe that all the time I was scheming to rob them of their savings?"[85]

"The dear boys", he concluded, "whether they are sleeping or still with us, know that I have not betrayed them, and you shall scour the country from east to west, from north to south, and you shall never empanel a jury which will say that Horatio Bottomley could be guilty of so cruel a crime against both God and man".[86] But the old magic did him no good and the magistrates committed him for trial.

On 29 April 1922, *John Bull* appeared with a new masthead: "Edited by W. Charles Pilley". In the following issue, its new editor wrote, "Since Mr Horatio Bottomley relinquished once and for all the Editorship of this Journal and all connection with it, we have worked unceasingly to bring about such a radical change in the policy of *John Bull* and in the methods of conducting the paper, that it would definitely begin a new era in weekly journalism". The sports coverage was increased to two pages, and articles were commissioned on the condition of the services and the financial situation, their authors the ultra-respectable figures of Field-Marshal Earl Haig and Sir John Ferguson of Lloyds Bank respectively. The following week the cartoon of *John Bull* himself was altered. His hair became darker, his face decades younger, his body leaner: the last link to the paper's founder Bottomley was being sundered.[87]

The sword of justice

Bottomley's trial at the Old Bailey before Mr Justice Salter[88] began on 19 May 1922. It lasted for eight days, Bottomley facing 24 charges of fraudulent conversion. Travers Humphreys conducted the prosecution, using evidence from Bottomley's bank accounts to show that the money from the Victory Bond Club had been frittered away on old debts, champagne and other extravagances. Witnesses included an out-of-work boilermaker, a widow, a builder and several servants: each had lost money from the demise of the Club.

The trial was expected to be great public theatre, as so many of Bottomley's trials had been. Among those attending was the 19-year-old writer Yvonne Kapp.[89] Her husband, the painter Edmond Kapp, had been commissioned to paint leading members of the legal profession, and the couple prepared for this commission by attending Bottomley's trial.[90]

Bottomley arrived in court, Seymour Hicks records, "all smiles". His friends were in the public gallery as usual, and he gestured to acknowledge them.

> As he was conducting his own defence, he took his seat at the solicitors' table. With the greatest possible confidence, he proceeded to take charge of the case as if he were judge and prosecuting counsel, and endeavoured to convey the impression that, much to his inconvenience, he had arrived to dispose rapidly of preposterous charges which had been brought against him with no other object than to take up his valuable time and interfere with his extremely busy life.[91]

Bottomley spoke for 90 minutes in his defence. He complained of the few witnesses that Travers Humphreys had called to demonstrate the suffering of Club members. Should he call in response, he asked rhetorically, the 100,000 members who had received their money back? They had not been disappointed. Yes, the Club had been in difficulty, but its sole problem was the impossibility of keeping up with the falling price of the government's war bonds, "I had foolishly, carelessly – recklessly perhaps – told subscribers that they should have their money in full at any time, and I soon discovered if I was to keep faith with them, I had involved myself in a very heavy financial responsibility".[92]

At one point, he claimed, he had been receiving letters at the rate of 35,000 a day. "It was no more possible to keep pace with the correspondence than for a man to jump over the moon". Some of the capital had been transferred to the Credit Lyonnais Bank in France, following letters which he "could not afford to ignore". Even today, he was receiving letters saying, "We know you were bad enough, but the receivers are much worse, and we would rather come back to you". There had been 200,000 subscribers to the Victory Bond Club, Bottomley said, and their contributions totalled £483,000. He had paid back £385,000 to them. There was a deficit, he accepted, but no fraud. The Club had cost him well over £50,000: "If that is not true, I can be charged with wilful and corrupt perjury".

Humphreys began where he reckoned Bottomley was weakest, with his unsuccessful campaign against Bigland. Humphreys trusted that these events would be familiar to the jury, that they would understand them and conclude from Bottomley's answers that the politician was lying. He then intended to move on to the Club. He knew he had to proceed with care. With his talent for lying without embarrassment, Bottomley could pluck figures from the air. Anything he said would sound credible. Claim by claim, it was nigh on impossible to show that he was lying. If the two traded figures, the jury would believe the defendant.

Humphreys began therefore by asking Bottomley for his account of the Bigland prosecution. Bottomley complained that Bigland had been libelling him for three years, worst of all over the past 12 months, when he "broke out on a very big scale".

"Did he charge you with fraud in connection with the Victory Bond Club?"

"Yes", said Bottomley, in the manner of the back-row pupil offering a teacher an opportunity to ramble, "and many other things – the whole of my career".

Travers dodged that trap. Instead he asked why Bottomley had not given evidence against Bigland. It would have been futile, explained Bottomley. When committing Bigland for trial the magistrate had said that he did not believe Bottomley on oath, a "most improper observation in sending a case for trial". After this complaint, Bottomley went on to say that he was glad that Bigland had been acquitted.

But this was one lie too far, and it gave Humphreys an easy chance to score with the jury: "You are glad he was! I daresay that was your object in prosecuting him".

The questioning turned to the duplicate certificates. Why had large numbers of subscribers received Victory Bond Club certificates bearing the same numbers? Bottomley explained that hundreds of subscribers had sent him letters demanding certificates with two sevens in their number, or excluding the number 13. This had prevented the club from issuing certificates with successive numbers reflecting the order of their arrival. He had left his staff to deal as best they could with these requests.

"I suggest to you", Humphreys countered, "that when £80,000 was entrusted to a person who is himself an undischarged bankrupt, he usually keeps some separate record?"

"My best record", Bottomley answered "was to keep a separate banking account which was done in this case. Thieves don't keep records against themselves".

Bottomley accepted taking money from the club but said he had done so only after advancing money to it first. If he took £10,000 to give to a friend, which he had, it was because he had given away £20,000 of his own money first. It was true that he had taken out £15,000 to pay for the submarine Deutschland, but it did therefore not become the property of the subscribers, because the club owed him more than £15,000. Bottomley claimed that the money spent by him on purchasing the *National News* and the *Sunday Evening Telegraph* was simply the club repaying a loan from him.

At that time, insisted Humphreys, "not a shilling was owing to you".

"I was bound to have a large sum of money", Bottomley said, to meet the "daily demands" of the club, "and the money was in my safe for this purpose".

"This is the best answer you can give?"

"It is a complete answer".

As the questioning moved onto the terrain of numbers, Bottomley's lies became more brazen. He joked when he could. He declined to answer questions, he digressed. Every device was an attempt to force the prosecution backwards. But in a context shaped by the failed Bigland prosecution, these tactics had less effect than hoped. At one point, Bottomley interrupted Humphreys, who rebuked him, "Answer my questions and do not argue".

Soon after, when the defendant was answering at length. Humphreys broke in: "All right, if you won't answer the question, I won't press it".

"I will answer it as best I can but I won't be tricked into an admission".

Later Humphreys passed Bottomley a document: "That comes from Bigland. Does that surprise you?"

The MP answered, "Nothing surprises me in regard to Bigland. I did not know you were working with him".

"Don't be insolent".

Bottomley stared back at Humphreys: "I am never insolent to counsel. I have been most forbearing in the face of many insults".[93]

Over the two days of the cross-examination Humphreys secured two damaging admissions from Bottomley. First, that his wartime lectures had earned him £27,000, which while not directly relevant to the hearings, must have been a shock to those who believed Bottomley's image. Second, that, as Bottomley told the court, since his income had stood at £40,000 a year, he could have no need to take money from the Victory Bond Clubs. Humphreys referred to a statement Bottomley had made, where he had estimated his income as £11,000 and his liabilities as over £100,000.[94] In short, he had every reason to commit fraud.

Houston saw Bottomley every morning. Even as he worked on the case his physical surroundings were being removed:

> After his committal for trial he was sold up at his flat, the brokers leaving him only a small bed in his bedroom. His elaborate dining room was stripped of all its contents, his telephone was cut off. One morning he sent for his solicitor, who arrived and found H. B. sitting on a plan wooden chair at a small folding card table, both of which had been borrowed. On the table was a bottle of wine and two glasses.[95]

The jury deliberated for just 28 minutes before reaching a unanimous verdict; Bottomley was found guilty of 23 of the 24 charges on the indictment. That left the sentence. "Horatio Bottomley", Mr Justice Salter began: "You have been rightly convicted of a long series of heartless frauds. These poor people trusted you, and you robbed them of £150,000 in ten months. The crime is aggravated by your high position, by the number and poverty of your victims". If Bottomley was expecting his wartime role to play in his favour, he was disappointed. The crime, he said, "is aggravated by the magnitude of your frauds, and by the callous effrontery with which your frauds were committed and sought to be defended.

I can see no mitigation whatsoever".[96] He sentenced Bottomley to seven years imprisonment.

Even in the depths of adversity Bottomley was determined that he should appear the master of his own destiny. He asked if he could discuss an appeal with his solicitor. Bottomley said, "I was under the impression, my Lord, that it was sometimes put to an accused person, 'Have you anything to say before sentence is passed on you?'" Salter replied: "It is not customary in questions of misdemeanour". Bottomley demanded the last word, "Had it been so, my Lord, I should have had something rather offensive to say about your summing up".

He was taken down from the court; a warder gripped his arms to his chest, perhaps to frustrate any attempt at escape, perhaps to prevent any attempt at suicide.

Notes

1 Houston, *The Real Horatio Bottomley*, p. 122.
2 Hyman, *The Rise and Fall*, pp. 193–4; Houston, *The Real Horatio Bottomley*, p. 122.
3 National Archives MEPO 3 302, file note by Chief Inspector Mercer, 30 March 1922.
4 Symons, *Horatio Bottomley*, p. 204.
5 Houston, *The Real Horatio Bottomley*, p. 126.
6 *Punch*, 17 November 1920.
7 V. Woolf, *Mrs Dalloway* (London: Wordsworth Classics, 2003), p. 54.
8 Woolf, *Mrs Dalloway*, p. 50.
9 Renton and Eaden, *The Communist Party*, p. 7.
10 R. Groves, *Sharpen the Sickle* (London: Merlin Press, 1981), p. 229.
11 S. Dorril, *Blackshirt: Sir Oswald Mosley and British Fascism* (London: Viking, 2006), p. 45.
12 I. Thomas, 'Confronting the Challenge of Socialism: The British Empire Union and the National Citizens' Union, 1917–1927', MPhil thesis, 2010, p. 112.
13 E. C. Hambrook (pseudonym), *The Red Tomorrow* (London: The Proletarian Press, 1920), p. 20.
14 Hambrook, *The Red Tomorrow*, p. 56.
15 Hambrook, *The Red Tomorrow*, pp. 221–3.
16 H. Hemming, *M: Maxwell Knight, MI5's Greatest Spymaster* (London: Penguin, 2017), p. 20.
17 Toczek, *Haters*, p. 196.
18 Tenax, *The Rise and Fall*, p. 381. At Bottomley's trial in 1922, the figure of £27,000 was used, but this covers only the patriotic lectures, not other grants from employers or the government.
19 J. Munson (ed.), *Echoes of the Great War: The Diary of the Rev. Andrew Clark 1914–1919* (Oxford: Oxford University Press, 1985), p. 239.
20 Symons, *Horatio Bottomley*, p. 209.
21 National Archives MEPO 3 302, file note by Chief Inspector Mercer, 30 March 1922.
22 National Archives MEPO 3 302, file note by Chief Inspector Mercer, 30 March 1922.
23 Felstead, *Horatio Bottomley*, p. 114; Tenax, *The Rise and Fall*, p. 156.
24 'The Stormy End of the Deutschland', *Manchester Guardian*, 24 March 1922.
25 National Archives MEPO 3 302, file note by Chief Inspector Mercer, 30 March 1922.

26 Bigland, *Bottomley!!!*, p. 58.
27 Felstead, *Horatio Bottomley*, p. 243.
28 Symons, *Horatio Bottomley*, p. 233.
29 Houston, *The Real Horatio Bottomley*, p. 258.
30 Bigland, *Bottomley!!!*, pp. 24–5.
31 Houston, *The Real Horatio Bottomley*, p. 253.
32 Minutes of a Conference of Ministers, 24 October 1919, CAB/23/44B.
33 *John Bull*, 17 September 1921.
34 Tenax, *The Rise and Fall*, p. 281.
35 It was listed in the bank's ledgers as the "Bottomley No. 2 account". National Archives MEPO 3 302, file note by Chief Inspector Mercer, 30 March 1922.
36 Houston, *The Real Horatio Bottomley*, p.223.
37 Symons, *Horatio Bottomley*, p. 212; Hyman, *The Rise and Fall*, pp. 196–7.
38 R. Bigland, *The Downfall of Horatio Bottomley MP* (Birmingham: Reuben Bigland, 1921); Hyman, *The Rise and Fall*, p. 180.
39 Bigland, *The Downfall*, p. 1.
40 Bottomley is arguing that Bigland cannot be entitled to keep this £1,000, if as he claimed it was fraudulently acquired (as it would then be the proceeds of crime). Bottomley of course insists that there was no fraud, which means that he is entitled to its return (because he had given it as a favour).
41 Houston, *The Real Horatio Bottomley*, p. 261.
42 Actually not quite a full score, since in at least one by-election two rival Anti-Waste candidates stood against one another. Some were also the official Conservative candidate, making Anti-Waste a kind of ginger group overlapping with the Conservatives from the right, partly within and partly outside, the rebels moving in and out of the main party as necessary, to maintain pressure.
43 G. C. Webber, *The Ideology of the British Right 1918–1939* (Abingdon: Routledge, 2016), p. 21.
44 Lowther was later among the majority of Unionist MPs who voted to end the coalition with Lloyd George at a meeting held at the Carlton Club on 19 October 1922.
45 The Conservatives in turn were pressuring rebels to stay loyal even if they objected to the coalition, but Anti-Waste mainly lost momentum as it became obvious the wartime truce was going to collapse, and also as Bottomley fell out with Rothermere.
46 Symons, *Horatio Bottomley*, p. 225.
47 Dorril, *Blackshirt*, p. 48.
48 "Richford": an imagined middle-class district which perhaps combines Richmond with somewhere like Chingford.
49 "Hoxditch": an amalgam of Hoxton and Shoreditch.
50 R. McKibbin, *Parties and People: England 1914–1951* (Oxford: Oxford University Press, 2010), p. 47.
51 R. McKibbin, *Classes and Cultures: England 1918–1951* (Oxford: Oxford University Press, 1998), p. 56.
52 M. Cowling, *The Impact of Labour 1920–4* (Cambridge: Cambridge University Press, 1971), pp. 58–9; J. Ramsden, *An Appetite for Power: A History of the Conservative Party since 1830* (London: Harper Collins, 1998), pp. 242–5.
53 Symons, *Horatio Bottomley*, p. 166.
54 Cowling, *The Impact of Labour*, p. 57.
55 Hyman, *The Rise and Fall*, p. 215; Bigland, *Bottomley!!!*, p. 83.
56 She had in fact been the designated prize-winner in the bogus sweepstake as engineered by Bottomley, where Bigland was claiming it had come straight to him.
57 Tenax, *The Rise and Fall*, p. 180.
58 This was not his only high-profile case. In 1928, Biron heard the prosecution of Radclyffe Hall's *The Well of Loneliness* for obscenity. His appointment was reported in the *Sun*, 5 April 1906.

59 Hyman, *The Rise and Fall*, p. 220.
60 Hyman, *The Rise and Fall*, p. 229; Minney, *Viscount Southwood*, p. 169; Symons, *Horatio Bottomley*, p. 241.
61Hyman, *The Rise and Fall*, p. 230.
62 Tenax, *The Rise and Fall*, p. 182.
63 Boulton, *Selected Letters*, p. 229.
64 D. H. Lawrence, *Lady Chatterley's Lover* (Cambridge: Cambridge University Press, 1993 edn), Chapter 1.
65 National Archives MEPO 3 302, witness statement, c. October 1921.
66 National Archives MEPO 3 302, file note, 8 October 1921.
67 National Archives MEPO 3 302, file note, 28 October 1921.
68 In the account being followed (Tenax: see next note), this official's name is nowhere given.
69 Tenax, *The Rise and Fall*, p. 192.
70 *John Bull*, 10 June 1922.
71 *John Bull*, 7 January 1922. The article went on to propose reforms of the inquest system.
72 *John Bull*, 18 February 1922.
73 Bowker, *Behind the Bar*, p. 103.
74Symons, *Horatio Bottomley*, p. 243.
75 Bowker, *Behind the Bar*, p. 103.
76 National Archives MEPO 3 302, letter, 24 January 1922.
77 National Archives MEPO 3 302, Inspector Protheroe file note, 24 January 1922.
78 Blathwayt, *Horatio Bottomley*, p. 25.
79 Kilday and Nash, *Shame and Modernity*, p. 79.
80 Hyman, *The Rise and Fall*, p. 244.
81 Symons, *Horatio Bottomley*, p. 248; Hyman, *The Rise and Fall*, p. 249; D. Barker, *Lord Darling's Famous Cases* (London: Hutchinson & Co., 1936), pp. 249–50.
82 Symons, *Horatio Bottomley*, p. 248.
83 National Archives DPP 1/69, Bottomley letter to DPP, 20 February 1922.
84 The initial charge was in the sum of £5,000 (i.e. just one of the payments Bottomley had made from the Victory Bond Club to the Receiver arising from his previous bankruptcy). By Bottomley's Crown Court trial, the police had had time to gather more information, and the indictment was amended to a fraud of £250,000.
85 Houston, *The Real Horatio Bottomley*, p. 147.
86 Houston, *The Real Horatio Bottomley*, p. 147.
87 *John Bull*, 29 April 1922, and 6 and 13 May 1922.
88 Previously elected to Parliament in the same year as Bottomley, at Basingstoke in Hampshire, a seat he held for the Conservatives until 1917.
89 Fifty years later, Kapp would publish the biography of Annie Besant's one-time rival, Eleanor Marx.
90 Y. Kapp, *Time Will Tell: Memoirs* (London: Verso, 2003), p. 115.
91 Hicks, *Not Guilty M'Lord*, p. 179.
92 The account of the trial which follows is based on Symons, *Horatio Bottomley*, pp. 230–56, and Hyman, *The Rise and Fall*, pp. 252–74.
93 'Mr Bottomley under Cross-Examination', *Guardian*, 25 May 1922.
94 Tenax, *The Rise and Fall*, p. 223.
95 Houston, *The Real Horatio Bottomley*, p. 99.
96 Hicks, *Not Guilty M'Lord*, p. 183.

11

VARIETY ARTIST

The journalist Filson Young, who was present at Bottomley's last trial, described the verdict as "like seeing an old horse pole-axed – but pole-axed for being a horse and for doing nothing other than what his nature bade him to do".[1] Those who had been Bottomley's closest companions, his fellow journalists of the right-wing press, turned on him. *The Times* termed him a "humbug… self-deceiving demagogue".[2] Labouchere's old paper *Truth* accused him of having displayed a "hypocritical pretence of patriotism": "That impression did much to swell the responses to his bond club prospectuses… [the people] decided to subscribe because his speeches and his articles seemed to prove that he had turned over a new leaf during the war".[3]

Bottomley's affairs were settled quickly. On 10 June, *John Bull* bade him farewell, with Charles Pilley expressing his sadness: "I would shake his hand again, cordially, and in the deepest sympathy I do not know, and do not care to know, the extent of his guilt".[4] On 13 June, Mr Hare, a trainer, applied for Bottomley's horses to be placed in the control of a Receiver. On 4 July, the courts heard a debt claim brought by Houston against Bottomley for £8,288.[5] On 11 July, the Senior Official Receiver took possession of his estate.[6] On 25 July he was ordered to attend Parliament. He wrote back: "I desire, first of all, to express my deep sorrow for having brought this slur on the House of Commons, which I have loved as I have loved my King and Country, and to be a member of which was the dream of my youth". Bottomley had run out of excuses. "All I can do is to ask Members of the House to judge me as they knew me".[7] For the second time in a decade, he was then stripped of his seat.[8]

In this same summer of 1922, Virginia Woolf was working on notes towards *Mrs Dalloway*, a novel of madness and self-sacrifice. We noted in the last chapter that the narrative used a central figure, Septimus, the veteran of 1914–18,

DOI: 10.4324/9781003306085-11

to comment on social change since the war. Though Woolf does not mention Bottomley's recruitment meetings, her protagonist had been "one of the first to volunteer". Septimus's friend Evans was killed on the Western Front. At first, he "congratulated himself upon feeling very little and very reasonably" – except from that moment fear burst on him in "thunder-claps".[9] His sense of doubt grows to self-loathing, until all that is left for him is to set in train the events that result in his own death. Bottomley was still alive, but his final defeat was no less self-inflicted.

His face grey, on Bottomley's arrival at Wormwood Scrubs, he was referred to the hospital. He was able to exchange greetings with his old co-conspirator Ernest Torah Hooley, recently given three years for an unrelated fraud.[10]

Bottomley was desperate for mercy. In 1923 or 1924 he wrote to former Prime Minister David Lloyd George, hoping he might intercede on his behalf: "I have no higher creed", Bottomley insisted, "than to live a decent life, play the game, love my friends (be they human or beast) and give a helping hand to the lame dog". Would not Lloyd George, as a Christian, take up his case? He also invited him to verify the truth or otherwise of the rumour that Bottomley had heard – that the sole impediment to his early release was a veto imposed by Labour leader Ramsay MacDonald.[11] A copy of this letter survives in Lloyd George's personal papers in Parliament, but not of any reply.

His prison conditions became a matter of public scrutiny. Journalists on the Labour newspaper the *Daily Herald* suggested that he was getting a better class of treatment than fellow inmates: "He not only enjoys a diet which would keep a navvy happy and which includes fish and grilled mutton chops, but he has actually got a valet to wash his back and lace his shoes". The author contrasted this with the arduous life faced by ordinary criminals, who exercised, had breakfast and were working by 8am. "Bottomley does not arrive at the printer's shop before 10am (and in winter time he is the only one to arrive in overcoat and gloves). He is accommodated with an armchair (with plenty of cushions) placed on a slightly raised platform, so that the soles of his shoes shall not rest upon the concrete floor.[12]

Gerold Clayton became Governor of Wormwood Scrubs in 1926: Bottomley had "mesmerised" the prison, Clayton complained, and inmates and prison officers all addressed him as "sir". Guards were bribed with cigars. Bottomley received a visit by his old friend, Sir Edward Marshall Hall. Passing through the printers' shop, the barrister was able to stop and blow his old friend a kiss. Though Clayton made it his business to "smash the strange authority of Bottomley", by his own account he failed. Their final conflict concerned the date of Bottomley's release, in July 1927. The former MP was planning a meeting to celebrate his liberty. To ensure that the cooks did not reveal the date, Clayton got his own wife to make Bottomley's last breakfast. Clayton then dressed Bottomley in Clayton's own silk shirt and gold cufflinks, a silk hat and cane, and told him that he was free. The old man refused to leave, so Clayton plied him with fresh coffee and slices of bread and ham. "All right, I'll go".[13]

The ghost of a career

"Liberty", wrote Theodore Felstead of Bottomley's release from Maidstone jail, "was an infinitely greater punishment than imprisonment. Nobody wanted to speak to him, friends of bygone days turned their heads as he came into view and, if they deigned to recognize him at all, did so with the barest of nods".[14] Bottomley's body had shrunk, his face had aged: he was nine-tenths broken. So much had happened while he was inside: the civil war in Ireland, Mussolini's march on Rome and Hitler's attempt to emulate it, the first Labour government – led by Bottomley's hated opponent Ramsay MacDonald – and the general strike.

First, he attempted to relaunch his career as an editor with a new magazine, *John Blunt*. But it was thinner than its predecessor, a sad publication that lasted until October 1929, when it was replaced by (the even less successful) *John Blunt's Monthly*.[15] On 7 February 1930, his wife Eliza died at the Dicker. The following week his daughter Florence married a planter, Gilbert Moreland, before leaving with him to live in his native South Africa.

Bottomley's dealings with the law were not at an end. Houston had sued him for debt during his incarceration, and Bottomley was determined to get his revenge, with an action for libel. Houston had told the press that Bottomley had obtained money by blackmail – as indeed he had. Nevertheless, Bottomley's claim was successful, and he was awarded £1,500 in compensation. But even this satisfaction was minimal: Houston had relied on a justification defence, bringing still more of Bottomley's past to public attention. As Houston's finances were no sounder than Bottomley's, the judgment debt was never paid.[16]

In spring 1930, Bottomley was before the bankruptcy courts again, where his liabilities were estimated at £115,000 and his assets £1,000.[17] He told the Deputy Official Receiver that he was earning £10,000–15,000 a year as a journalist[18]; in truth his income was just a few pounds a month. He had gone back to promoting companies – such as the Phoenix Press, which held the rights to *John Blunt* and collapsed when it folded. Helen Vacquier, a creditor in New York, wrote to Scotland Yard asking for help in obtaining £612 owed to her. But she was also corresponding directly with Bottomley, and in a second letter to Scotland Yard asked the police to investigate no further: "It is just a question of time for the party to be in a position where the debt can (and I believe it will be) honourably discharged".[19]

In 1931, Bottomley ate at the Quo Vadis restaurant on Dean Street. The meal cost £18 and the owner agreed to accept a promissory note for £25, paying Bottomley the £7 difference. The note was not honoured. In January 1932, Bottomley ordered £22 of wines from the Soho Wine Supply and again did not pay.[20]

Most people assumed that Bottomley had hoarded an enormous trove of savings, and that his complaints of poverty must therefore be false. Felstead tells of an encounter at the Dicker between Bottomley and a bookmaker seeking payment of an old debt of £500: "What about paying me that monkey you owe me?" Bottomley called him a skunk and refused to pay a penny.[21] Such was the Freemasonry of the Turf.

In the five years following his release it is estimated that Bottomley netted £5,000 from compromised claims for libel.[22] Like many in the public eye who are then disgraced, he had skirted a lifetime's-worth of shady dealings, so that journalists making much of his conviction in the Victory Bond trial could often not resist the temptation to recount his entire life story as a sequence of cases in which justice had been the loser.[23] And perhaps the truth was being served by such tales – yet this is not the attitude the law will take, at least in theory. Having served their sentence, even someone convicted of fraud is presumed to regain the right to a good reputation. And then as now, newspapers prefer to compromise rather than fight a lengthy legal battle. Besides, there was small prospect of getting costs back from this bankrupt. He had sent out many writs for libel on his release, and most often a newspaper or a proprietor or a distributor would offer to settle. This income was enough for Bottomley to get by.

In 1932 his bluff was called. Woolworths had an agreement with manufacturers of American pulp magazines to sell remaindered publications, around 50,000 copies a week, buying them by the ton. The department store took no steps to check them before sale, and Bottomley found himself bringing a libel action against the outlet in Kingsway, over an article in *Detective Story Magazine*, published soon after his release, titled "Horatio Bottomley, Editor and Embezzler". "By putting this magazine on the English market", Bottomley told the court, "at a time when I am endeavouring to lead a clean and honest life, Woolworths have done me a great wrong... In my 50 years' experience of these Courts I have never known a libel case in any way akin to the present one with regard to the cruelty and cowardice of the libellers".[24] He protested that the store had threatened in pre-trial correspondence to question him about his character. He described his sufferings in prison. And he avoided the indignity of cross-examination by declining to offer any evidence himself. Which must have been a sad moment, questions being beside the point when the answers were known to every juror.

The jury held that the managers of the store had been negligent in not checking the magazines to see if they contained libels, and ruled that Bottomley should receive damages of £250. As a matter of principle judgement should have been entered at this point, with £250 handed to Bottomley. Yet the jury also ruled that the defendants had been innocent of any knowledge of the libel contained in the magazine, and the trial judge ordered that this judgment be entered for Woolworths. The Court of Appeal found the jury's verdict contradictory and two-faced, "absurd" even, but nevertheless also upheld it.[25]

For a short while, his last public role was being paid to tell anecdotes in the intervals at the Windmill Theatre. Biographer Theodore Felstead watched him there: "There he was, a broken, tottering old man, stumbling on to the stage on the glare of the footlights with a drop curtain at the back of him... It was not much that he had to tell a few lukewarm anecdotes, nothing to what he could have told". Bottomley admitted nothing. "He just strung together imitation pearls, promised a few more, and then hobbled off, to the accompaniment of a few hand-claps given by the more sympathetic section of his hearers".[26]

In April 1933, he applied for a state pension. Bigland, of all people, offered to come to his old adversary's assistance, but was rebuffed. Bottomley could endure any other adversity but not Bigland's charity.[27] In his last weeks, he was in Middlesex Hospital with Peggy Primrose: "I have been several kinds of a fool", he told a journalist. "But I might not have come off so badly had I not been so loyal to my friends".[28]

He died on 26 May 1933, the cause of death given as cerebral thrombosis caused by arteriosclerosis, [29] and was cremated at Golders Green. For four years his ashes were left unclaimed, until in 1937 Peggy Primrose and Bottomley's nephew Bertie Dollman drove out together and scattered his ashes on the Sussex Downs.[30]

Notes

1　F. Young, 'Bottomley', *Saturday Review*, 3 June 1922.
2　Kilday and Nash, *Shame and Modernity*, p. 82.
3　Kilday and Nash, *Shame and Modernity*, p. 81.
4　*John Bull*, 10 June 1922.
5　*R v Bottomley* (1922) 16 Cr App Rep 184; Houston, *The Real Horatio Bottomley*, p. 12.
6　Tenax, *The Rise and Fall*, p. 239.
7　Symons, *Horatio Bottomley*, p. 258.
8　HC Deb 25 July 1922 Vol. 157 cc212–3.
9　Woolf, *Mrs Dalloway*, pp. 64–7.
10　Felstead, *Horatio Bottomley*, p. 289.
11　Bottomley to Lloyd George, undated but 1923 or 1924, Parliamentary archives, LG/G30/2/62.
12　Felstead, *Horatio Bottomley*, p. 297.
13　G. F. Clayton, *The Wall is Strong: The Life of a Prison Governor* (London: John Long, 1958), pp. 92–4.
14　Felstead, *Horatio Bottomley*, p. 302; there is a similar passage in Symons, *Horatio Bottomley*, pp. 270–1.
15　The copy for 15 October 1929 is in the National Archives at MEPO 3 510.
16　Symons, *Horatio Bottomley*, p. 270.
17　National Archives MEPO 3 510, file note, 21 May 1930.
18　*Morning Post*, 22 March 1930.
19　National Archives MEPO 3 510, letters, 7 May, and 4 June 1930.
20　National Archives MEPO 3 510, file note, 2 December 1932.
21　Felstead, *Horatio Bottomley*, pp. 56–7.
22　Dean, *Hatred*, p. 169.
23　The posthumous biographer is protected by a rule that the dead may not sue for libel.
24　Dean, *Hatred*, p. 171.
25　*Bottomley v Woolworth (W. F.) and Co., Limited*, 48 T. L. R. (Ct. App.) 521 (1932).
26　Felstead, *Horatio Bottomley*, p. ix.
27　Houston, *The Real Horatio Bottomley*, p. 289.
28　'Death of John Bull', *Time*, 5 June 1933.
29　Symons, *Horatio Bottomley*, p. 272.
30　Morris, 'Bottomley, Horatio', *Dictionary of National Biography*; Houston, *The Real Horatio Bottomley*, p. 292.

12

IN RETROSPECT

In his closing speech at Bottomley's last – and decisive – trial at the Old Bailey, the barrister Travers Humphreys remarked that the defendant's undoing was a product of his personal vanity. Had he not pursued Bigland, his own criminal trial would have been most unlikely: "He so cleverly did conceal his tracks in regard to the War Stocks Combination that we never could have charged him with misappropriating these two sums, for there is not in existence a scrap of evidence, except his own admission in cross-examination in the Bigland prosecution".[1]

To the extent that is true, Bottomley belongs to a category of people – including Oscar Wilde a generation before – brought low by legal suits they themselves had initiated.[2] So one question becomes obvious: what might have happened had he followed his friends' advice to ignore Bigland, and *not* pursued him? His careers in politics and in journalism could not have been maintained indefinitely. He was committed to unsustainable habits of consumption. The scale of his debts compelled him to always be looking for new ways to fund his spending. He dreamt of a future in which he controlled an entire industry: whether the press, or printing, or finance, or company promotion, or the importation of gold from Australia.

Yet Bottomley had no experience of the emerging media of radio or the cinema. Even the press was dominated by others. The sum that set Bottomley on his way had been the £150 he took in payment for employing Harmsworth as an apprentice. Five years Bottomley's junior, the apprentice went on to found the *Daily Mail* and *Daily Mirror*, to own the *Observer* and *The Times*, to be Lloyd George's Director of Propaganda. Harmsworth had also kept half an eye on Bottomley's career; the *Sunday Pictorial* column he gave him had brought the older man a larger audience than he'd ever established for himself at *John Bull*. Harmsworth contributed almost as expansively as Bottomley to the anti-German sentiment of 1914–18. As Viscount Northcliffe he had died a rich and successful man in summer 1922.

DOI: 10.4324/9781003306085-12

The reason why Bottomley settled on fraud is because the opportunities to sustain his press empire were narrowing, and because it seemed obvious that any criminality on his part would go unpunished. For a decade, Bottomley had warned that politics was corrupt, and the main parties indistinguishable. He had insisted that the greatest hypocrites of all were the Labour leaders and those Liberals who claimed to stand for anything different. By the early 1920s, the increased reporting of corruption seemed to prove all his warnings true. Lloyd George was in government, and selling honours to the highest bidder: convicted South African diamond miners, meat-importing tax evaders and fraudsters accused of war profiteering had all been named in the Honours Lists.[3]

The real injustice, Bottomley could tell himself, was that other people were cheating on a massive scale, and *he was not*. If they were corrupt and their friendships and connections protected them then surely, he told himself, he deserved his chance too.

As for politics, Bottomley had long broken all ties with the Radical Liberalism of his parents' circle. His hatred for the socialist left became the defining story of his political career. He was an early example of a phenomenon that would become widespread as the interwar years wore on, the former leftist gone bad. Such figures would play a recurring role on the far right with fascist parties in Italy, Britain and France all led by former socialists (Mussolini, Mosley and Doriot). Anti-democratic movements were springing up across Europe. More talented political figures than Bottomley, the likes of Rothermere and Lloyd George, were to waste the 1920s and 1930s admiring these newly governing parties.

Here was the same anti-political mood, the same sense that ordinary politics had broken down, the same logic of national and racial exclusion as could be seen in Bottomley's journalism. As for his specific group of Independents, Sir George Makgill of the People's League had operated at the furthest edge of Conservatism, for example urging members of the Anti-Socialist Union to merge with the British Fascists. During the 1926 general strike, he managed the day-to-day operations of the Organization for the Maintenance of Supplies, dying that same autumn a respected member of the establishment. When the strike ended, the miners were still locked out.[4] Admiral Sueter had re-joined the mainstream Conservative party, and despite being a member of the Anglo-German Fellowship advocating peace with Germany in the 1930s, held his Hertford seat for them until the Labour landslide of 1945.[5]

Yet the likes of Mussolini or Hitler went further than Bottomley. He had supported the Great War and made speeches defending it; they sought with all their power to remake society in the image of the trenches. He called for the shooting of strikers and Labour politicians; they not only called for the murder of political and racial enemies, they also organised the gangs to carry out the murders, equipping them and sending them into battle. They did not stop at launching new parties of the right; they took them from the margins into government.[6]

It is, in this sense, accurate to consider Horatio Bottomley's politics not fascist but far right. Bottomley had no intention of leading a street movement against liberals and the left. He wanted to be a member of the existing elites, not to shake up the very system of authority. Any violence he employed was limited to threatening his opponents with shooting. He did not organise the destruction of union or Labour halls, or the killing of his opponents. In recent years, we seem to have lost the ability to see or still less describe a far right that falls short of fascism. But the left and right distinction goes back to 1789; in other words, it predates fascism by 150 years. In all that time, there has always been a political left and a right, a moderate right and a far right. For most of that time, the far right has been content to dream of the past rather than imagine a future of tanks and prison camps.[7] Seeing Bottomley close up enables us to grasp how such non-fascist far-right politics recurs – in history and today.

What would it have required to convert Bottomley into a fascist? He would have needed to swap his deference to parliamentary politics for the street. Beyond that he would have needed the sorts of opportunities that supplied themselves in abundance as the decade wore on, the example of fascism in power for him to emulate. He did not have the flair to be the world's first fascist, but he could have stood in the second rank.

One reason we can place him on the near side of the fascist/far right distinction is that Bottomley was not at odds with the Edwardian ruling class, but trying to become part of it. In 1924, the horse-riding barristers of the Pegasus Club had held their first annual ball. Among the 500 attendees were Sir Patrick Hastings, Attorney General for the new Labour Government, who had rushed over from a meeting with George V still dressed in the modified court dress (of "ordinary dress coat, cloth breeches, and silk stockings") that Prime Minister Ramsay MacDonald insisted be the maximum show permitted of Labour ministers in their dealings with the King. Lord Darling, who had acquitted Bigland, was present as the club's former president, dressed in the blue coat of the Badminton Hunt.[8] Others were unable to attend: Sir Henry Hawkins was long dead, and so was Sir Charles Russell, but the latter's sons were carrying on both conjoined family traditions, in the law and in horse-racing. One of them, Frank Russell, who had in the past cross-examined Bottomley, had become a judge.

F. E. Smith appears to have missed the ball. As Lord Birkenhead, he was concentrating his energies on defeating the country's new government. Four days before the 1924 general election Lord Northcliffe's *Daily Mail* had published the Zinoviev letter. This forgery purported to show the head of the Communist International proposing to mend diplomatic relations with Britain's Labour government, as part of a secret plan to foment insurrection in Britain, and in her colonies. The Conservatives won the election, after which a cabinet committee, with Smith on it, declared the letter genuine.[9]

Henry Osborne O'Hagan died in 1930. He had been Bottomley's backer in the affairs which led to the Hansard Union trial, and became the dominant figure in the British cement industry.[10] Julius Elias, Bottomley's ally until the Bigland trial, continued to publish *John Bull* after the conviction, and negotiated with the unions to purchase a half share of the *Daily Herald*, which had been the voice of the anti-war left. Though he died a Labour peer in 1946, the Viscount South-wood,[11] its politics under his ownership would be diluted.[12] Renamed *The Sun* in 1964, it was bought in 1969 by Rupert Murdoch – who made it the paper it is today.

None of the above had their reputations tarnished by their association with Bottomley. But the ordinary men and women who had relied on him went on to less glittering futures. His secretary Henry Houston, for example, died in East London, poor and alone.[13]

Bottomley had been a newspaper proprietor. He knew how his life's story was likely to be written and he tried in his last years, with such force as he still had, to fight the descent into cliché. "We are all familiar", he began one piece, "with the newspaper interview with the robust octogenarian, or nonagenarian, who attributes his longevity to a course of living held up as an example to all. Early rising, daily walks, simple diet, abstention from alcohol and tobacco, and a list of virtues are paraded for our inspiration, however contradictory and inconsistent they may be".[14] His life, he well knew, would be employed in the opposite way – as a litany of vices, culminating in his humiliation. Bottomley insisted that such stories told you more about the author than they did about him, and on that one he was correct. He loved the best food and drink, he thrilled to watch his horses win a race. No doubt his longing to possess was such that he bought in his time everything and everyone that he could. Perhaps, as many said, he was a sensualist. Had he not spent so much time drunk he might never have ended up in jail. But nor would he have dared attempt those extraordinary swindles which formed the substance of his triumphs. Without his glass of Pommery to hand, many of his dupes would never have believed him. Had he not spent so recklessly, he would never have been caught – but he would also never have begun his ascent. As a former orphan, he would never have been permitted (however precariously) to join the governing classes of Imperial Britain.

We should pause before we turn the tale of his decline into a simple morality tale, of speed of ascent, personal corruption and eventual demise. Bottomley's need to acquire was not just the cause of his downfall. It was also the cause of his rise. It was how he acquired an entourage. It was where he wooed politicians and financiers and how he made millions. "Bottomley's life is the greatest romance of our times", wrote one early biographer, "there is no parallel to his career in the whole history of England".[15] If this goes too far; Bottomley was not without talent. We do not need to admire him, but we can acknowledge his success.

We have seen the compliments with which Bottomley showered himself: the "finest orator in the Kingdom... the first lay lawyer in the land... a fearless and independent politician". The truth is that Bottomley was a first-rate jingo and an accomplished propagandist. He had a skill for summoning into being new ways of delivering nationalist politics. In these respects he was a performer – even an artist. We revolt against that admission, but that revulsion is misplaced. Hasn't the last decade taught us that such quicksilver types can evade earnest liberal attempts to contain or counter them? We can accept that, on Bottomley's own terms, he prospered. He meant to make himself seem large and he succeeded. If others suffered as a result of his cruelty, Bottomley himself avoided those consequences for many years.

The superficial truth that Bottomley grasped is that deferring the moment of gratification does not convert lust into virtue. The deeper truth, which he never dared to express, is that something is amiss in the very thinking by which righteous ambition is supposed to be crowned by the personal acquisition of wealth. Bottomley was a patriot, and he was neither the first nor the last of that kind to act on his supporters' loyalty to their country by enriching himself as best as he could at their expense. If he stole more than others it was because better opportunities provided themselves to him. The true lessons of Bottomley's life will only have been learned when our society makes itself immune to the charms of people like him.

Notes

1 Bigland, *Bottomley!!!*, p. 93.
2 Bottomley knew Wilde's *Ballad of Reading Gaol* and on release from imprisonment published his own book of poems loosely based on it, *Songs of the Cell* (London: William Southern, 1928).
3 Following the collapse of Lloyd George's government, the Honours (Prevention of Abuses) Act 1925 made it a criminal offence to sell peerages or other honours.
4 Hemming, *M*, p. 59.
5 For the Fellowship and its politics more generally, R. Griffiths, *What Did You Do During the War?* (Abingdon: Routledge, 2017).
6 The British Union of Fascists reported Bottomley's death with some sympathy: "Bottomley was a poor, emotional, careless creature – the ideal meat for Capitalist justice", *Blackshirt*, 8 to 14 July 1933.
7 The themes of this paragraph are developed, on the terrain of political theory, in my book, *The New Authoritarians: Convergence on the Right* (London: Pluto, 2019).
8 Hawkes, *Bench and Bar*, p. 165.
9 "Smith, Frederick Edwin", *Dictionary of National Biography* (Oxford: Oxford University Press, 2004), Vol. 51, pp. 116–17.
10 R. Davenport-Hines, 'O'Hagan, Henry', *Dictionary of National Biography* (Oxford: Oxford University Press, 2004), Vol. 41, p. 619.
11 H. Richards, 'Elias, Julius Salter', *Dictionary of National Biography* (Oxford: Oxford University Press, 2004), Vol. 18, p. 47.
12 P. Foot, 'How the TUC Killed Workers' Paper', *Socialist Worker*, 15 September 1973.
13 Symons, *Horatio Bottomley*, p. 273.
14 Felstead, *Horatio Bottomley*, p. 7; Hyman, *The Rise and Fall*, p. 283.
15 Felstead, *Horatio Bottomley*, p. 273.

INDEX